M. Louis Hughes

Mediterranean

Malta or undulant fever

M. Louis Hughes

Mediterranean
Malta or undulant fever

ISBN/EAN: 9783742830647

Manufactured in Europe, USA, Canada, Australia, Japa

Cover: Foto ©Andreas Hilbeck / pixelio.de

Manufactured and distributed by brebook publishing software
(www.brebook.com)

M. Louis Hughes

Mediterranean

Fig. I

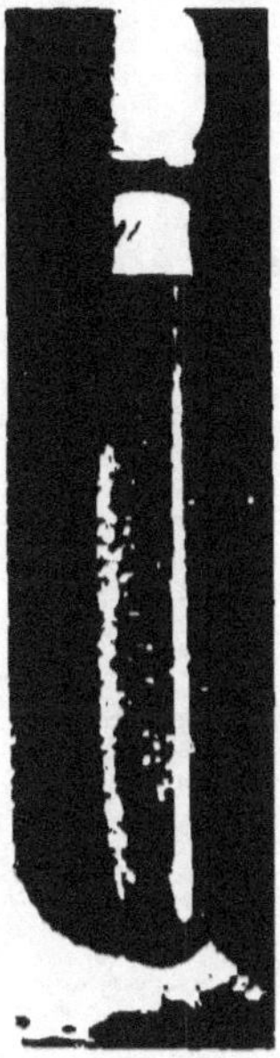

Fig. II.

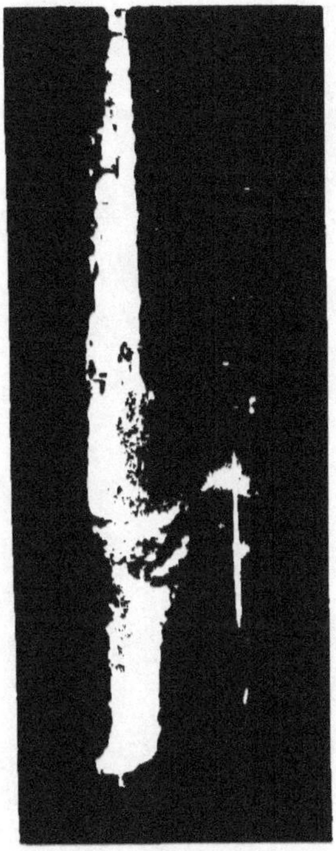

Fig. III.

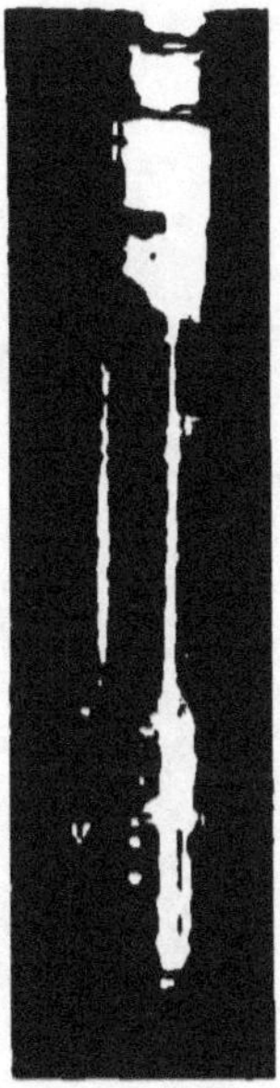

Fig. IV.

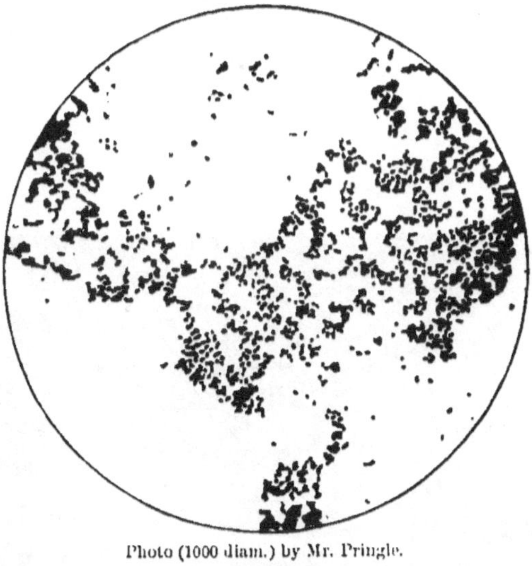

Photo (1000 diam.) by Mr. Pringle.

Fig. I.—Micrococcus Melitensis *vel* Brucii, colonies from human spleen about 14 days old, less than one-half natural size.

Fig. II.—Mic. Mel. from spleen of monkey (Exp. III. Chap. II.), colonies full grown, almost natural size.

Fig. III.—Mic. Mel. from human spleen, colonies full grown, about half natural size.

Fig. IV.—Mic. Mel. from colony on agar (× 1000), microphotograph.

PREFACE

When the writer arrived in Malta towards the end of the year 1890, for a six years' tour of service in that place, he found that his medical work would chiefly consist, during the greater part of the year, of treating a fever about which no two medical officers appeared to agree, respecting its cause, treatment, or even name. Some even doubted its specific nature, calling it a variety of enteric or malarial fever, and until the writer had been present at a post-mortem examination on a fatal case, he was himself prejudiced in favour of all serious cases being of an enteric nature. The fallacy of this theory soon became apparent, and extended clinical and pathological experience showed how much there was to learn, and how little to guide anyone, in the study of this important fever. The majority of medical officers, naval and military, gain much valuable knowledge during their service in the Mediterranean, but in most cases this goes away with them on the expiration of their tour of service, and new medical officers have to take up the work *ab initio.* Could these latter but begin where their predecessors left off, we should in course of time, by accumulated knowledge, really know much about this disease. It is with the idea of placing such little knowledge as the writer has gained, during six years of almost constant hospital and other practice amongst such fever cases, at the disposal of those coming after him, that this small book has been compiled. Let us hope that it will form a nucleus for a more extended and accurate account at some future date, in which case, crude and disjointed as it is, it may prove of service. Only the hours that could be spared from a busy life, at the headquarters of a large station, were available for the compilation of these notes, which are therefore far from being as systematic or complete as could be wished, and leave much for others to correct and work out. Further, during the last summer of the author's service in the Mediterranean, he contracted this fever himself, and had to be invalided to England. Though this proved a most practical if unwelcome experience, it precluded him from carrying out research into many points of interest, more particularly with reference to the blood and the bacteriology of the urine and fæces.

Few but medical officers of the Army and Navy meet with this fever in its endemic area, and all our present knowledge about it has been drawn from the accounts of the experiences which they have been able to publish. Unfortunately their shifting and busy life affords but little opportunity for systematic research. One of the greatest advances towards gaining a knowledge of the fever, namely, its recognition as a distinct disease, by the Committee appointed by the Royal College of Physicians of London, by whom the last edition of the *Nomenclature of Diseases* has been drawn up, has been acknowledged by that august body, in their preface, as being "in consequence, more especially, of representations made by officers of the Medical Department of the Army." This is not only a proof that such work has not been wasted, but is a matter for which those who have the honour of the Army Medical Staff at heart, may be pardoned for feeling some pride.

The etiology and treatment of this fever are of considerable importance to Great Britain, for the Mediterranean is not only a winter resort and important commercial centre, but is also a training-ground for a large fleet, and a half-way house in which regiments are acclimatised before proceeding to India. It contains a permanent force of over 25,000 soldiers and sailors, and may at any time become the seat of warlike operations, when every available man may become of vital importance. All these troops are at present more or less exposed to the effects of this endemic fever, both in the garrison towns and in the various ports which our fleet visit. Its lengthened duration causes an enormous yearly financial loss, from non-effective pay and invaliding, while it may be said to be the most important, and next to venereal diseases, the most prevalent form of sickness affecting our Mediterranean forces.

To the French, Italian, and other Mediterranean nations, this subject cannot but be of importance, while the limits of its geographical prevalence have yet to be fixed.

The author, who together with his wife and two sisters have suffered from the disease (average pyrexial duration, 140 days), feels only too strongly the need that exists for discovering and removing its cause, it being to Englishmen at present the scourge of the Mediterranean.

In the text, a date enclosed in brackets, following a name, refers to the bibliography, a section of the work which the author has endeavoured to make as complete as possible. All the matter he has been able to collect has been included, without reference to the particular views of the individual writers, so that it may be a guide to those who wish to make a systematic and exhaustive study of the disease. The author will always be grateful for further references, particulars of which any reader may be willing to furnish him.

Though the writer has had an opportunity of seeing cases of this fever in many parts of the Mediterranean, his practical experience has been gained in Malta and among soldiers and their families. The greater part of this book must therefore refer to that place, and to the prevalence of the fever in the Army. He has, however, collected as much general matter as may have come to his knowledge, and doubtless the experiences gained in Malta will be found to apply in great part to this fever as it occurs elsewhere.

In conclusion, the writer has to especially thank Surgeon-Major-General O'Dwyer, Surgeon-Majors Bruce and Manché, Surgeon-Captain Ritchie, Dr. Thin of London, Prof. Wright of Netley, Drs. Pisani, Carruana Sceluna, and T. Zammit of Malta, and many others, for much valuable help and kind encouragement in his work. Also Mr. Pringle and Mr. Rosser for their excellent photographs.

M. L. H.

c/o Holt & Co.,
17 Whitehall Place, London, S.W.

CONTENTS

CHAPTER I

CHAPTER II

CHAPTER III

CHAPTER IV

CHAPTER V

INDEX TO CLINICAL DESCRIPTIONS OF CASES

INDEX OF TABLES

INDEX OF CHARTS

CHAPTER I

Definition.—Synonyms: (*a*) From its supposed resemblance to enteric (typhoid) or malarial fevers; (*b*) from its remittent character; (*c*) from the occurrence of gastric derangements or other symptoms; (*d*) from its lengthened course and indefinite duration; (*e*) From its geographical prevalence; (*f*) from its supposed origin.—*Short description.—Specific nature:* Supposed resemblance to enteric and malarial fevers; Differentiation from these fevers.—*Nomenclature:* Necessity for a suitable name; geographical names unsatisfactory; fallacy of names connected with other fevers; consideration of other suggested names.—Undulant fever suggested as a suitable name.—*Historical Sketch:* Accurate history begins A.D. 1859; (*a*) occurrence prior to 1859; Hippocrates, B.C. 460; Demarco and Howard, A.D. 1722-87; Fauverge, 1798-1800; Cleghorn, 1744-49; Heastie, 1825-28; Burnet, 1800-10; Hennen, 1816-25; Davy, 1833-35; Parliamentary statistical reports, 1817-59; Crimean War period. (*b*) More accurate history, Marston, 1859; Mackay, 1862; Pottinger, 1862; Royal Navy, 1872; Boileau, 1865; Chartres, 1866; Guilia, 1871; Donaldson, Oswald Wood, and Lane Notter, 1876; Veale, 1879; Turner, 1884; Maclean, 1885; Bruce, 1886, etc., Discovery of a specific micro-organism; Moffet, 1889; Articles in text-books on medicine and inclusion in the nomenclature of the Royal College of Physicians of London, 1893-97; Italian and other writers. Summary.—*Geographical Distribution*—Malta and Gibraltar; Sardinia; Balearic Isles; Italy and Sicily; Greece; Turkey; Cyprus; Crete; Jerusalem; North African coast; Red Sea; France. Somewhat analogous or possibly identical forms of fever occurring in China, India, and America.—*Bibliography.*

Definition.—An endemic pyrexial disease, occasionally prevailing as an epidemic, having a long and indefinite duration, an irregular course with an almost invariable tendency to undulatory pyrexial relapses. It is usually characterised by constipation, profuse perspirations, and accompanied or followed by symptoms of a neuralgic character. Often accompanied by swelling and effusion of the joints and other rheumatoid symptoms. After death, the spleen is found to be enlarged and often softened, many of the organs congested, but Peyer's glands neither enlarged nor ulcerated, nor is ulceration present in other parts of the small intestine. There is a constant occurrence in certain tissues of a definite species of micro-organism.

Synonyms.—(*a*) *From its supposed resemblance to enteric (typhoid) or malarial fevers.* Febbricola tifiodea (Grimaldi, 1872, etc.); Intermittent typhoid (Borrelli, 1877); Adeno-tifo (Cantani, 1878); Febbricola tifosa (De Renzi, 1884); Febbre tifoidea atipica (Capozzi, 1885); Ileo-tifo a forma sudorale (Jaccoud, 1885-86); Pseudo-tifo (Guiffré, 1893); Recurrent typhoid; Typho-malarial fever (Maclean, 1875, Rho, 1895, etc.); Fæco-malarial fever (Donaldson, 1876); Subcontinuous malarial fever (Baccelli, 1875, 1894; Drummond, 1888); Fièvre typhoïde sudorale italienne (Jaccoud, 1897); Tifo atassico.

(*b*) *From its remittent character.* Mediterranean gastric remittent fever (Marston, 1861; Chartres 1866; Boileau, 1865); Bilious remittent fever; Remittent fever (so returned by Royal Navy and Malta Civil Government up to 1896, and by Army from 1871 to 1885).

(*c*) *From the occurrence of gastric derangements or other symptoms.* Mediterranean gastric remittent fever (Marston, 1861; Boileau, 1865; Chartres, 1866); La febbre gastro-biliosa (Guilia, 1871); Febrile dyspepsia; Bilious remittent fever; Febris sudoralis (Tomaselli, 1880); Febbre miliare (Frederici, 1885, etc.); Recurrent fever; Febris complicata (Veale, 1879); Bilious continued fever (Typhaldos, 1882); Biliosa dei pæsi caldi; Undulant fever (Author, 1896).

(*d*) *From its lengthened course and indefinite duration.* Febbre subcontinua (Torti, 1712; Baccelli, 1866); Common continued fever (Hennen, Davy, etc. 1817-35); Simple continued fever (Military returns, 1885-96); Febbre continua epidemica (Tomaselli, 1886).

(*e*) *From its geographical prevalence.* Mediterranean fever (Burnett, 1810; Guiffré and others); Mediterranean gastric remittent fever (Marston, 1861; Boileau, 1865; Chartres, 1866); Rock or Gibraltar fever (Turner, 1884; Moffet, 1889, etc.); Malta fever (Oswald-Wood and Notter, 1876; Bruce, 1889); Neapolitan fever (Borelli, 1887; Fazio, 1879; Galassi, 1883); Febbre delle fogna (Dominicis, 1875, etc.); Febbre urbana; Cyprus fever (Carageorgiades, 1891); Levant fever; Cretan fever; Syriac fever.

(*f*) *From its supposed origin.* Fæco-malarial fever (Donaldson, 1876); Febbre infetiva atipica (Rummo, 1881); Pythogenic septicæmia (Moffet, 1889); Febbre climatica (Pasquale, 1889, etc.); Sewage, mephitic or cesspit fever; Febbre da idrotionemia.

(*g*) *Other designations.* Febbre innominata (Guiffré, 1888); New fever (Crete); Febricola nostrana (Fazio, 1879).

Short description.—This endemic fever of the Mediterranean, both clinically and pathologically, has very definite and constant features, which enable it to be distinguished from other diseases; more particularly from enteric and paludic fevers. It has, however, a close clinical relationship with these two febrile conditions, and occurs in many localities side by side with one or both of them.

Clinically, the fever has a peculiarly irregular temperature curve, consisting of intermittent waves or undulations of pyrexia, of a distinctly remittent character. These pyrexial waves or undulations last, as a rule, from one to three weeks, with an apyrexial interval, or period of temporary abatement of pyrexial intensity between, lasting for two or more days. In rare cases, the remissions may become so marked as to give an almost intermittent character to the febrile curve, clearly distinguishable, however, from the paroxysms of paludic infection. This pyrexial condition is usually much prolonged, having an uncertain duration, lasting for even six months or more. Unlike paludism, its course is not markedly affected by the administration of quinine or arsenic. Its course is often irregular and even erratic in nature.

This pyrexia is usually accompanied by obstinate constipation, progressive anæmia, and debility. It is often complicated with, and followed by neuralgic symptoms referred to the peripheral or central nervous system; arthritic effusions; painful inflammatory conditions of certain fibrous structures, of a localised nature; or swelling of the testicles.

Though the rate of mortality is very low, the invaliding rate is high, and the duration prolonged, so that the average stay in hospital is from seventy to ninety days.

The fever is endemic in certain places, and may become epidemic within a limited area. It does not appear to be contagious directly from man to man.

Pathologically, the spleen becomes at first much enlarged and softened, though subsequently it may shrink again. The alimentary tract may be the seat of irregular patches of arborescent venous congestion, which, though often excessive in the large intestine in rapidly fatal cases, have otherwise no special localisation. They have no relation to Peyer's patches, which are macroscopically unaffected. The microscopical appearances of the tissues are those brought about by the continued action of an irritant poison. Altered blood pigment is not deposited in the tissues, as in paludism.

A specific micro-organism has been isolated from the tissues after death, which when introduced into the tissues of healthy monkeys, produces in those animals a similar pyrexial condition. From the bodies of such inoculated monkeys, after death, the same micro-organism has been isolated in a pure state and cultivated artificially. Moreover, the micro-organism obtained from such monkeys has, when introduced into the tissues of other healthy monkeys, again produced a form of prolonged pyrexia, similar in character to that of undulant (Mediterranean) fever in man.[1]

[1] In the countries in which the author has had an opportunity of studying this fever, a large number of cases of pyrexia of short duration have occurred side by side with this and other continued fevers. These cases were most commonly met with during epidemics of undulant or enteric fevers, and while coming from the same locality, were most numerous at the beginning and towards the end of each epidemic. The majority of these short attacks lasted but a few days, and appeared to belong to that class of fever known as simple ardent fever or febricula, a most common affection in those countries. Other cases, lasting from seven to twenty days, had in some instances the characteristics of undulant fever, in others those of enteric fever. That they may be mild or abortive attacks of these fevers is possible and even probable, but we have no data on which to base any definite theory. Under these circumstances, the writer has, in this work, based his descriptions and conclusions only on those cases which have lasted long enough, or in which post-mortem observation has proved sufficient for him to be sure of a diagnosis. In the statistics of admission rates, etc., all cases of under three weeks' duration have been excluded, with the exception of fatal cases with post-mortem verification.

Specific Nature.—That undulant fever is a specific disease there can be no doubt. There are, however, both in England and on the Continent, members of our profession who still regard this disease as a variety of either enteric or malarial fevers. Many of these have served in India, and are among those who, until a comparatively recent date, refused to recognise the existence of enteric fever as an endemic Indian disease. Certain of these would even go so far as to call undulant fever by the misleading and unscientific term "typho-malarial fever," about which the writer will have more to say in the section dealing with the nomenclature of this disease. Many of these men belong to a class termed "germ sceptics," and hold that the clinical manifestations of this disease are those of enteric or malarial fevers modified by climatic conditions, or a mixture of both these fevers produced by peculiar climatic conditions acting upon the human body.. Others, more orthodox and advanced in their views, accept the necessity of a casual and living virus, but attribute the peculiar clinical characteristics of undulant fever to either an altered mode of entrance to the body in the case of enteric fever or to altered climatic conditions to which the malarial virus may be subjected where this undulant fever exists. Newcomers to the Mediterranean are often sceptical on arrival as to the specific nature of this fever, especially as they are usually advised, as a matter of safety, to treat these cases as enteric until they have become more experienced in diagnosis and treatment. They soon, however, especially after a post-mortem examination of an acute case, recognise the peculiar nature of this fever. A few of the less scientific, however, cling to that common opposition to new theories which characterises many who are unwilling to acknowledge truths they have failed themselves to discover and demonstrate.

The clinical resemblance between undulant fever and other pyrexial conditions will be dealt with in detail under the question of diagnosis; it will merely be necessary at this stage to discuss its resemblance with its closer neighbours, enteric and malarial (paludic) fevers.

Undulant fever has been classed with *enteric fever*, because—

(*a*) Cases of both diseases may occur side by side, and be even attributed to a similar fæcal origin. On the other hand, on careful investigation it is found that the general and individual distribution of cases, and the apparent life history of the poisons, is considerably and markedly different.

(*b*) Severe cases of undulant fever have a tendency to assume the so-called typhoid state, in which case, even if diarrhœa be not present, they may closely resemble enteric fever of a somewhat uncommon type. Under these circumstances, and especially near the commencement of an attack, sure diagnosis is often difficult and even impossible, as is not uncommonly the case in the initial stages of other febrile diseases. The number of these cases having a close clinical resemblance to enteric fever, even during the early stage of an attack, is both small in proportion and confined to severe and fatal cases. Even these at a later stage, if not fatal, and the vast majority of cases at all stages, have very distinct and characteristic differences, while a large number are so utterly different as to preclude their having any connection whatever with enteric fever. That the diseases have often some clinical resemblances there can be no doubt, for if not they would long ago have been differentiated. The same difficulty was met with in the cases of typhus and enteric fevers, until their separate nature was clearly laid down by Murchison, who himself says: "With regard to the specific distinctness of typhus and enteric fever it is right to state that I was taught to regard them as mere varieties of one disease, and that with this impression I commenced their study in the London Fever Hospital." The writer's acquaintance with typhus fever is limited to one epidemic, which occurred at Benghasi (North Africa) in the spring of 1893, but he is of opinion that, if the contagiousness of that fever is put aside, it resembles enteric fever much more closely than undulant fever does.

Besides these points of resemblance, there are other differences which must be mentioned:—

Firstly, in undulant fever there is a total absence of those morbid changes in Peyer's glands so characteristic of enteric fever in England, the Mediterranean, and indeed all the world over.

Secondly, there is usually present in the spleens of fatal enteric fever cases,the bacillus of Eberth and Gaffky, a micro-organism believed by many to be the proximal cause of the disease. This bacillus the writer has isolated from the spleens of the only nine cases of enteric fever, in which he has sought for it in Malta; but it has been invariably absent from the spleens of fourteen fatal cases of undulant fever that the writer has had the opportunity of investigating. Bruce also found this to be the case. Moreover, this bacillus has been replaced by a definite micrococcus in the twenty-five instances of fatal undulant fever in which Bruce, Gipps, and the writer have been enabled to investigate the spleen soon after death. This micrococcus, when introduced in a pure state into the tissues of healthy monkeys, has been found to produce a similar pyrexial condition to that observed in men when suffering from undulant fever. It has also satisfied those tests laid down for the establishment of the specific nature of pathogenic organisms.

Lastly, the serum-reactions of these two fevers, with respect to their casual micro-organisms, are such as could only exist in two distinct and specific forms of fever.

To call this disease a variety of enteric fever would necessitate a belief in the polymorphism, not only of the individual virus, but of the clinical and pathological phenomena that this virus is said to produce in the human subject, a belief which, if true, would alter and even upset the whole basis on which bacteriology and nosology at present rest.

Undulant fever has been classed as a *malarial fever* (*i.e.* as paludism), because—

(*a*) The remittent, and at times the intermittent character of the pyrexial curve has led to its being returned as "remittent fever," both by naval and civilian practitioners. In this way it came to be included in the malarial group of fevers under the 1885 edition of the *Nomenclature of Diseases.* This remittence and intermittence is, however, of a non-paroxysmal nature, and is not markedly affected by the administration of quinine. It is more like the remittence met with in some cases of enteric fever, or the intermittence of phthisis, or of the hectic fever of suppuration.

(*b*) The irregular course, uncertain duration, and tendency to relapses after apparent subsidence, have been urged as betokening its malarial nature. Whereas, however, in the case of true paludism, the irregularity of course has a certain periodic and paroxysmal nature, this is not the case in undulant fever. Again, a patient who has once become infected with true paludism, may be subject to subsequent attacks on but slight provocation, even years after he has totally removed from all chance of re-infection. In the case of undulant fever, however, when once really convalescent, a patient is completely free from febrile relapses of a like nature; nor does one attack appear to specially predispose to a subsequent one, but in the opinion of some writers it even confers immunity.

(*c*) The two fevers may exist side by side in the same locality, and so lead to ambiguity. In Malta, however, paludism does not exist, in these days, as an endemic disease, but only occurs in the form of relapses in men who have been previously infected in India, Mauritius, or elsewhere; whereas undulant fever is endemic, and unfortunately very prevalent. There exist therefore in Malta special facilities for studying this fever, apart from, and uninfluenced by paludic infection; and any one who has had the opportunity of seeing and treating cases of these two fevers side by side, the one imported and the other endemic, must at once be struck by their great clinical differences. Again, Dr. Thin,[1] the writer, and others who have sought for it, have failed to find Laveran's hæmatophyllum in the blood of cases of undulant fever, nor has deposition of altered blood pigment been observed. Laveran's discovery has cast a flood of light on what has heretofore been chaos, with regard to malarial fevers. The terms "remittent" and "intermittent," used in the official nomenclature of diseases (1885), have become most inapplicable. Such terms classify together, by one clinical characteristic common to various febrile disorders, various as yet undifferentiated but specific diseases. At the same time they place apart, under separate sub-headings, cases of a single disease, which (on account perhaps of the quantity, quality, or variety of its virus; some resistance peculiar to the patient, or other cause) may exhibit even in the same attack a pyrexial curve varying from an intermittent to a remittent or even a continuously high type. Even those who habitually return undulant fever as "remittent fever," agree that it is not strictly a malarial disease, but justify their action by pointing out that no better heading is available in the nomenclature of diseases. By the word "malarial" the

[1] Report of meeting of Roy. Med. and Chir. Soc., London, in *Brit. Med. Jour.* or *Lancet* for 18th April 1896.

writer refers to those diseases believed to result from infection by the amœboid bodies first discovered by Laveran, and not to its literal derivation of mal aëria. Now that the heading "Mediterranean Fever" has been added to the new nomenclature (1896) there is no excuse for returning this fever as "remittent fever."

Finally, the seasonal prevalence of these three fevers under discussion is not identical.

It may therefore be said that there are strong clinical, pathological, and etiological reasons for believing undulant fever to be distinct from either enteric fever or paludism, and though they may, scientifically and geographically speaking, be somewhat near neighbours, it is impossible that they can all three be one and the same disease. There are no other diseases described at present in the leading works on medicine that can be confounded with undulant fever.

Moreover, if our experiments are what we believe them to be, its specific nature has been proved on the lines laid down by Professor Koch, with a bacteriological completeness attained in few other instances. For while this fever has such distinct and constant features, both clinically and pathologically, as enables it to be identified from other diseases, a micro-organism, distinguishable from all others by its appearance and mode of growth, has been discovered in those parts of the body where, from clinical symptoms and post-mortem appearances, one would expect to find it. This micro-organism would appear to be present in every case; neither has any other organism been found under similar circumstances, nor is any other disease known in which this micro-organism is present. It has been passed artificially through six generations of pure cultures without change; and when introduced in a pure state and with due precautions into the tissues of healthy monkeys, has produced febrile phenomena similar to those occurring in man, without causing any local changes at the seat of inoculation. From the tissues of these monkeys after death a similar micro-organism has been obtained, which also has been passed through six generations of pure cultures, and which, when introduced into the tissues of other healthy monkeys, has caused a similar train of febrile symptoms.

All this points conclusively to the fact that this undulant fever is a specific disease.

Nomenclature.—Having arrived at the conclusion that this fever is a distinct and specific disease, the very important question of a suitable and generally acceptable name, under which it may be returned, arises. This has proved a most difficult subject; for, to come into general use, the name should be so stamped with the identity of the disease as to at once recall to the mind that disease and no other; while at the same time it must not be based on any theory which later knowledge may explode. Many names have been suggested, but none of them has proved wholly satisfactory. At this early stage in the public literary existence of this disease the choice of a suitable name is of great moment, as when once in general use, however undesirable it may prove, it will be exceedingly difficult to change.

Hitherto, for want of a better name, the writer has always termed it the "Endemic Fever of the Mediterranean," or more briefly "Mediterranean Fever." For a similar reason, the committee appointed by the Royal College of Physicians of London, in revising the official nomenclature of diseases, has termed it "Mediterranean Fever" (synonym, "Malta Fever"). This name implies a theory of geographical limitation which is neither an established fact, nor in the opinion of the writer a probable condition. While cases of so-called climatic or typho-malarial fever, of long duration and irregular course, neither enteric nor paludic in nature, exist in the coast towns of the Red Sea and China, and even in parts of India and America, it would be unwise to lay down any geographical limitations for the prevalence of this fever, until the exact nature of these cases is ascertained.

Bruce has always called it "Malta Fever," while others have given it equally local names, such as "Gibraltar or Rock Fever," "Neapolitan Fever," "Cyprus Fever," etc. To give it the name of a single town or country, is to rather unfairly saddle that place with the responsibility of a fever by no means peculiar to that special part of the world.

The excuse, that to call it "Malta Fever," is to shed a scientific radiance upon the island where first it was accurately studied, carries more weight with a scientist than an hotel proprietor. The name micrococcus Melitensis, given by the writer in 1893 to the specific micro-organism of the disease, and since adopted by others, has not the same objectional characters.

Geographical names have in the past been responsible for much of the confusion concerning "fevers," which for so many years retarded the progress of scientific medicine, preventive and therapeutical. Sir William Aitken, when advocating the use of the first general nomenclature of diseases in 1872, wrote: "Except as matters of history and as beacons to warn us from a greater danger to science, let these (geographical) and such-like names be consigned to oblivion." Such names are as a rule picked up, in the first instance, by newcomers from the empirics of the places where these fevers exist, and are never retained after the disease has been carefully studied. Though it has been a great advance to have this fever recently included in the leading text-books on medicine, and in the official nomenclature of diseases, even as "Mediterranean or Malta Fever," it is unlikely that these names will prove permanently satisfactory.

In the returns of the Royal Navy, of the Maltese Civil Government, and of the Army between the years 1871 and 1885, all cases of this fever were described as "Remittent Fever," a term which has necessitated their being included among the malarial group of fevers, together with all cases of paludic infection. In the military returns before 1871, and from 1886 to 1896, these cases have been included, together with all febrile attacks of indefinite and doubtful nature, under the heading "Simple Continued Fever," a disease then officially defined as "continuous fever having no obvious distinguishing character." This name was applied to very many and various febrile disorders, varying in their duration from two to two hundred days, which were not diagnosed, or which, though correctly diagnosed, could not be placed under any more definite heading. Now this fever has some most "obvious distinguishing characteristics," and the only excuse for so misnaming the disease, was that while military regulations lay down that every case of sickness must be returned under some official heading, that of S. C. Fever interfered least with the statistics of other better defined diseases. It therefore follows that the returns of the last hundred years throw but little statistical light upon the prevalence of this fever. The introduction of the disease into the new third edition of the nomenclature of diseases has removed this difficulty, and will in time provide us with much valuable information.

The British soldier, on account of its long and tedious course, with unconscious punning upon the shortened term in common use (S. C. Fever), has christened this disease "slow continued fever," a cumbersome though not inappropriate name.

Various names connected with enteric and malarial fevers have been suggested, more especially by continental writers, such as "continuous or subcontinuous malaria," "fæco-malaria," "pseudo-typhoid," "pseudo-enteric," "intermittent" or "adeno-typhoid," and last but by no means least often, the name "typho-malarial fever." All such hybrids are hopelessly misleading. The last term, which has been even recently advocated, though contained in the second (1885) edition of the nomenclature of diseases, has been happily omitted from the new edition (1896).[1] The term in English works has been used to denote:

(1) Atypical enteric fever occurring in hot climates.

(2) Enteric fever affecting a patient also infected with the virus of paludism, the latter poison being supposed to modify the effects of the former (Woodward, etc.) Or malarial fever simulating enteric fever.

(3) Fevers identical with or resembling this undulant fever.

If these fevers are either enteric or paludic in nature, they should be returned as such. If they are cases of acute enteric fever, occurring with and modified by concurrent paludism, they should be included in returns under that condition which at the time appeared the more serious; and though it might perhaps be more accurate to include them under both headings, this would scarcely be advisable from a hospital accommodation point of view, leading as it would to a variance between the number of men in hospital, and the number of cases of sickness admitted. The condition is comparable to that in which a syphilitic[2] or

[1] See Squire (1886), Maclean (1875, 1876, and 1885), Duncan (1888), and Davidson (1892), *Geo. Path.* (*America*).

[2] For such a case see report of Surg.-Capt. MacNaught, A.M.S., *Indian Med. Gazette*,

tubercular[1] subject contracts enteric fever or sustains an injury. In such instances it is not thought necessary that compound names like typho-syphilis, or tuberculo-enteric should be used, nor is any difficulty complained of in such cases. If, on the other hand, as we believe, this endemic fever of the Mediterranean is neither enteric nor malarial in nature, but is due to an entirely different cause, it would be a most unscientific and retrograde step to apply a term to it, which when literally translated implies "a fever of malarial origin resembling typhus (exanthematicus)."

We must remember, however, that in Italy, where the term "pseudo-tifo" is used, the nomenclature of diseases differs from ours. There the term tifo (typhus) refers rather to a group of fevers, than to any one disease; individuals being distinguished by an additional qualification such as "tifo enterico vel abdomenale," and "tifo petecchiale vel esantematico." We may, however, in England, put away from our nosology such hybrid names and variations on the word "typhus," and by an accuracy of nomenclature keep pace with our extended and definite modern pathology.

The term recurrent fever is descriptive, but it has too close a resemblance to the Italian "febbre ricorrente," and the German "typhus recurrens," both synonyms for our relapsing fever.

Pythogenic septicæmia (Moffet) is, in the present state of our knowledge, rather a leap into the darkness of its supposed origin.

Professor Veale suggested the name complicate fever, as he thought that the attribute adjunct complicate, stated at once the most salient feature of the disease, but implied no theory as to its nature or cause. Like the term febbre sudorale (Tomaselli) it is descriptive, but neither of these has been accepted as satisfactory.

It is one thing, however, while drawing a lesson from history, to discard unsuitable synonyms and call for a new name, and quite another to suggest a suitable substitute. The writer has had many discussions and correspondences on the subject with Surgeon-Major Bruce and others interested in this fever, but without result. For six years, while seriously considering the question, he has waited in hope that a suitable name would be forthcoming, but in vain.

As the writer has taken upon himself the responsibility of placing this book before the public, he feels keenly that it is his duty to deal with this difficult subject if he possibly can. At the same time he knows, as only those who have worked at the subject are able, how little there is to guide one in the right direction. He has determined to call the fever, in this work at least, by the name "UNDULANT FEVER." If this is a good name it will stand the test of time and use, if the reverse, the sooner it is condemned the better. That it is not a perfect name is self-evident, for to be so it "should be so characteristic and

vol. xxxi. No. 7, p. 252, 1896, and Sir Dyce Duckworth, *Brit. Med. Jour.* vol. ii. p. 896, 11th April 1886.

[1] See Chantemesse, *La Semaine Medicale*, Année 17, No. 30, p. 240, 23rd June 1897.

significant that a person but slightly acquainted with the language and subject should, on hearing it, immediately understand what is the nature of the disease it designates" (Plouquet). Sir William Aitken says: "It should be composed out of the same elements as the definition of the disease, in fact it ought to be the definition converted into a name, and derived either from the symptoms of the disease or from the supposed proximate cause." Now, in the definition of this peculiar blood infection, the only constant features we meet with are pyrexia of uncertain duration and peculiar undulating and relapsing course; certain changes in the spleen; and the occurrence in certain tissues of a micro-organism. Of its supposed fæcal origin we scarcely yet have sufficient data on which to base a name, while one derived from a leading clinical characteristic, while appealing to the ordinary mind, is less liable to error than one derived from a supposed proximate cause. Either relapsing or splenic fever are terms which would have referred to definite characteristics, but both names are already in use. It has therefore appeared to the writer that the term undulant fever, by referring to the peculiar pyrexial curve so characteristic of the disease, might prove a usable name. The name appeals forcibly to the clinical observer, who, standing in a ward surrounded by cases of this fever (as one may do on any summer day in the military hospitals of Malta), gazes at the temperature charts upon the walls, and notices the way in which the recorded pyrexial curves undulate across the paper in waves of varying size; especially when the temperature is allowed to run its course unchecked by artificial means.

The advantages of the term "undulant fever" may be briefly summarised—

(*a*) It describes one of the most constant and characteristic clinical features of the disease, namely the pyrexial undulations so apparent upon the ordinary temperature records.

(*b*) The term appears to be grammatically correct.

(*c*) The term is not one which can be applied to other febrile diseases, which is the weak point with the terms remittent and intermittent fever.

(*d*) It need not (as is the case with the heraldic term "wavy") be held to mean a definite quantity or amount of intensity; but as in nature, undulations vary from the gentle ripple or broader swell to the chopping wave or overwhelming breaker, so may the expression be applied to the various pyrexial waves of this fever, however much they vary in length and magnitude.

(*e*) Its Latin synonym (febris undulans) renders it comprehensible to scientists all over the civilised world, while it is easily translatable into their various individual languages, in most cases with but little change.

(*f*) While the term is descriptive, has a familiar sound, and slips easily and lightly from the tongue; and as it has not previously been used by scientists in such a manner, its use should not give rise to ambiguity.

Historical Sketch.—The accurate history of undulant fever commences from the year 1859, when Marston wrote the first description of the fever as a distinct disease. This was published in the *Army Medical Report* for 1863, and has been the basis of most of the papers written since that date.

A careful study, however, of the literature of the fevers of the Mediterranean prior to 1859, leads one to believe that this particular fever must have prevailed in many of the towns on its coasts during the last century if not at an earlier period. Until the commencement of the present century, and, indeed, during its first quarter, "fevers" were a very indefinite quantity. We find, however, on comparing those at present prevailing in the Mediterranean with those of the past, so close a similarity in their general type and seasonal prevalence, as to raise a strong presumption, in the absence of evidence to the contrary, that new types have not been introduced. Thus the presence or absence of true malarial fevers in certain localities is well indicated; the occurrence of enteric fever is apparent, either directly or indirectly, before it was separately returned, by the number of cases of peritonitis, perforation of intestine, etc., which disappeared from the returns when enteric fever came to be considered as a definite disease. We find also a large number of cases of "simple or common continued fever" (including fatal ones), and others returned under various symptomatic headings, which appear to have been much like those fevers of the present day, which we are in the habit of calling simple ardent fever, Mediterranean or undulant fever, etc. Like the malarial and enteric cases, these seem to have occurred at the same period of the year, and under similar favouring circumstances as these fevers do now, except that they appear to have been more severe, fatal, and on the whole more prevalent than at present. The following extracts from authors, besides other references in the bibliography, appear to throw some light on this subject.

B.C. 450. As far back as Hippocrates (of Thasus, off the coast of Thrace, *circa* B.C. 450) we find in his *Epidemics*, in the words of Prof. Veale, two passages "which, making allowance for the difference between his modes of thought and expression and those of our time, might almost pass for a brief description of this disease."[1] Adams, in his translation (A.D. 1849), at page 351 says: "The conclusions to which a patient study of modern authorities on the subject have brought me, amount to this, that the fevers described by Hippocrates in his *Epidemics* are exactly the same as those which are now described as still prevailing in the land of Greece; and that they correspond very well with those described by Cleghorn as occurring in Majorca" (presumably meant for Minorca). Until the present century, we find few works in which clinical facts are so carefully and accurately recorded as they are in the case descriptions ascribed to Hippocrates. Now, at pages 408, 415, and elsewhere in the same translation, we find full accounts of cases of protracted fever (duration up to 120 days), which are not unlike undulant fever. The first

[1] See trans. by Adams, pp. 355 and 359.

of these (p. 408), after four pyrexial waves, suffered from irregular and intermitting fever. After the fortieth day "apyrexia at times, at others not; for if the fever intermitted and was alleviated for a little, it immediately relapsed again." Death occurred upon the 120th day. Of this case Adams says: "This is an example of one of those protracted fevers of an intermittent type which, as I have been informed by an intelligent physician who practised for several years in the Ionian Isles, are common in the climate of Greece." Others of his recorded cases are like enteric fever (pp. 411, 412, 418, and 420) and simple ardent fever (p. 413) of the present day, whereas the malignant cases are similar to those described by Cleghorn, Davy, and other more modern authors.

During the eighteenth century we find references to the occurrence 1722-1800.
of continued and remittent fevers in Malta (Demarco, etc., 1722-1787). Howard (1786), in his Report on the Continental Hospitals, mentions that fevers were prevalent in Malta, and describes a low form of fever prevalent in the wards of the Great Hospital of the Knights of St. John. Bonamici, who died in 1680, and Boisgelin, who was present in Malta before and after the French and English occupations of the island, both describe an indigenous fungus, which was held to be a sovereign remedy for "fever," and a valuable monopoly of the Grand Masters.[1] Fauverge (1803), who served as a military surgeon during the French occupation of Malta (1798-1800), says: "Les maladies bilieuses, les fièvres intermittentes, les affections catarrhales et les hémorrhoïdes, affectant plus particulièrement les habitans de Malte."

Cleghorn (1751) describes cases of non-paroxysmal continued fever in Minorca, occurring between the years 1744 and 1749. These were of irregular type, incurable by "bark," marked by excessive perspirations, and followed by relapse after relapse. After death the spleen was "so excessively soft and rotten, that it had more the appearance of congealed blood wrapt in a membrane than of an original part." Some of his cases may have been of a paludic nature, others were distinctly enteric in character, while such cases as those above described closely resemble undulant fever.

The majority of the early medical writers of Gibraltar were so taken up with the subject of yellow fever, that they neglected such homely themes as their common endemic fevers (see Rey,[2] Pym, Gilkrest, Wilson, Chervin, Amiel, Bancroft, etc.).

During the early part of the present century we find that the same classes of fever prevailed at Malta, Gibraltar, and Minorca (Port Mahon), whereas in the Ionian Isles "malarial fevers" occurred "in addition" (see Burnett, Hennen, Davy, etc.).

[1] Fungus Melitensis, or Cynomorium coccineum, Balanophoraceæ, Ord. Rhizantheæ, mostly used as a styptic and astringent. See J. F. Bonamici, *Dissertatio de Fuco Spicato Coccineo Melitensi.* MSS. vol. xviii., Public Library, Malta. Also, Louis de Boisgelin, *Ancient and Modern Malta*, 2 vols. 1805.

[2] Rey, H. J., M.D., *Essai sur la topographie médicale de Gibraltar.* Paris, 1833. (With references to the other authors.)

Dr. Heastie (1830), who served in various parts of the Mediterranean from 1825 to 1828, says: "It is notorious, and well ascertained from a series of practical observations, that the yellow fever, which lately proved so fatal at Gibraltar, and occasionally appears in various parts of the Mediterranean, has succeeded to the mild remittent which was long ago known to exist in these places before the populations increased, and the exciting local causes became so numerous, formable, and aggravated."

1800-1810. Sir William Burnett, writing in 1810, and describing ten years' experience of Mediterranean fevers affecting sailors, returns a very large number of cases of a continuous nature. The high mortality and comparatively short duration of most of these cases point rather towards an enteric origin. In some instances, however, the enteric element is, at least from his description, not so conspicuous. Thus in the case of ships fitting in Malta dockyard (pp. 169-180), we find an admission rate of 777 cases, with a mortality of only 2·50 per cent; and that in days of most heroic treatment. Again, on page 180, the same is found in an account of fever at Palermo. Nearly all his cases occurred while ships were fitting in port.

It is still more interesting to note, that his general description of fever cases occurring during the autumn and winter months, agrees essentially with that of enteric fever; whereas his description of cases occurring during the summer months agrees more with that of undulant fever; a seasonal distinction which prevails to the present day. Thus in cases met with towards the end of June and onwards, he says: "Considerable headache, deep-seated in the orbits, nausea and prostration, epigastric uneasiness, and even vomiting; through the whole course a loathing for food, a bad taste in the mouth, tongue white and moist; there is commonly constipation of the bowels and loss of appetite. Pains in the joints, back, and calves of the legs, profuse perspirations, but skin usually dry; much head symptoms." During the winter months, however, he says: "Affection of the brain is not at all times so prominent a symptom, nor the bowels so constipated, and there is often a more anxious look at the beginning and severe pain on pressing the abdomen. In some cases epistaxis, subsultus tendinum, picking at the bed-clothes, and involuntary stools." The post-mortem descriptions of these latter also point to enteric fever. None of the cases were contagious, they occurred mostly among those who went on shore, while in his opinion the administration of quinine did more harm than good.

1816-1825. Dr. Hennen (1816-25), in his Medical Topography of the Mediterranean, states that the mortality from fevers amongst the native population of Malta, from 1818 to 1823, was 1 in 66·71 of the total population (96,404), for the six year period, being over a tenth of the total mortality from all causes. Though his detailed descriptions leave much to be desired, especially with regard to case description, his statistics are clearly arranged. These show a very small admission-rate for malarial fevers (and even these cases are stated to have been mostly imported from the Ionian Islands); and a very large admission rate for common continued fever, intestinal inflammatory diseases, pneumonia, bronchial catarrh, and rheumatism among the troops.

Dr. Davy (1842-62) who served in Malta from 1833-35, publishes, especially in his later work, graphic clinical and post-mortem accounts of the fevers he had met with there. Many of the fatal cases, with intestinal Peyerian ulceration, must undoubtedly have been enteric in nature, while others closely resembled undulant fever as met with in these days. He gives the following admission rate per thousand, among the troops, from 1837 to 1847:— 1833-1835.

Diseases.	Gibraltar.	Malta.[1]	Ionian Islands.[2]
Feb. intermit.	3·95	2·17	44·91
Feb. remit.	1·53	·66	26·29
Feb. com. contd.	73·76	202·50	75·29
Typhus	1·60	...	...
All other diseases	857·10	909·80	883·89

If we study the official parliamentary statistics of sickness among the troops serving in the Mediterranean, for the years from 1817 to 1846, we find much the same classes of fevers prevailing as at the present day, though in greater amount. Thus in Malta we find malarial fevers confined to certain years in which a number of men were transferred from malarious countries, such as the Ionian Islands, while in certain years no entries for these diseases occur. For common continued fever some 10,644 admissions are recorded, for synochus 125, for rheumatic affections 2352, for non-tubercular pneumonic affections 2413, and for intestinal complaints of a symptomatic nature a very high rate. From these fevers, equal to an annual admission rate of 185·3 per thousand of strength, 2·87 per thousand of strength died annually. To 1846.

It is stated in these reports (1817-36), that of these fevers "common continued fever was the cause of by far the greater proportion of deaths from this class of disease." And later (1837-46) we find "there was a high fever rate, of which the chief is common continued fever." See also remarks by Captain Smyth, R.N. (1854) referring to the years 1830-36.

In 1859, in a parliamentary sanitary report on barracks and hospitals, as follows: "During the entire period which has elapsed since the first hospital records were kept in Malta, the prevalent type of fever has been common continued fever. Out of 22,969 cases of fever admitted to hospital, of which we have accounts, 21,122 have been registered as of this type (1817-59), and though most were slight, still five-sixths of the fever mortality has been caused by this disease. The type next in frequency has been remittent fever, which has supplied about 5·50 per cent of the fever admissions, and about 9 per cent of the To 1859.

[1] Malarial cases imported. [2] Malarial fevers endemic.

fever deaths. Intermittent fevers have been so rare as to make it probable that they were imported. . . . Natives and British troops suffer alike from the usual zymotic diseases, and both suffer from the same classes of disease."

The actual quantity and severity of these continued fevers, taken as a class, and of those symptomatic diseases under which they were often returned, was proportionally much greater in those days than now; but the seasonal prevalence of both periods, as quoted in the various official returns and private publications, has not varied since the beginning of the century. These statistics bring us into the period of the Crimean War, at which time Malta became a military base of some importance. Soon after this time (1860), enteric fever was first diagnosed and returned officially in the records of military hospitals, and we find that fever at once replacing such diseases as peritonitis, hæmorrhage of bowel, perforation of intestine, enteritis, and pneumonia. At this time also Marston published his paper upon enteric and other fevers prevalent in Malta.

1854. The fact that during the Crimean War there was a very large temporary increase in the admission rate for enteric and other continued fevers in Malta, there being a largely increased number of troops of a susceptible age there at the time, besides numbers of convalescents and sick from the seat of war, has given rise to the belief among the Maltese that the English imported both enteric and undulant fevers into the island at that time from the Crimea. Marston in 1859 refers to this theory: "Of late years, it has seemed to me, that the prevalence of this three days' fever has considerably diminished, while other febrile diseases, of a severer character and longer duration, have made their appearance. The civil surgeons practising here consider that a very marked change has taken place in the type of fevers generally. They are in the habit of referring the date of such alteration to the period of the Crimean War. However this may be, typhoid and fevers of long duration appear to be more common than they were six or eight years ago." It must be noted that in 1859 continued fevers were more prevalent than they have ever been before or after. The fact that these fevers were "more common (in 1859) than they were six or eight years before," *i.e.* previous to the Crimean War, is not surprising when we also take into consideration that while so many more susceptible persons were present in Malta at that time, the years from 1855 to 1859 were those when, from statistical experience of the past seventy-eight years, we should expect the prevalence of these continued fevers to be on the increase (see table 10).

Oswald Wood (1876) writes: "Some twenty years ago cases of Malta fever were comparatively unfrequent and mild in their type; indeed it was by no means the formidable disease which it is now." He does not, however, mention any authority for his statement, and as he was not many years in Malta, it is probable that his information was derived from Marston's paper. Notter, the same year, in the same periodical, states: "That it has long existed is evident to anyone who will study the history of this fever. It appears to have been especially prevalent in Her Majesty's Royal Navy half a century ago, for, on turning to the medical history for that period, we find that rheumatism was common and often extremely intractable, and that two-thirds of all the invalids were classed under the head of inflammation with fever,—a vague term, I acknowledge, but one easily understood by anyone who has studied the disease."

Whether or not these diseases became permanently more prevalent after the Crimean War, not only did they exist in Malta before that time (Davy), but since then there has been a steady decrease in the admission-rates for continued fevers and their allies, which descredits the theory that these fevers were first introduced during the Crimean War. The following statistics are available :—

Simple Continued and Remittent Fevers from 1871-1885 in Malta.

1817-36	Admission-rate per mille, 173·3	Mortality 2·90
1837-46	,, ,, ,, 210·0	,, 1·80
1847-56	,, ,, ,, 256·0	,, 2·50
1857-59	(The years 1857-58 are not available.)	
1860-69	Admission-rate per mille, 181·5	Mortality 3·08 [1]
1870-79	,, ,, ,, 168·1	,, 2·60
1880-89	,, ,, ,, 128·5	,, ·93

This is not due to the separation from these figures of enteric fever (returned as a separate disease since 1860), for if we add the enteric fever cases to the above it does not materially alter the admission-rates, though it increases the death-rates. The increase in the death-rate is due to enteric and undulant fever cases being included as such, instead of under such headings as perforation of intestine, pneumonia, etc. It is still more significant that during the periods under discussion there has been a still more marked decrease in the number of cases returned under the various symptomatic headings allied with these continued fevers. This is specially marked in the respiratory and intestinal diseases :—

Admission and Mortality per Mille, Malta.

Non-tubercular Respiratory Diseases.			Symptomatic Intestinal Diseases.	
Years.	Admissions.	Mortality.	Admissions.	Mortality.
1817-36	111·0	2·90	109·2	3·40
1837-46	130·3	1·40	170·5	·84
1847-56	81·0	1·10	95·3	·40
1859-68	42·0	·68	Not differentiated, and almost all included under enteric fever.	
1869-78	42·4	·66		
1879-88	...	...		

[1] Enteric fever first diagnosed in military returns, and undulant fever recognised.

The exception to this general decrease in prevalence occurs in the case of the "rheumatic affections," which in Malta are usually to a great extent the results of this fever. These increased slightly until 1877, but this was accompanied by a marked decrease in the corresponding death-rate :—

Rheumatic Affections per Mille, Malta.		
1817-36	Admissions 34·0	Mortality ·20
1837-46	,, 46·0	,, ·14
1847-56	,, 38·0	,, ·10
1859-68	,, 49·0	,, ·04
1869-78	,, 50·1	,, nil
1879-88	,, 33·3	,, ,,

During the time that the Crimean War was going on we have to take into consideration the fact that not only was the material—*i.e.* the cases—more abundant for purposes of clinical observation, but also there were a much larger number of skilled observers in Malta at that time, leading to a concentration of public interest in these continued fevers, more particularly in those of a severe and fatal nature. It was at the time also when enteric fever was being generally recognised and separated from other fevers, and the clinical thermometer was coming into use. There is a great tendency on the part of some medical men to believe a disease must have recently appeared, because they themselves have previously failed to recognise it. Indeed, the author has met with well-educated Maltese physicians who have informed him quite recently that this undulant or Mediterranean fever was not known in Malta ten years ago, but that it *originated* when the new drainage was laid down in 1885!

Lyons and Aitken mention, in their account of the pathological appearances met with in fatal cases of fever in the Crimea during the war, cases of typhoid or common continued fever in which no ulceration was present. These cases, together with typical enteric ones, were called "Crimean Fever," and although some of the long cases of remittent fever, in which quinine was said to have been of no avail, might be held to have some clinical resemblance to undulant fever, it would be jumping at conclusions to use these facts as an argument in favour of the disease having been imported from the Crimea to Malta. Malta was certainly a depot for the Crimea in those days, and the disease might as easily have been transported from there to the Crimea as in the opposite direction. We find that the statistics of Gibraltar, which go back into the last century, closely resemble those of Malta with the same prevalence of similar types of fever. Moreover, although the disease does not appear to have been recognised in Italy until after papers had been published in 1861, 1865, and 1866 by Marston, Boileau, and Chartres, still it seems to have been present as an endemic disease before that time. Where, then, did places so much nearer Malta, and in consistent intercourse with that place for centuries, such as Sicily, Italy, Crete, Greece, and Gibraltar, obtain this fever? If they did not obtain it from Malta, but possessed it before the Crimean period, Malta could scarcely have escaped contamination from these sources. We do not find that change in the admission and death rates and in the seasonal prevalence of fevers in Malta that would be expected, had either undulant or enteric fever appeared there for the first time between 1855-57, and still less than if both had appeared together. We have, on the contrary, direct evidence that one or both existed in Malta in 1833-35 (Davy). Lastly, had they appeared for the first time so recently, the native Maltese population could scarcely have acquired the amount of immunity from these fevers they at present possess. Many of the foregoing remarks, doubtless, have bearing on other places in the Mediterranean less well known to the author.

The author is therefore of opinion that undulant fever has existed as an endemic disease, in Malta and Gibraltar at least, since the beginning of the present century, and probably for much longer, but that it was not recognised until 1859 as a distinct type of fever.

The accurate history of this undulant fever, therefore, dates from 1859. 1859, when Marston, who graphically describes his own sufferings from this fever, published in the *Army Medical Blue-Book of* 1863 a most excellent and exhaustive account of the fevers which he had met with previously in Malta. He states that he "had as far as possible made a point of seeing all the cases of fever—whether occurring among the troops or inhabitants—and of being present at the post-mortem examinations." First of all he gives a very clear and detailed account of enteric fever, stating that it always commenced (as in these days) about autumn; then reaching its acme of prevalence soon after that season, continued through the winter, but towards the spring ceased to prevail to any extent. After a description of simple ardent fever, which he called "Maltese Fever," he described a form of fever which he termed "Mediterranean remittent or gastric remittent fever." This latter, from the clinical and post-mortem reports, cannot have been other than the fever with which we are dealing. It has, he says, a very long course of from three to five or ten weeks, marked by irregular exacerbations and remissions, great derangement of the assimilative organs, tenderness in the epigastric region, splenic enlargement, and no exanthematous eruption. Pathologically it is marked by congestion or inflammation, with softening of the enteric mucous membrane, particularly that of the stomach and duodenum; but without any lesion of the Peyerian follicles, but with hypertrophies of the liver and spleen. He adds: "The disease prevails particularly during the spring and summer months (less so during the autumnal months); it is not contagious; and is comparatively nonfatal." At the end are detailed accounts of special symptoms, cases, and post-mortem reports.

About this period we find in the Annual Medical Blue-Books of the Navy descriptions of cases of pyrexia similar to those of undulant fever, but included under the names remittent fever, rheumatism, cachexia, and bronchial catarrh, etc.

1862. Thus in 1862 Dr. A. Mackay states: "In the Mediterranean the term fever is not unfrequently applied to a train of symptoms of so anomalous and obscure a nature as would justify their being classed rather as cases of climatic cachexia than of fever so called." Again, Surgeon R. Pottinger states, when speaking of some typhoid cases: "Rheumatism accompanied and very much retarded convalescence in a large number of these cases. Convalescence from this disease was exceedingly slow, and a peculiarity connected with it was a gradual coming on of a rheumatic affection, which sometimes attacked several joints, but for the most part settled in one of the hips. This sequela of fever was very intractable, and resisted the use of all the remedies employed in the cure of rheumatism." The admission-rate for rheumatism was, in 1862, 104·8 per 1000, and in 1861 as much as 112·8 per 1000; and in the general remarks for the former year we find: "In last year's Report it was observed that rheumatic affections very frequently followed in the train of the various fevers common in the Mediterranean, whether periodic or continued. The returns of this year confirm that observation in the strongest manner. The disease appeared in a large number of cases either as a direct sequela of fever, or it occurred in persons who had at some recent period suffered from febrile disease. It is a very prominent feature also in that peculiar form of cachexia which is liable to be begotten in the Mediterranean, and not unfrequently, in one form or another, it was the most decided symptom which that condition exhibited."

Even later, in 1872 (pp. 51, 52), we find "cases of continued fever with relapses. In no instance was fever attended by diarrhœa, or followed by tertian or quartan sequelæ. In all cases more or less obstinate constipation coexisted, with a white, flabby, indented tongue. No individual appeared in the slightest danger, and nourishment could always be given; but convalescence, even in the mildest cases, was very tediously protracted, and rheumatic sequelæ nearly invariably followed. In a few instances the curious form of muscular rheumatism referred to attracted attention; in four individuals the disease terminated favourably in an unusual form of orchitis. . . . In three the right testicle suffered; in one the left was attacked. Duration of cases 81, 51, 77, 136, 36, 131, 89, 94, 107, 103, 117, 78, etc., days." Such cases seem to have been similar to undulant fever cases of the present day.

1865-1866. The next articles, published in English, were those by Boileau and Chartres, also in the Army Medical Blue-Books, about 1865-66. The paper of the former professes "to contain only carefully-observed facts, faithfully set down"; and is based on 450 cases of "fever." While eliminating enteric fever and slight cases of febricula, he gives an accurate account of undulant fever, under the name of Mediterranean gastric remittent fever, together with reports of cases and temperature charts. He defines the disease as "a fever, most irregular in its course and most protracted in duration; characterised by dyspeptic symptoms; accompanied by profuse diaphoresis or sudamina; eventually and almost invariably ending in complete recovery. . . . Its alliance with the paroxysmal fevers appears to me very doubtful. It has not the characteristics of any of the intermittents or remittents that have ever been correctly described as such. There is no alternation of cold, hot, and sweating stages. It is as monotonous in its course as it is insidious and gradual in its onset. . . . There is not even an approach to the erratic forms of periodic fevers."

Chartres gives a detailed account of an epidemic of "Mediterranean gastric remittent fever," which attacked the 100th Regiment when quartered during the year 1866 in Verdala Barracks in Malta, a barrack to this day infested with this fever. The men attacked had an average service of 2·50 years in Malta, and seven in the army. The clinical and post-mortem details are undoubtedly those of undulant fever.

Guilia, the only modern Maltese physician who has written on the 1871.
subject, published in 1871 a short account of the fever locally, adding nothing, however, to previous reports.

In 1876, in the *Army Medical Report*, Donaldson describes the fever 1876.
as it prevailed at that time in Verdala Barracks; and during the same year Oswald Wood and Notter, army surgeons, published short descriptions of the fever in the *Edinburgh Medical Journal.*

In 1879, Surgeon-Major Veale, in the *Army Medical Report*, published 1879.
a paper, which, with those of Marston and Bruce, may be termed one of the three classics concerning undulant fever. He graphically describes the symptoms seen, at the Royal Victoria Hospital at Netley, in febrile relapses, occurring in cases which had been invalided home from Gibraltar, Malta, and Cyprus. Besides an accurate account of undulant fever, he draws a clear line of distinction between cases of this fever and cases of malarial fever from the Mediterranean and elsewhere.

Turner, on an experience of two years' practice in the Civil Hospital 1884.
at Gibraltar in 1884, endeavoured but very unsatisfactorily (as was pointed out by Professor Maclean in 1885) to prove the enteric nature of "Rock fever." He says that he was "led to believe that the bulk of the cases differ in no essential respect from enteric fever as it is met with in England and elsewhere; that although the mode of expression and the severity of the fever may be modified by surrounding influences, the extent of variation is not so great as would at first appear; and that the idea of a specifically distinct 'Rock fever' cannot be entertained." Though his clinical descriptions show that some of his cases may have been Rock or Mediterranean fever, the special cases he mentions in detail and one of his two post-mortem descriptions are undoubtedly accounts of enteric fever cases and of nothing else. As these cases of enteric fever are described by him as "a few samples of Rock fever," it is easy to see how the error arose. Enteric fever, unfortunately, is also an endemic disease in Gibraltar, but undulant fever is less prevalent there than in Malta.

With the exception of short articles more or less based on the papers already mentioned, little else of importance appears to have been published in England, until Bruce discovered the specific and causal
1887-1889. organism in 1886, to which the writer later gave the name of "Micrococcus Melitensis." In 1889 Bruce published in the *British Medical Journal* the first really detailed account of the fever. In the same year Moffet of Gibraltar described its prevalence in that place.

Since that time the disease has been recognised in England as a separate form of fever; and during the last three years it has been
1895-1896. given a place in such standard works as Quain's *Dictionary*, Allbutt's *System of Medicine*, and Davidson's *Hygiene of Tropical Diseases*, etc., and also in the 1896 edition of the *Nomenclature of Diseases.*

From the above account, and from a study of the literature of the subject, it will be seen that the isolation and description of undulant fever, and its acceptation as a separate and specific disease in England, and indeed on the Continent also, has been brought about, the author is proud to say, entirely by the exertions of various medical officers of the British Army [1] and Navy.

In Italy its existence was first definitely described by Tomasi in 1874, since which many observers have published accounts of the fever, among whom may be mentioned Copozzi, Rho and Galassi of Rome; Borelli, Fazio, De Renzi, and Rummo of Naples; and in Sicily, Tomaselli of Catania and Guiffré of Palermo. Other writers, there and elsewhere, are mentioned in the bibliography.

It is interesting to note that as early as 1879 Prof. Eugenio Fazio not only described this fever as it then occurred in Naples, but while referring its cause to insanitation (more particularly to sewer emanations), laid great stress on the distinct and specific nature of the disease, and on the probability of its proximate cause being some micrococcus or other microphyte ("micrococco, microfito," etc.)

There is therefore unimpeachable evidence that undulant fever existed in Malta in 1859, and was then established as an endemic disease. Moreover, the writings of Davy (1833-35), the similar character of the statistics of sickness and of the seasonal prevalence of continued fevers in Malta and Gibraltar as far back as 1817, and the tone of the medical reports of the fevers which prevailed in the Mediterranean during the whole of the present, and to a less definite extent during the last century, lead one to believe that this undulant fever probably has existed as an endemic disease in the Mediterranean (or at least in Malta and Gibraltar), as far back as the last century, if not a great deal longer. Whether the occupation of Malta by the French and then by the English caused any change in character of the prevailing fevers it is impossible to say. There has been, however, but

[1] See memorandum of sub-committee on classification in *Nomenclature of Diseases*, Royal College of Physicians of London, 3rd edit. 1896, p. xxv.: "In consequence, more especially, of representations made by officers of the Medical Department of the Army, Mediterranean or Malta fever has been admitted as a distinct disease."

little change in the nature of the inhabitants, as the natives were as now, Maltese; the garrison of the Knights of St. John being recruited from the various countries of Europe, north of the Mediterranean, were (from 1530-1798) strangers to the place. Their vows of celibacy also prevented the establishment of a residential alien population, which might have in time acquired a hereditary immunity. Moreover, the Order came to Malta from Crete, where the same fever exists, and individuals were constantly going backwards and forwards between Malta and the various Mediterranean ports where the fever is now endemic. The old buildings that they constructed in Malta, now utilised in many cases as barracks, have been during the English occupation the seats of the greatest and most regular prevalence of this fever since it has been recognised, and of "continued fevers" before that time. We know from documentary evidence that "fevers" prevailed in Malta during the middle and latter end of the last century.

From all accounts the sanitary condition of these buildings in the time of the Knights must have been terrible, whereas modern improvements have altered little of the stone or of the foundations originally used in their construction. Malta has never been in an independent position, but has for centuries been ruled by various alien races, and been a sort of half-way house in the Mediterranean. There is evidence to show that continued fevers existed there in the time of the Knights, and subsequently during the occupation by the French; and ample evidence that such fevers existed amongst both the natives and the English garrison, similar in character to those of the present day, but in greater abundance in proportion to the number of those present in the island. It seems highly improbable, therefore, that the introduction of undulant (and enteric) fever into Malta was reserved for the English, considering the greater facilities and opportunities that our predecessors possessed.

Geographical Distribution.—*Malta and Gibraltar.*—The author can state definitely, from personal observation, that undulant fever exists as an endemic disease in both these places; and that Rock fever and Malta fever are synonyms for the same disease. These facts are amply confirmed by the writings of Marston, Veale, Bruce, Moffet, and others, and by the similarity of symptoms of fever cases invalided to Netley Hospital from these two places.

Sardinia.—Dr. Luigi Zauda, quoted by Bruce, states that this fever is well known in Cagliari and elsewhere in the interior of the island. Guiffré also notes its occurrence.

Balearic Isles.—The writer has been informed on good and recent authority that this fever is endemic in Minorca. There was a large naval hospital at Port Mahon during the early part of the century, where cases of fever from the fleet, contracted in various parts of the Mediterranean, were treated. Fevers contracted at this place were described by Burnett (1800-1810) as being similar to those met with in

Malta.[1] Gaston Vuillier, describing Iviza, says: "Fever is endemic at Iviza. Besides such obvious causes as putrefying vegetable matter, stagnant water, filthy streets, drain gutters which are no better than open sewers, there is no doubt that the confined and sedentary life led by the people helps to foster epidemics."[2]

Italy.—Its occurrence in Rome is described by Capozzi, Galassi, Drummond, etc. In Naples by Borelli, Fazio, Capozzi, De Renzi, Rummo, etc. Guiffré states that it is endemic in Naples, and other places in the neighbourhood (Caserta, Benevento, Campobasso, etc.); and in middle and upper Italy (Rome, Ariccia, Terano, Fermo, Padua), with a frequency decreasing as the latitude increases towards the north. The fever became epidemic in Naples in 1872. Cardarelli described its occurrence in southern Italy (Cittanova) in 1879.

Sicily.—Tomaselli describes its common occurrence in Catania, where it prevailed in epidemic form in 1872, 1878, and in 1884. Guiffré states that it occurs as an endemic disease in Palermo and Catania, and is also to be met with in Taormina and other villages on the south side of Mount Etna. Prof. Cassiola also informed the author, when at Taormina, that this fever occurred at that place.

Greece.—Prof. P. Typhaldos (1882) describes a similar form of fever to be met with in Athens. Dr. G. Inglessis (of Naples), in 1882, stated that he had observed in Cephalonia cases of fever likely to be identical with "Neapolitan fever."

Turkey.—Guiffré mentions its occurrence in Constantinople and Smyrna. Dr. Paterson describes it as common in the former place. Dr. Moore, R.N., describes cases of fever similar to this contracted at Smyrna in 1872. Dr. Davids, of the German cruiser *Loreley*, quoted by Bruce, stated that he had the opportunity of observing fifteen cases of this fever at Constantinople and three at Smyrna.

Cyprus.—Dr. J. G. Carageorgiades, of Limasol, has published a small monograph on the subject, proving the existence of this endemic fever in the towns of Cyprus. Guiffré also mentions its occurrence. Malarial fevers are also met with.[3]

Crete.—Dr. A. Capetanakis, of Candia, reports that it has become frequent in occurrence in this place since 1880. Guiffré also quotes this place.

Jerusalem.—Dr. Thomas Chaplin, in 1864, described cases of fever in Jerusalem very like this undulant fever. He also gave a graphic account of the insanitary condition of the "Holy City," built, he says, upon the rubbish of 3000 years. Later, in 1885, he published a paper on cases of "Malarial Typhoid Fever" occurring in the same place, and appearing similar to undulant fever. It is, he says, uninfluenced or but

[1] See also Cleghorn (1744-1749).

[2] *Impressions of Travel in the Balearic Isles*, by Gaston Vuillier (trans. by Frederic Breton), London, 1897.

[3] See also Davidson's *Geographical Pathology*, Cyprus, p. 261 *et seq.*; Veale (1879); *Lancet*, 20th July and 8th December 1878; *Med. Times and Gazette* and *Health of the Navy* both for 1878; Heidenstein (1886); and Sullivan (1878).

slightly influenced by quinine or other drugs; severe and fatal cases last from 30 to 120 days, mild ones from 4 to 8 weeks; non-contagious and non-exanthematous; onset like enteric fever, but the course differing from that disease in the infrequent occurrence of diarrhœa and tympanites, the tendency for the temperature to run on for many weeks, and to show during the second month great diurnal ranges of temperature without there appearing to be much the matter with the patient. The temperature of one case is given, but though it is of an undulant fever character it is not of sufficient length to be of much value. Unfortunately he was unable to make any autopsies, so that his remark that "Peyer's glands are apparently not affected" is an unconfirmed surmise. He states that in this place both malarial and enteric fevers exist in their typical form, and that enteric fever attacking malarial subjects is proportionally modified, but that "malarial typhoid fever" is apparently a separate form of fever from these two. Whatever this fever is, it has the seasonal prevalence and many of the characteristics of undulant fever, and as Jerusalem is not an unlikely place in which to find the disease this evidence is valuable.

North Africa.[1]—The author has frequently been informed that cases of this fever occur in Alexandria, but has failed to gain reliable information on this point. Most of the cases prove to be relapses in men transferred from Malta, where they have suffered from the fever. Surgeon-Captain F. G. Morgan (1892), however, mentions a few instances of this fever attacking men in Alexandria who had not served previously in other parts of the Mediterranean.

Guiffré mentions its occurrence in Tunis and Algiers. Dr. Perini, from twenty years' experience in Tunis, informed Bruce that in 1879 he had the opportunity of observing the first case of this fever which occurred there. He further states that when the French occupation took place an epidemic of this fever broke out at Golletta, a muddy seaport in the vicinity, and that since that time it has become endemic. Bruce says: "This fever does not appear to be known at Tripoli." A Maltese doctor, with long experience in that place, had not met with the fever there. When visiting Benghasi and Derna, on the same coast, in 1893, the author failed to find evidence of its occurrence in these places, but at the same time evidence gained in such primitive places is unreliable.

Red Sea.—Dr. Hutchinson-Milnes states that he met with this type of fever at Suakim and Massowah, where it differed in no way from that met with in Malta, Naples, and Crete. Drs. Pasquale, Rho, and other Italian physicians, describe somewhat similar cases as occurring at Suakim and Massowah. Recent discussions in the medical journals on the subject of whether Aden is really malarious, point to the likelihood of this fever being endemic in that place.[2] Dr. Squire has also described

[1] In South Africa cases of typho-malarial fever were reported during the Zulu War, but without much foundation, *A. M. D. Report*, 1879, Appendix; also recently in Matabeleland, *Brit. Med. Jour.* vol. i. p. 1105, 1st May 1897.

[2] Surgeon-Major Colson, *Brit. Med. Jour.* vol. i. p. 1019; 1896.

cases of typho-malarial fever in Suakim in 1885, which might seem similar to undulant fever attacks elsewhere.[1]

France.—Jaccoud states that it is only met with in Paris as an imported disease in persons lately from Italy. The exact northern limits of the geographical distribution of this fever have yet to be fixed. From information the author has received from various towns on the French Mediterranean coast, and from Genoa, Venice, and Trieste, he is of opinion that the disease is not of common occurrence in these places, but is unable to either exclude or definitely confirm its existence in these latitudes.

China.—Fevers of a somewhat similar type have been described as occurring in Hong Kong by Durand-Fadel and Mitford-Atkinson. At a recent discussion on this subject, at the Royal Medico-Chirurgical Society, Dr. Patrick Manson said that he had probably seen cases in China similar to those described.[2] Army medical officers have met with cases in Hong Kong they consider similar to this fever. Prof. Wright, of Netley, has met with a case of continued fever from Hong Kong, which showed a serum reaction to the micrococcus Melitensis similar to that met with in the blood of cases of undulant fever from the Mediterranean.[3]

India.—In various reports upon the diseases of India we read accounts of cases of fever which, without being either malarial (paludic) or enteric in nature, have a certain clinical resemblance to both these diseases. Such cases are, however, unaffected by quinine. In the belief that they were caused by a combination of the malarial and enteric poisons in the human body at one and the same time, they have occasionally been termed "typho-malarial fever."[4] Many of these cases, in both India and Burmah, have a number of the clinical characteristics of this undulant fever. As the climatic and topographical conditions in many parts of India and Burmah are apparently suitable for the existence of this fever, it is worth while discussing the question that others may be led to go into the subject locally. Our reasons for believing in the possibility of its existence in these places may be briefly mentioned.

(1) These cases are described in published works either as anomalous forms of continued fever which can be placed under no definite type; as atypical enteric fever; or as typho-malarial fever, a disease which in the Mediterranean has proved to be undulant fever.[5] The clinical accounts of these cases are quite as much like undulant fever as those written in the Mediterranean before that fever became an established disease.

Thus Surgeon-General Moore, in his *Manual of the Diseases of India*, describes "undefined climatic fever." Such cases, he says, "begin like other fevers until the temperature rises to 101° or 102° F., from which period until the date of death or recovery is from a fortnight to three

[1] See also *Health of the Navy*, 1884, pp. 104-7.
[2] *Vide Brit. Med. Jour.* (18th April) vol. i. p. 973; 1896.
[3] *Lancet*, vol. i. p. 656; 1897.
[4] See back, section on nomenclature, typho-malarial fever.
[5] *Ibid.*

weeks ordinarily, occasionally shorter, but often much longer, extending even to 120 days. During this time there are always morning and evening variations, the range of temperature being sometimes as much as 9°, frequent but variable remissions, and often amelioration about every ninth day, when the appetite may return and the inexperienced be led to believe there is little the matter. . . . Thus, in the thermometric range the fever somewhat resembles remittent, in the duration of the febrile stage it most resembles typhoid, while in the tendency to periodical amelioration and the occasional abrupt cessation it simulates relapsing fever. . . . The disease may sometimes most resemble remittent, at others typhoid or relapsing, yet not be found fairly distinguishable as either, according to the dicta enunciated by the exponents of fever types, but yet a blurred image of all. Any complication or sequelæ which occur during or after any other phase of fever may be present during or after undefined climatic fever, but pneumonia is the most common complication."

See also Surgeon Lieut.-Colonel Crombie, I.M.S., in the presidential address at the recent Indian Medical Congress;[1] Dr. Mitra in the last number of the *Medical Annual;* Sir Joseph Fayrer in his work upon the *Climate and Fevers of India;* and Dr. P. Rho in 1894.

(2) In an account of two outbreaks of fever, by Marston, in 1879 (*Army Med. Reports*), one of true enteric fever at Ranikhet, the other, in close vicinity, of so-called remittent fever at Choubattia, we find accurate clinical and post-mortem accounts and temperature charts. The cases at Ranikhet were similar to enteric fever elsewhere.

As pointed out by the writer in 1892,[2] the clinical and post-mortem descriptions of those from Choubattia are indistinguishable (to one who has not actually seen the cases) from cases of undulant fever in Malta.[3] Squire mentions a similar occurrence at Dinapore, Lower Bengal, in the 70th Regiment in 1883.

(3) The writer has met with a case of acute fever, landed in Malta from a troopship homeward bound from India, which was said to be at the beginning of the second week of enteric fever (see Case 1). The disease had commenced seven days after leaving Bombay. Though many of the symptoms were severe and adynamic in character, they resembled those met with in severe undulant fever more than those of enteric fever. Quinine had no beneficial effect. The case proved fatal on about the fourteenth day of the disease. At the post-mortem examination twenty-four hours later no signs of enteric lesion were present, but the appearances were those met with in acute and fatal cases of undulant fever. Unfortunately the writer did not have an opportunity of making any bacteriological experiments, nor of examining the blood for malarial organisms.

Case 1.—*Case of fever, said to be of the Indian remittent type.*— Sergt. S., age 30, service 10 years. Admitted to hospital (10-11-1892)

[1] *Lancet*, vol. i. p. 187; 1896. [2] *Lancet*, vol. ii. p. 1265; 1892.
[3] See also remarks on these outbreaks by Squire in 1886.

on board ship soon after leaving Bombay, with fever of asthenic type. No abdominal symptoms or diarrhœa. Said to be due to residence in the climate of India. The case was diagnosed enteric fever, and transferred from the ship to Valetta Hospital, when passing Malta, in an adynamic condition (17-11-92). As the case progressed the symptoms became more grave and typhoid in character, but were not, in the opinion of the medical officers of the hospital, in keeping with the diagnosis of enteric fever. Delirium set in, and was succeeded by coma, and he died at 12.10 P.M. much cyanosed (24-11-92).

Treatment.—Milk, eggs, and beef-tea. Brandy. Ice to suck and externally to the head. Quinine without effect, antipyrin and salicylate of soda.

Post-mortem.—Twenty-four hours after. Body well nourished and covered by a good layer of adipose tissue. Heart 11·5 ounces, normal, but with much external fat. Lungs 19 and 20 ounces, with slight hypostatic congestion. Kidneys enveloped in fat, but normal. Liver and brain normal. Spleen very small, but soft and diffluent (rotten). Intestines normal, no congestion nor inflammation of Peyer's patches. Mesentery contained much fat.

Account extracted from the records of the hospital. Though the author was not in medical charge nor present at the post-mortem examination he had frequent opportunities of seeing the case up to the last moment; also the intestines and spleen were kept in spirit for his inspection.

(4) A large number of medical officers who have served in India and Burmah before coming to Malta have expressed decided opinions, when questioned by the writer, that many cases of fever they had met with in the former places were identical in nature with undulant fever. These had been returned as enteric fever, though in fatal cases the specific lesions had been absent from Peyer's patches, and in some instances the primary attack had been followed by as many as five relapses. For the powers of clinical observation of many of these medical officers the writer can vouch.

A medical officer, whose knowledge of clinical medicine is sound, wrote to the author in 1892 from Lucknow as follows:—

"I send you an assortment of charts. We get cases here evidently not malarial, which run on for weeks, which get very debilitated, lose flesh, hair, etc., but don't die. These sort of cases are not mentioned in any work. Quinine, arsenic, etc., have no effect, and they simply get well in process of time, and are rarely complicated. The senior medical officers generally call them enteric modified by malaria, and going on to malarial fever, but none of the juniors believe in this, but are of an opinion that they resemble 'Malta fever.' I have seen half a dozen cases of over 100 days' duration, and I now have a case of 79 days. He eats a most liberal diet and is very anæmic and thin, gets evening headache, but complains of nothing. He has been twice badly cinchonised, has taken enormous doses of arsenic, iron, and opium, but is none the better."

It is only right to mention also that other medical officers, in whom reliance can be placed, deny this resemblance between Mediterranean and Indian fevers, but these will generally be found to have served in different parts of India from those previously mentioned. India has, as we well know, a large variety of climates and topographical conditions in the million and a half square miles of its territory; and we must expect to find as many variations of disease prevalent. The existence or otherwise of this fever in India and Burmah is, however, a subject which is worthy of investigation.

(5) Lastly, but by no means of least importance, are the experiments recently carried out at Netley by Professor Wright and others.[1] They have obtained a serum reaction in relation to the micrococcus Melitensis, with the blood of cases of so-called enteric fever invalided from India (Subathu), the reaction being similar to that met with in cases of undulant fever invalided from the Mediterranean. Many of these cases, having had no previous Mediterranean service, suffered at Netley from febrile relapses, swollen testicles, etc., which symptoms were indistinguishable from those met with in cases of undulant fever.

America.—As we have drawn attention to the possibility of the existence of undulant fever in India, it is equally important for us to discuss the occurrence of certain types of fever which occur in America. These cases have been termed "typho-malarial fever" by Woodward (1876), Maurel (1879), Bartlett (1881), and Webb (1883). In the valley of the Mississippi they were called "malarial continued fever" by Maury (1881), who has published some interesting temperature charts. At the General Medical Congress (1893) at Washington, fevers occurring in Venezuela were described which Dr. Rho (1895) has compared with the fever of Malta and Gibraltar, as described by English military doctors. See also remarks by Stewardson (1841), Fife (1888), accounts of continued fever in the *Medical History of the War of Rebellion*, and in Davidson's *Geographical Pathology*.[2]

In the parts of America mentioned we again find a suitable climate for the existence of this fever, and without theorising further, would draw the attention of our American colleagues to these at present undefined forms of fever, which to a certain extent resemble this undulant fever.

BIBLIOGRAPHY

460-357 B.C. HIPPOCRATES. *Epidemics.* Translated by Adams, Syden. Soc. vol. i. London, A.D. 1849.

1709. BATES, T., Naval Surgeon. *An Enchiridion of Fevers incident to Seamen in the Mediterranean*, 2nd edition, London.

[1] *Brit. Med. Journal*, 1897, vol. i. p. 911. See also Freyer, Welch, and Macartney, 1897.

[2] Typho-malarial fever in the valleys of the Mississippi, Potomac, Ohio, and Chickahominy rivers, p. 830; Remittent fever, U.S.A., p. 829; Mountain fever by Koher of California, p. 833.

1712. TORTI. *Theraputiee spec. ad febres pernieiosas, periodicas, etc.* (Febbre subcontinua.)

1744-49. CLEGHORN, G., Army Surgeon. *Epidemical Diseases in Minorca.* London, 1751.

1763-87. DEMARCO, GUISEPPE, M.D. *Fasti Morborum Melitensis;* also *Disertatio Academica de Febre,* vol. xxxvi. MSS. Pub. Lib. Valetta; also *De Febribus Acutis,* May 25, 1786, vol. xxxvii. MSS. Pub. Lib. Valetta; also Inglott MSS. No. 2, 1722-1737, same library.

1786. HOWARD. *The Lazaretos of Europe,* Section on Malta, p. 58.

1798-1800. FAUVERGE, J. P., Chir. Major. *Des maladies qui ont règne à Malte, pendent le Blocus,* Paris, 1803. He also quotes ROBERT, "Mémoire sur la topographie physique et médicale de Malte . . . . parmi les troupes françoises," pub. in the 4th vol. of *Mémoires sur l'Egypte,* by Prof. Desgenettes, Paris, 1803.

1800-10. BURNETT, Sir W., M.D. *A Practical Account of Mediterranean Fevers.* London, 1816.

1810. IRVINE, W., M.D., Army Physician. *Observations upon Diseases in Sicily* (Continued Summer Fevers). London.

1816-25. HENNEN, J., M.D., Inspector of Mil. Hosp. *Medical Topography of the Mediterranean,* London, 1830; also quoted in Montgomery Martin's *History of the British Possessions in the Mediterranean.*

1820. BURN, G., Naval Surgeon. *De febre Mediterranea.*

1821. BAXTER, A., Military Surgeon. *De febre Remittente (Mediterranei),* Edin. Univ. Graduation Essays. Also CLARK, J., Military Surgeon, similar essay on same subject.

1824-35. DAVY, M.D., F.R.S., Insp.-Genl. *Notes on the Ionian Islands and Malta,* vol. ii. p. 262 *et seq.* *On the Fevers of Malta,* London, 1842. Also see *Diseases in the Army,* article on Malta, 1833-5, London, 1862.

1825-28. HEASTIE, A., Naval Surgeon. *Observations on Fever as it generally occurs along the Coasts of the Mediterranean and on Shipboard,* being Part ii. of a work on yellow and other fevers. Edin. 1830.

1836. MAILLOT. *Traite des fièvres, Ajaccio, Algiers, and Bona.* Paris. See also Boudin, 1842, and Bonnet, 1853.—CRAIGIE. *Elements of the Practice of Physic,* vol. i. 'Fevers." Edin.

1817-36. *Parliamentary Statistical Reports on the Diseases of the Army, including Mediterranean Stations.* London, 1840.

1830-36. SMYTH, Capt., R.N. *The Mediterranean.* London, 1854.

1830-36. } *The Health of the Navy.* Annual Parliamentary Return.
1856-95. }

1837-46. *Parliamentary Statistical Reports on the Sickness, Mortality, and Invaliding among the Troops in the Mediterranean, etc.* London, 1854.

1841. JOHNSON, J., M.D., and MARTIN, J. RANARD. *The Influence of Tropical Climates on European Constitutions,* 6th edit. pp. 390-399.—STEWARDSON, *American Journal* for April.

1849-59. *Parliamentary Report on the Sanitary condition of the Mediterranean Stations,* drawn up by Capt. Douglas Galton, R.E., and J. Sutherland, Esq., M.D., Including tables of fever prevalence. London, 1861.

1852. HASPEL, A. *Maladies de l'Algeria,* Paris. See also *Brit. and For. Med. and Chir. Gaz.* October, p. 349.

1856. LYONS and AITKEN. *Parliamentary Report on the Pathology of the Diseases of the Army in the East.*

1857. *Parliamentary Report on the Medical and Surgical History of the Crimean War,* vol. ii. part i. sect. vi.; also review in the *Brit. and For. Med. and Chir. Gaz.* for July.

1858. ARNAND. *Hist. méd. chir. de la guerre de Crimée.*—JACQUOT. *Du typhus de l'armée d'Orient.* Paris.

1860. CAZALAS. *Maladies de l'armée d'Orient.* Paris.

1859-95. *Army Medical Reports.* Published annually for the War Office by Harrison and Son, London.

1861. MARSTON, J. A., M.D., Assist. Surg., R.A. "Report on Fever (Malta)." *Army Medical Report,* pub. in 1863, vol. iii. p. 486.

1862. *Health of the Navy.* Parliamentary return, pp. 41 and 59.

1863. CASORATI. *Tratato delle febbri intermittenti.* Pavia and Milan. See also *Brit. and For. Med. and Chir. Gaz.* 1864, vol. ii. p. 34.

1864. CHAPLIN, T., M.D. "The Fevers of Jerusalem," *Lancet*, 27th Aug., 3rd Sept., and 10th Sept. *Syriac Fever*, vol. ii. pp. 236, 263, and 289, see on 1885.

1865. BOILEAU, J. P. H., Assist. Surg. 29th Regt. "Remarks on Fever in Malta, with Cases," *Army Med. Report*, pub. in 1868, p. 478.

1866. CHARTRES, Surgeon 100th Regt. "Gastric Remittent Fever," *Army Medical Report*, pub. in 1867, p. 527.—BACCELLI. *Delle febbri subcontinua*, Rome, and again in 1875 and 1894.—GUIDICI. *Sulla febbre tifoidea.* Torino.

1868. GRIESINGER. *Infectionskrank.* Italian edition pub. in Milan. *Delle malattie d'infezione*, p. 90 and seq.—DUTROULAN, A. F. *Traité des maladies des Europeans dans les Pays Chauds*, p. 15.

1870. BORRELLI, Prof. D. *Della febbre.* Napoli.

1871. GUILIA, G., M.D. "Sulle febbri Endemiche di Malta," *Il Barth, Gazzetta di Medicina*, No. 1, Lugio 25th. Malta.

1872. BORRELLI, D. "Della febbre a tipo intermittente," *Revista clin. di Bologna.*—GRIMALDI, G. *Sul tifo*, Napoli.—AITKEN, Sir W., M.D. *Practice of Medicine*, vol. i. p. 595 (Simple Continued Fever).—MOORE, Staff-Surgeon, R.N. *Health of the Navy*, p. 49.

1873. CANTANI, A. "Sull' Infezione da Malaria," *Lezione cliniche* (Qualunque febbre non-malarica), *vide Il Barth*, Nov. 15th, Malta.

1874. TOMASI, S. *Notarella sulla cura del tifo*, Morgagni.

1875. MACLEAN, Prof., C.B., M.D., I.M.S. "On Malta Fever, with a Suggestion," *Brit. Med. Journ.* vol. ii. p. 224, August.—TOMASI, S. *Nota sul tifo*, Morgagni.

1876. MACLEAN, Prof. (see above). "Sequel to a Note on Malta Fever," *Brit. Med. Journ.* vol. i. p. 190 (February).—WOOD, OSWALD, M.B., Surgeon, A.M.D. "Malta Fever," *Edin. Med. Journal* for July, xxii. p. 40.—NOTTER, LANE, B.A., M.S., D.P.H., Surgeon A.M.D. "On Malta Fever," *Edin. Med. Journal* for October, xxii. p. 289.—DONALDSON, J. Y., Surgeon-Major, A.M.D. "On the Diagnosis and Causation of Fæco-malarial Fever" (Malta), with note by Prof. Maclean, in *Army Med. Report*, published in 1879, p. 238.—DOMINICIS, N. *La febbre da fogna*, Napoli, 1876 and 1883 (v. pure il suo Trattato di Pathologia e Therapia speciale medicale, Napoli, 1887. p. 633).—WOODWARD. *Outlines of the Chief Camp Diseases; Typho-malarial Fever*, Philadelphia.

1877. BORRELLI. "La febbre di Napoli," *Rivista Clinica di Bologna*, No. 225, Argosto.

1878. AITKEN. "Malarial Fever at Rome," *Brit. Med. Journ.* April 27th, vol. i. p. 597.—CANTANI, A. *Intorno ad un caso di adeno-tifo*, Morgagni, p. 395.—SULLIVAN, J., M.D., F.R.C.P. "The Malarial Fevers of Cyprus," *Med. Times and Gazette*, vol. ii. p. 539, Nov. 9th.

1879. FRANCO, Dr. D. "Febbre di Napoli," *La Scuola Medica Napolitana*, fasc. 3, anno ii. See also *Giornale Internaz.* Naples, 1880.—VEALE, H., Surgeon-Major, M.D. "Remarks on the Cases of Fever from Cyprus, Malta, and Gibraltar, treated at Netley," *Army Med. Report*, vol. xxi. p. 260, published in 1881.—FAZIO, Prof. E. "Febbre napolitana," Associazione Naturalisti e Medici, 8 Maggio, *Movimento medico-chirurgico*, p. 239. Napoli.—MARSTON, J. A., Brig.-Surg., A.M.D. "Remarks on Enteric (and Remittent) Fever, Bengal," *Army Med. Report*, published in 1881, vol. xxi. p. 238.—MAUREL. "Typho-malarial Fever in the French Convict Settlement, Cayenne," *Gaz. hebd. de méd.* No. 4.—DURAND-FADEL. "Typho-malarial Fever in China," *Bull. de l'Acad. de méd. de Paris*, No. 5.

1880. CANTANI, A. *La diversita dei quadri clinici nelle malattie da infezione.* Also, *Un caso di adenotifo di difficile diagnosi*, Morgagni.

1881. RUMMO, G. *Una forma di febbre infettiva*, Napoli.—MAURY, R. B., M.D. of Memphis, Tennessee. "Fevers of the Mississippi Valley," *American Journal of Medical Sciences*, April, vol. clxii. art. 9.—BARTLETT. *History and Treatment of the Fevers of the United States of America.* Philadelphia, 1842, 1856, and 1881.

1882. CARAGEORGIADES, J. G., M.D. *Aletheia Journal*, January, No. 58, published in Limasol, Cyprus.—TYPHALDOS, Prof. P. "On Bilious Continued Fevers," *Galen*, Nos. 48-51, pp. 337-418; and in 1883 in Nos. 20, 21, pp. 305-330, published in Athens.—FAYRER, Sir J. *On the Climate and Fevers of India.* London.

1883. GALASSI, L. "Sulla considdetta febbre napolitana," *Rivista clinica e terapeutica.*—*El Genio Medico Quirurgico* for January 15th (Davidson).—INGLESSIS, G. *Galen* for April, p. 268, published in Athens.—WEBB. "Typho-malarial or Continued Malarial Fever," *American Journal of American Sciences* for April.

1884. TURNER, W., M.A., M.D. "On the Nature of the so-called Rock Fever of Gibraltar," *Practitioner* for April, vol. xxxiii. p. 305.—DE CHAUMONT, Prof., M.D. "Lecture on Military Hygiene," *Journal of the United Service Institution*, p. 762, London.—DE RENZI, E. "Sulle febbricola," *Rivista clinica e terapeutica;* and *Riforma Medica*, 1885, n. 165.

1885. MACLEAN, Prof., M.D., C.B. "The Fever of Malta and Gibraltar," *Practitioner* for January, xxxiv. p. 78.—CHAPLIN, T., M.D. "On Malarial Typhoid Fever" (Jerusalem), *Lancet* for September 19th (see **1864**, p. 31), vol. ii. p. 518.—CANTANI, A. "Ancora dell' ileo-tifo, della cosiddetta febbre napoletana," *Riforma medical*, n. 127.—CAPOZZI, D. "Della febbre tifoidea atipica," *Lezioni nel Medico practico contemporaneo*, 1885-1887.—FEDERICI, C. "Sulla febbre miliare di Palermo," *Sperimentale*, 1885, ii.—GALASSI, L. "Della febbre napoletana o febbricola del Prof. de Renzi," *Sperimentale* 1885, ii.—JACCOUD, S. *Leçons de clinique médicale*, 1883-84. Paris, Delahaye et Lecrosnier.—LEPIDI-CHIOTI, G. *Sulla cosiddetta miliare di Palermo*, Morgagni.—CRAIG. "Rock Fever," *Lancet* for November 28th, vol. ii. p. 1028.—HIRSCH. *Handbook of Geographical and Historical Pathology*, New Syd. Soc. vol. i. p. 620 (Typho-malarial Fever).

1886. MOORE, W. J., Surg.-Genl., C.I.E. *Manual of Diseases of India*, 2nd edit. p. 275 ("Undefined Climatic Fever"). See also editions of 1841, p. 145 ("Rheumatism").—TOMASELLI, S. "La febbre continua epidemica dominante in Catania dal settembre 1878, all' Aprile 1879," *Negli Atti del' Accademia Gioenia*, vol. xiv. 1879, 3rd edit. 1886, 4th edit. 1895.—JACCOUD, S. *Leçons d'overture*. Paris, Delahaye et Lecrosnier.—HEIDENSTEIN, M.D. "Cyprus Fevers" in *Colonial Report for Mediterranean*, No. 23 (Carageorgiades and Davidson).—SQUIRE, J. E., M.D., F.R.C.P. "Typho-malarial Fever," *Transactions Epidemiological Soc. London*, vol. vi. p. 24. Also *Lancet* for January 1887 (abstract).

1887. JAGOE, H., Surg.-Major. "Notes on Enteric and Typho-malarial Fever," *Lancet*, vol. i. p. 119, Jan. 15th.—BRUCE, D., Surg.-Captain, M.D. "Note on the Discovery of a Micro-organism in Malta Fever," *Practitioner* for September, xxxix. p. 161.

1888. BRUCE, D. "The Micrococcus of Malta Fever," *Practitioner* for April, xl. p. 241.—DUNCAN, A., Surg.-Major, I.M.S. *The Prevention of Disease in Tropical Climates* (Typho-malarial Fever), London.—DRUMMOND, E., M.D. "Fever at Rome," *Practitioner* for October, vol. xli. p. 256.—DE BLASI. "Le febbri continue epidemiche di Palermo," *Giornale della R. Accademia di Medicina di Torino*, Nos. 4 and 5.—GUIFFRÉ, L. *Sulle febbri continue epidemiche, etc.*, Torino, Ermanno Læscher.—FIFE. *Report of the 51st Ann. Sess. Med. Soc. of Tennessee.—Medical and Surgical History of the War of Rebellion*, Part III. vol. i. pub. at Washington.

1889. BRUCE, D. "Observations on Malta Fever," *Brit. Med. Jour.* 18th May (also leading article in same), vol. i. p. 1101; *Riforma Medica*, 1° semestre, p. 811.—SINCLAIR, J., Surg.-Genl. "Diseases Prevalent in Malta," *Brit. Med. Jour.* 5th January, vol. i. p. 9.—MOFFET, G. E., Surg., A.M.S., M.B., C.M. "Notes on the Endemic Fever of Gibraltar," *Army Med. Report*, pub. in 1891, xxxi. p. 403.—PASQUALE. "On the Fevers occurring at Massowah," *Giorn. Med. del R. esercito R. Marina, Maggio, e giugno. Ibidem*, luglio 1891. Also quotes Fiorani, 2° semestre 1885; marzo 1886; Panara, maggio 1886; Rho, dicembre 1886; Cognetti, luglio 1887; Barbatelli, ottobre 1888.—DE CONCILIIS. "Contributo allo studio della febbri climatiche di Massaua," *Ibidem*, febbraio 1889.—KELSCH and KIENER. *Traité des maladies des pays chauds*. Paris.

1890. BRUCE, D., Assist. Prof., Netley. "On the Etiology of Malta Fever," *Army Med. Report*, pub. in 1892, vol. xxxii. p. 365.—GIPPS, A. G. P., Surgeon, R.N. "On Malta Fever," *Trans. of the Epidemiological Society of London*, vol. ix. p. 76.—ELLIS, H. M., Staff-Surgeon, R.N. *Note in Naval Annual Report*, p. 41.—BOZZOLO, C. Communication to the International Congress of Berlin.

1891. CHANTEMESSE. Article in vol. i. *Traité de médecine*, Charcot, Bouchard, and Brissaud. Paris.—GODDING, C. C., Staff-Surgeon, R.N. "Malta (Remittent) Fever," *Brit. Med. Jour.* 16th May, vol. i. p. 1065.—BRUCE, D. "Note on Malta Fever," a criticism of the last in *Brit. Med. Jour.* of 13th June, vol. i. p. 1281.—CARAGEORGIADES, J. G., M.D. *Cyprus Fever or Febris Complicata*. Limasol, Cyprus.—RHO. "Delle febbre predominanti a Massaua," *Riv. Clin. Arch. Ital. di clin. med. puntata* 2° 1891.—MARAGLIANO. "Febbre simulanti la febbre Typhoidea e Genova," *Riforma Medica*, 1891, ii. p. 181 (Guiffré).

1892. PASQUALE. See **1889**, p. 32, and *Lancet*, 25th May 1892.—MILNES, H., M.D., R.N. "Note on the Fevers prevalent on the Shores of the Mediterranean and Red Seas," *Lancet*, 18th June, vol. i. p. 1359.—OLIVER, T., M.D., F.R.C.P. "Danubian (?) Fever," *Lancet*, 18th August, vol. ii. p. 361.—BOND, C. Knox. "Danubian Fever," *Lancet*, 27th August, vol. ii. p. 507.—HUGHES, M. LOUIS, Surg.-Captain A.M.S. "Investigations into the Etiology of Mediterranean Fevers," *Lancet*, 3rd December, vol. ii. p. 1265.—PETELLA. "Le febbri climatiche de Massaua," *Giorn. Med. del R. esercito e R. Marina*, Agosto, and Suttembre.—DAVIDSON. *Geographical Pathology*, Edin. (section on Spain and Gibraltar) vol. i. p. 198.—MORGAN, F. T., Surg.-Capt. A.M.S. "Notes on the Fevers of Alexandria," *Army Med. Report*, pub. 1894, vol. xxxiv. p. 380.

1893. BRUCE, D. "Sur une nouvelle forme de fièvre rencontrée sur les bords de la Mediterranée," *Annales de l'Institut Pasteur*, avril, vol. vii. p. 289.—HUGHES, M. LOUIS. "Sur une forme de fièvre fréquente sur les côtes de la Mediterranée," *Annales de l'Institut Pasteur*, aout, vol. vii. p. 628, and in *Riforma Med.* vols. i. and iii.—*Idem.* "Natural History of Mediterranean Fevers," *Medit. Naturalist*, Jan. Feb. and March, vol. ii. No. 20, p. 299, No. 21, p. 325, and No. 22, p. 332.—BRUCE, D., HUGHES, M. LOUIS, and WESCOTT, SINCLAIR. "Notes on Mediterranean or Malta Fever," *Brit. Med. Jour.* of 8th July, vol. ii. pp. 59 to 62.—BRUCE, HUGHES, and FAZIO. "La febbre mediterranea e la febbricola nostrana," *Rivista internazionale d'igiene*, Octobre, No. 10, p. 394; also *Riforma Medica*, Nos. 1 and 3, Napoli.—GUIFFRÉ, L., and SILVA, B. "Febbre Mediterranea, pseudo-tifo," *Trattato di Medicina di* Charcot, Bouchard, and Brissaud, 22° del, vol. i. Paris and Milan.—BRUCE, D. "Malta Fever," article in Davidson's *Hygiene and Diseases of Warm Climates*, Edin. p. 1265.—KLEIN, E., M.D., F.R.S. "Malta Fever," article in the *Treatise on Hygiene and Public Health*, by Stevenson and Murphy, vol. ii. p. 170.

1894. BACCELLI. "La subcontinua tifoide," 1875, republished 1894 in *Le scuole ital. di clin. medica*, Milano, vol. i. p. 138.—MITFORD-ATKINSON. "The Malarial Fevers of Hong Kong," *Lancet*, 28th April, vol. i. p. 1054.—MACARTNEY, J., M.D., Surg.-Col. "Mediterranean Fevers," letter to the *Brit. Med. Jour.* 16th June, vol. i. p. 1332.—HUGHES, M. LOUIS. "The Diagnosis between Enteric Fever and the Remittent Fever of the Mediterranean," *Medical Magazine* for August, vol. iii. No. 2, p. 152; *Brit. Med. Jour.* 28th July, etc.—BRUCE, D. Article in Quain's *Dictionary of Medicine*, vol. ii. p. 10, "Malta Fever."—RHO, F. *Sguardo Generale sulla Patologia di Massua, etc.*, Rome, Tipografia Nazionale di G. Bertero, Via Umbria (especially note appendix).—RHO, F. "Delle febbri tifoidee atipiche e della cosiddetta febbre tifomalarica," *Sperimentale*, fasc. 28° and 29°, anno xlviii. p. 545.—*American Journal of Medical Science* for September.

1895. CROMBIE, Surg.-Lt.-Col., I.M.S. Presidential Address, Indian Medical Congress, *Lancet*, 9th Jan. vol. i. p. 187.—HUGHES, M. LOUIS. "The Fevers of India and the Mediterranean," *Lancet*, 2nd March, vol. i. p. 574.—CLIMO, H., Surg.-Col., A.M.S. "Malta Fever in relation to Local Sanitary Conditions and the Hermite Process," *Lancet*, 18th June, vol. i. p. 1510.—RHO, F. "Malattie predominanti nei paesi caldi e temperati," *Annali di Medicina Navale.* Rome.—*International Medical Magazine*, vol. iii. p. 740.

1896. MITRA, M. C., M.A., M.D. "Indian Remittent Fever," *Medical Annual.* Bristol.—HUGHES, M. LOUIS. "The Endemic Fever of the Mediterranean," *Trans. of the Royal Med. and Chir. Society, London*, 14th April, vol. lxxix. p. 279.—*Nomenclature of Diseases*, drawn up by a committee appointed by the Royal College of Physicians of London, 3rd edit., 17(a).—HUGHES, M. LOUIS. "Undulant (Malta) Fever," *Lancet*, 25th July, vol. ii. pp. 239 and 518.—STERNBERG, M.D., LL.D. Note on "Malta Fever" in a *Text-book of Bacteriology*, pp. 528 and 597; see also *American Year-Book of Medicine and Surgery*, p. 53.

1897. WRIGHT, A. E., Prof., M.D., and SEMPLE, Surg.-Major, A.M.S. "Note on the Technique of Serum Diagnosis of Acute Specific Fevers," *Brit. Med. Journ.* 16th Jan. vol. i. p. 139; also 30th Jan. vol. i. p. 258; also "On the Employment of Dead Bacteria in the Serum Diagnosis of Typhoid and Malta Fevers," *Ibid.* 15th May, vol. i. p. 1214.—JACCOUD, Prof. "De la typhoïde sudorale," Clinique médicale, Hôpital de la Pitie, *La Semaine médicale*, Février 10, 1897, 17° année, No. 6.—WRIGHT, A. E., Prof., M.D., and SMITH, F., Surg.-Capt., A.M.S. "On the Application of the Serum Test to Differential Diagnosis of Typhoid and Malta Fevers," *Lancet*, 6th March, vol. i. p. 656; also "A Note on the Occurrence of Malta Fever in India," *Brit. Med. Jour.* 10th April, vol. i. p. 911.—MACLEOD, G. E. "Case of Purpura Hæmorrhagica following

Malta Fever," *Lancet*, 22nd May, vol. i. p. 1410.—FREYER, Surg.-Major, A.M.S. "Occurrence of Malta Fever in India," *Brit. Med. Jour.* 22nd May, vol. i. p. 1319.—NOTTER, Prof. LANE, A.M.S. Article in *A New System of Medicine*, Clifford Allbutt, F.R.S., London.—MACARTNEY, J., Brig.-Surg.-Lt.-Col., A.M.S. "On the Occurrence of Malta Fever in India," *Brit. Med. Jour.* 29th May, vol. i. p. 1384.—"Mediterranean Fever in Gibraltar," *Brit. Med. Jour.* 29th May, vol. i. p. 1381.—WELCH, Surg.-Col., A.M.S., F.R.C.S. "The Occurrence of Malta Fever in India," *Brit. Med. Jour.* vol. i. p. 1512, 12th June.—GROCCO. "Sul decorso della febbre nelle infezione tifoidea," *Settimana med. dello sperimentale*, Jan. 9th and 16th.

CHAPTER II

Etiology.—Bacteriology: Discovery of a micrococcus; its isolation from the tissues after death; Method of isolation; Description of the micrococcus; Inoculation experiments on animals; Pathogenic nature of micrococcus.—*Predisposing Causes.—Method of propagation and dissemination:* Non-contagious; Elimination of such causes as inoculation, polluted aqueduct or well water, milk, mineral waters, grog-shop and canteen drinks, ice, and food; Discussion of fæcally polluted air as a cause, in connection with insanitation; Extracts from authors; Factors usually present; Examples of outbreaks connected with insanitation; Fæcal pollution of harbour water as a suggested cause; Non-fæcal telluric exhalations and dust considered in relation to cause; Micro-organisms in air; Soil zones; Micro-organisms in sewer gas; Effects of climatic conditions upon prevalence; Drainage of Valetta; Air-borne enteric fever; Reaction of fæcal matter, Difficulty with plate cultivations; The cesspit populations of Malta; Mode of entrance into the human subject.—*Age and sex.—Incubation period.—Seasonal prevalence.—Influence of rainfall and temperature.— Immunity from subsequent attacks considered.—Changes in type (quantitative and qualitative):* Need for statistics to cover a sufficiently long period; Rumoured increase in prevalence since 1885 discussed; Difference between urban and rural prevalence; Its limited occurrence in Gozo; Recent increase in the number of susceptible persons exposed to infection; A discussion on the past military statistics for simple continued and remittent fevers, the only available ones procurable, which deal with the past prevalence of this fever.

Bacteriology.—Although undulant fever has existed in the Mediterranean as an endemic disease for so many years, it was not until 1886 that a micro-organism was discovered, to the effects of which the phenomena of this disease could be attributed. This has been owing partly to the fact that naval and military medical officers are seldom long enough in one place to be able to undertake scientific investigations; partly that early post-mortem examinations are rarely attainable by civilian medical men, on account of the religious tenets of the nations inhabiting the Mediterranean littoral; and partly on account of the comparatively recent date of recognition of this disease as a separate and specific form of fever.

The discovery of this micro-organism at Malta was the result of the researches of Surgeon-Major David Bruce, A.M.S., since Assistant-Professor of Pathology in the Army Medical School at Netley.

In a case of this fever, which died on the 15th day of the disease, Bruce found, nine hours after death, in splenic sections, "enormous numbers of single micrococci" scattered through the tissues. This led him to believe that a micrococcus might be the cause of this fever, and in May of the following year (1887), with Dr. Carruana Sccluna, he made between thirty and forty inoculations into sterilised agar-agar with blood aseptically taken from the fingers of ten cases of this fever, but without result. One of these cases, however, proved fatal, and less than one hour after death eight tubes of agar-agar were inoculated with the usual precautions. These were kept at the temperature of the air (25° C.) for 16½ hours, after which six were placed in an incubator at 37° C. Colonies of a micro-organism, which the writer has called the Micrococcus Melitensis, appeared in all the tubes; in those placed in the incubator sixty-eight hours after inoculation, but in the remaining two tubes not until after 168 hours.

In his next case Bruce was unable to make an autopsy, but seven hours after death, by means of a sterilised trochar and canula, he obtained some splenic pulp with which he inoculated six tubes of agar-agar. In four of these tubes, placed next morning in the incubator, colonies of the micrococcus Melitensis appeared in eighty-four hours. In one tube kept at the temperature of the air, but somewhat higher than in the preceding instance, the same micrococcus appeared in 110 hours, while the remaining tubes proved contaminated. In his fourth case of six tubes of agar-agar inoculated directly from the spleen and placed at once in the incubator, colonies of the same micrococcus appeared in sixty-seven hours in four of the tubes, the remaining two proving contaminated.

The next case gave positive results in all six tubes inoculated, in ninety-seven hours—the greater length of time being accounted for by the fact that the gas burner of the incubator was accidentally turned out for twenty-four hours. These growths were cultivated through generations of pure cultures. A fragment of fresh splenic pulp, in sterilised water and × 500 diams., showed "the field of the microscope literally crowded with myriads of micrococci dancing in about in the most active manner."

The sixth case was somewhat peculiar (see on p. 171, Chapter IV.) and out of six tubes inoculated from the spleen, liver, and kidneys, and kept at a temperature of 25° C., but one contained a growth, and that not until after 336 hours. Bruce, however, states: "This growth was subjected to a most rigorous examination microscopically and by staining reactions, with the result that I fully convinced myself of its identity with the micrococcus of Malta fever."

Details of the above cases may be found in the *Practitioner* for September 1887 and April 1888.

Three more cases, in which this micrococcus was obtained from the spleen after death, were published by Bruce in the *Annales de l'Institut Pasteur*, in 1893, making nine cases in all.

In 1890, Surgeon Gipps, R.N., described two cases in the *Trans. of the Epidemiological Society*, in which he believed that he had isolated a similar micrococcus, of which he gives a drawing. He does not appear, however, to place much confidence in its causal connection with the disease.

In 1891 Bruce was able in two cases to cultivate the micrococcus from blood aspirated from the spleen during life.

In one fatal case only did Bruce (in 1891) fail to obtain the characteristic micrococcus. This was subsequently proved to be due to the excessive alkalinity of the culture media. Colonies subsequently obtained by the writer from other cases refused to grow on this alkaline agar.[1]

In 1891 the writer began to work at the bacteriology of this fever, since which time he has been able to cultivate artificially, from the spleens of fourteen fatal cases of undulant fever after death, pure colonies of a micrococcus similar in every respect to that discovered by Bruce. In no cases has the micrococcus been absent.

DETAILS OF FOURTEEN CASES

Case 2.—Illustrating a fatal result during a relapse.—Admitted 27th July 1891. Age 22; service two years. Previous health good. Admitted with the usual febrile symptoms, onset being sudden. On the 10th day the symptoms partook of a typhoid character, the tongue became dry and brown, the pulse quick and feeble, the abdomen tympanitic, there was also subsultus tendinum and abundant crops of sudamina. This continued until the 24th day, when he began to improve, the disease being characterised by constipation and rheumatic symptoms to the end, whereas from the 13th to the 26th day there had been a tendency to diarrhœa. From the 40th to the 45th day there was an apyrexial period, after which there was a severe relapse. The condition gradually became worse, tympanites set in and was a prominent symptom. There were signs of hypostatic congestion at the bases of the lungs at the back. He died much exhausted, at 2.30 A.M., on the 73rd day of the disease. The pyrexial curve was similar to that of Case 3, except that the first or primary wave lasted 39, and the second (fatal) wave 27 days.

Treatment.—No solid food; stimulants, antipyrin, salicylate of soda, diaphoretics. Quinine in various doses from two to fifteen grains three times a day.

Though not in clinical charge of the case, the writer had constant opportunities of visiting it during life, and there was no doubt as to the diagnosis of undulant fever. At the post-mortem examination four hours after death, six army and three civilian medical officers were present, who all confirmed the diagnosis. The body was fairly well nourished and the heart normal. The lungs showed some hypostatic congestion of both bases, with sero-purulent exudation in the bronchioles.

[1] See Davidson's *Diseases of Warm Climates*, p. 267; and *Army Medical Report* for 1890, published in 1892, vol. xxxii. p. 365.

Liver weighed 74 ounces, was slightly fatty. Kidneys normal. Spleen, 12 ounces, enlarged and dark, but firm in texture. Stomach and duodenum normal; the jejunum had a patch of congestion, 4½ inches long, a foot below the duodenum. The ileum, Peyer's patches, and the solitary glands were all normal. In the large intestine the cæcum was normal, but just below this for one foot in extent, and again for six inches at the upper part of the sigmoid flexure, were patches of congestion and exudation. There was no sign of ulceration along the whole extent of the alimentary tract.

Experiment.—The spleen was removed as aseptically as possible, and without tearing its capsule, at once wrapped in a towel soaked in a solution of perchloride of mercury, and removed to the laboratory. There three cuts were made in the spleen with three sterilised knives, each cut being through and at right angles to the plane of the preceding one. The innermost cut being used for inoculation purposes, the cuts being allowed to fall together between each operation. Three tubes of agar-agar were inoculated by a small drop of blood removed on a sterilised platinum ooze, two tubes were at once placed in the incubator at 99° F., and one left at the temperature of the air (about 75° F.) Characteristic colonies of the micrococcus Melitensis appeared in both the tubes placed in the incubator after 124 hours, but the tube left at the temperature of the air remained sterile. These growths were passed through six generations of pure cultures on agar-agar and were used for inoculation of monkeys. One primary and two secondary cultures forwarded to Bruce at Netley were identified by him as the same micro-organism that he had found.

Case 3.—Was somewhat similar in character, proving fatal during a relapse, on the 54th day of the disease. (For details and chart see Chapter III.)

Cover-glass preparations of fresh splenic substance showed micrococci here and there. Three tubes of nutrient agar-agar were inoculated from the spleen with the same procedure as in the last case, and were placed in the incubator at 99° F. Characteristic growths appeared in every tube within 120 hours from inoculation.

Case 4.—A malignant one, proved fatal on the 23rd day from hyperpyrexia. He was the only fatal case that occurred in the epidemic mentioned on p. 59. At post-mortem examination the lungs were found to be much congested at the bases, the spleen congested, friable, and weighing 15 ounces, the liver congested, but Peyer's patches and the mesenteric glands normal. Inoculations were made in broth and on agar-agar; characteristic colonies appearing on the seventh and sixth days respectively at 99° F.

Case 5.—Also a malignant case in a delicate subject which proved fatal from cardiac failure on the 12th day. At the post-mortem there were mitral vegetations with fatty degeneration and infiltration of the heart. The spleen weighed 13 ounces and was extremely congested, liver enormously enlarged (88 ounces), but Peyer's glands and the mesenteric glands normal. The spleen was removed one hour after death, and three tubes of agar-agar inoculated, characteristic growths appearing on the fifth day at 99° F.

Case 6.—Died on the 18th day of continuously high pyrexia in a comatose condition. At the post-mortem examination seven hours after death the lungs showed basal congestion, the liver (73 ounces) was congested and friable, the spleen (21 ounces) was almost in a state of liquefaction, its substance breaking up on the slightest pressure. The mesenteric glands were slightly enlarged, but Peyer's patches were normal. The great gut for 18 inches, including the cæcum, was deeply congested, somewhat swollen and thickened, and the solitary glands were prominent. Characteristic growths were obtained from the spleen on agar-agar in five days.

Case 7.—Died of collapse, vomiting and exhaustion on the 35th day of the disease, the temperature having fallen the day before death only to rise again. After death the bases of the lungs and the spleen (18 ounces) were found to be congested; the mesenteric glands slightly enlarged, but Peyer's patches and the intestines normal. Characteristic growths on agar-agar were obtained from the spleen in 130 hours at 99° F. (See Chapter III.)

Case 8.—Died of heart failure and pericardial effusion on the 19th day of a very remittent case, see on p. 144. This and the preceding case are mentioned in the instances of outbreaks. After death the lungs showed lobular consolidation of the lungs, the spleen (12 ounces) congested, the liver nutmeg, and the heart with mitral vegetations; Peyer's patches and the mesenteric glands normal. The micro-organism was visible in cover-glass specimens of splenic substance, and was obtained from the spleen on agar-agar in pure growths on the 6th day. (See Chapter III.)

Case 9.—Died of hyperpyrexia on the 24th day of continuously high pyrexia, after admission to the hospital. After death there was basal congestion of both lungs, the spleen (12 ounces) was congested, the large gut much congested, the mesenteric glands slightly enlarged, but Peyer's patches normal. One hour after death the micro-organism was visible in cover-glass preparations of fresh splenic substance, and characteristic growths were obtained on agar-agar on the 5th day.

Case 10.—A long case with short undulations (see Chart No. XVII.) died of sudden hyperpyrexia on the 57th of the disease. After death the lungs were œdematous and congested at the bases; the liver (80 ounces) intensely congested; spleen (11 ounces) congested, but firm; mesenteric glands and Peyer's patches normal. Micrococci visible and growths obtained as in the last case. (See Chapter III.)

Case 11.—A somewhat unique case, was admitted to hospital for three weeks' fever, and then discharged apparently cured. Four months afterwards he was again admitted with fever of a typically intermittent character, which proved fatal from cardiac failure on the 154th day of this attack. After death the heart was flabby, there was a small aneurysmal dilatation above the posterior left semilunar valve, and all three of these valves had vegetations on them. There was much serous fluid in the pleural cavities, the bases of the lungs being congested and œdematous. The liver (76 ounces) was nutmeg, the spleen (14 ounces) congested, but Peyer's patches, the mesenteric glands, and intestines were normal. Six tubes inoculated from the spleen all showed characteristic growths on the 6th day.

Case 12.—Died of hyperpyrexia on the 24th day of acute fever. After death there was considerable congestion of the bases of both lungs; the liver was nutmeg; the spleen (14 ounces) engorged with venous blood; there were patches of congestion here and there in the intestines, most marked in the colon. Peyer's patches and the mesenteric glands were normal. Characteristic colonies were obtained from the spleen as in the other cases.

Case 13.—Had served for three years in Gibraltar and for five months in Malta. He died suddenly of cardiac failure, after a slight mental excitement, on the 111th day of the disease. At the post-mortem examination warty vegetations were found on the mitral valve, there were recent pleuritic adhesions at the base and posterior parts of the right lung, the lower lobe of which was consolidated. The spleen (15·5 ounces) was congested, soft and friable, the liver congested. The kidneys showed the characteristic appearances of "large white kidney." The intestinal walls were attenuated, but were otherwise healthy. The spleen was removed three hours after death, and from it characteristic growths were obtained, while sections were made of portions of the different organs. (See Chapter III.)

Case 14.—Died somewhat suddenly, on the 62nd day of the disease, of effusion into the pericardium, during a relapse, and after his temperature had been normal for 17 days. (For details see on p. 145.) At the post-mortem examination 17 ounces of fluid were found in the pericardium, the right pleura was obliterated by organised lymph, the right lung œdematous and congested, the liver nutmeg, the spleen (15 ounces) congested, but the intestines, Peyer's patches, and the mesenteric glands normal. Characteristic growths were obtained from the spleen on the fifth day after inoculation. (See Chapter III.)

Case 15.—Died on the 117th day from cerebral symptoms. (For details see under nervous symptoms, Chapter III.) Characteristic growths were obtained from the spleen and brain.

These cases, together with those of Bruce and Gipps, make altogether twenty-five instances in which this micrococcus has been successfully isolated from the spleens of fatal cases of undoubted undulant fever. From the clinical symptoms and post-mortem appearances met with in this fever, the spleen, in the last case the brain, and in other cases the kidney, are, moreover, the places where it might be expected to be present. No other micro-organism has been found present under similar circumstances, nor has a similar organism been found present in the tissues of fatal cases in Malta, which have died from causes other than undulant fever. Thus Bruce states[1] that the micrococcus Melitensis was absent in several cases of enteric fever, dysentery, tuberculosis, pneumonia, and other diseases in which he sought for it. The writer has isolated from the spleens of nine fatal cases of enteric fever occurring in Malta pure cultivations of Eberth's bacillus; but in no case was there present any organism at all similar to the micrococcus Melitensis.

The micrococcus has not been isolated from the blood of cases suffering from this fever, a condition met with in enteric fever (Roux in Epitome, *British Medical Journal*, May 23rd 1896, vol. i. p. 84, also Stern, Jan. 15th, 1897, vol. i. p. 9, etc.). The writer has not sought for it in the kidney of man, but it has been isolated from this organ by Bruce once (see *Pract.* vol. xl. p. 244). The organism has been twice isolated from the spleen during life.[2] In only one case has it appeared absent from the spleen, when sought for after death, and in this case there existed ample reason for the failure in isolation of the micro-organism artificially, even if it had been present in great quantity.[3]

It would therefore appear to be reasonable for us to believe that this micro-organism is invariably present in the spleen, and possibly other organs, of cases suffering from undulant fever.

Method of procedure.—The following procedure has been adopted in obtaining the micro-organism from the spleen (or other organ) after death. A clean towel is first soaked in a solution of corrosive sublimate (1 in 1000), wrung out, and doubled over once. This doubled towel is folded three times upon itself and placed on a plate, previously washed with the same solution. After rendering the hands aseptic, a median incision is made with sterilised instruments in the cadaver, as soon after death as practicable, through the abdominal wall from the ensiform cartilage to the left of and a little below the umbilicus. The hand is thrust into the abdominal cavity (the operator standing on the cadaver's right and using the right hand), and passed along the inner surface of the abdominal wall to the spleen. This organ is then firmly grasped and brought forward and through the opening in the abdomen, any adhesions being easily broken down by the fingers. The vessels are then severed, and the spleen at once placed within the folded towel and conveyed to the laboratory. Inoculations have not often been made in the dead-house on account of the impurities present in the air, and the absence of the various adjuncts suitable for such experiments; but with the aid of a spirit lamp they can and have been so conducted on two occasions.

Three incisions are now made in the spleen by means of a pair of forceps and three new knives, which have not been used for such a purpose before, and which have been previously sterilised in the naked flame of a Bunsen burner. The first incision is made vertically, longitudinally, and to one side of the middle line, through the splenic substance. The second horizontally through the plane of, and at right angles to the first cut, and in the direction of and through the middle

[1] *A.M.D. Report*, 1890. [2] See Davidson (art. by Bruce), 1893, p. 267. [3] See back.

line of the organ. The third is made vertically through the middle of the plane of the second. Each cut is made with a freshly sterilised and different knife. The centre of the third cut at some distance from the capsule is used for inoculation purposes. A drop of splenic blood is taken in the loop of a sterilised ooze and transferred to the broth or to the surface of the nutrient agar-agar in the usual way. The surface of the cuts in the spleen are allowed to fall together and the ooze is sterilised between each inoculation, so as to be exposed to accidental contamination as little as possible. The inoculated tubes are then placed in an incubator at 99°-100° F. When the tubes are inoculated, cover-glass smears may be made by taking a cover-glass, previously cleaned in alcohol, with a pair of forceps and lightly touching the surface of the inner cut with it. This must then be laid, face downwards, on a similar cover-glass, the two slid apart, one placed on a filter-paper under a sterilised glass shade to dry, and the fellow placed face downwards on a slide, and the edges painted with petroleum (to prevent evaporation) when it is ready for immediate microscopic examination. The former when dry can be fixed, stained, and examined at leisure. Any number of these can be prepared by even an unskilled operator and forwarded to experts for examination.

Small portions of the organ may next be removed with sterilised instruments, and placed in alcohol for future investigation.

Other organs may be similarly examined.

This detail which to the bacteriologist is but simple every-day technicality, has been given in detail for two reasons. Firstly, to show that the element of doubt which might arise from want of simple precautions against contamination has been eliminated; and, secondly, as a guide to others who, as beginners, may wish to carry on the good work of investigation here initiated.

In five of his cases[1] Bruce extracted the spleen ten minutes after death, in four the writer removed the organ within an hour of death. In other cases the interval varied up to eight hours. In one case the author obtained the micro-organism from the brain, together with other but slight contaminations as late as twenty hours after death, but from the spleen of the same case he had been enabled to obtain pure cultivations from inoculations one hour after death.

Description of the micro-organism.—This minute micro-organism the author in 1893 named the "Micrococcus Melitensis," to which he would add the name "vel Brucii." It grows best in nutrient material, the alkalinity of which is slightly less than that of the human blood, and at a temperature of about 37° to 38° C. At temperatures between 40° and 42° C. growth is suspended; above 42° C. artificial growths die. Below 18·5° C. growth is also suspended, while if they are kept at a moist heat of 15·5° C. for long they die. Colonies that were allowed to dry completely were found to be dead when tested three years after. Cultivations forwarded to England during the winter died on the way.

[1] *Annales de l'institut Pasteur*, 1893, vol. vii. p. 289.

On the sloping surface of 1·5 per cent peptone agar-agar, at a temperature of 37° C., its colonies become visible to the naked eye in from 120-125 hours from the primary inoculation from the human spleen. They appear first as minute transparent colourless drops on the surface of the agar, but slightly different in colour from the agar itself. In about 36 hours more they become of a transparent amber colour, and increasing very slowly in size, on the fourth or fifth day of their appearance become opaque. At this stage they most resemble split pearls lying upon the agar surface. Under a low power and by transmitted light such colonies appear to be orange in colour, quite round, with a definite but granular margin. If kept on moist agar they slowly increase in size, and, while retaining their circular shape individually, may gradually coalesce. In the course of three months these colonies turn to a buff or even orange colour in naked-eye appearance; and at the same time increase in thickness by heaping up material in the centre of the colony. Individual colonies do not attain to any great size, when compared with other growths, ceasing to increase when little larger than a split pea, which old colonies often resemble. No liquefaction takes place. Though they do not increase in size after two months' growth, the colonies retain their vitality at a suitable temperature for over three months. When a comparatively large amount of living material is transferred from a primary growth on agar, with an ooze, to the surface of a new portion of agar, a streak appears in from two to three days, composed of innumerable small colonies. These are barely visible to the naked eye at first, but soon coalesce, and form a flat, slightly opaque gray streak, which does not, however, tend to spread to any extent beyond its original boundaries. Not only does the large amount of growth transferred mathematically increase the apparent rate of growth, but at the same time the micro-organism seems to acquire by education a slightly increased power of growth on artificial food. This readiness of growth does not, however, continue to notably increase with subsequent cultivations.

The micrococcus will not grow on agar, the alkalinity of which is much in excess of that of the human blood, nor would it grow on acid agar which had not been neutralised with alkaline solution. If cultivated on successive media of increasing alkalinity, they can be educated to grow on very alkaline media. In such case, however, they are longer in appearing and grow more slowly, and in very diffuse manner on the agar surface, with only abortive attempts at the formation of definite colonies. Such diffuse growths, however, when transferred to agar, having a suitable alkalinity, again revert to their original characteristic mode of growth.

In making primary inoculations on agar, the best success is obtained with new material that has not had time to dry off its moisture. When old dry agar is used, the blood transferred from the spleen, by drying in a small clot, occasionally interferes with the growth of the colonies. With new agar, in which there is a residue of moisture at the lowest point of the sloping surface, we often find that while only a few colonies appear on the upper and drier portion, very numerous small colonies appear on the lower portion as the moisture dries up, from evaporation in the incubator. The most successful method of obtaining growths from the spleen and other tissues is to make the primary inoculations into broth, and to make secondary ones from this to agar a few days later.

The micrococcus grows also on gelatine and in bouillon. On the former it grows very slowly at 22° C. without liquefaction. In the latter it gives rise to a general and increasing opaqueness, commencing on the fifth or sixth day, afterwards forming a white precipitate consisting of these cocci, but without forming a surface pellicle. On potatoes at 37° C. no apparent growth takes place (Bruce).

Microscopically in the hanging drop they appear as very minute cocci, measuring ·33 μ in dried specimens (Bruce), ovoid in shape, and in rapid molecular (Brownian ?) motion. Many are seen in pairs, and a few in temporary short chains of four, the latter more especially when they have been grown on alkaline agar. No chains are visible in cover-glass or dried specimens. They stain very readily with all the usual aniline dyes, but lose their colour very rapidly when treated with alcohol or other decolorising agent. The absence of a fixation agent makes the bacteriological examination of tissue sections at present an impossibility. Serum from the blood of patients recently attacked with this undulant fever, or of monkeys that have been experimentally inoculated with the micrococcus Melitensis, has been found by Prof. Wright to have an agglomerating effect on pure cultures of the micrococcus Melitensis in a fluid medium, an effect not possessed by the serum of other persons or uninoculated monkeys (*vide* "Diagnosis," Chap. IV.).

The slow growth, peculiar appearance of colonies on the surface of nutrient agar, the small size that the individual colonies attain, the minute size of the coccus, and the readiness with which the micro-organism stains and decolorises, serves to differentiate it from others.

Having proved the constant presence of this micro-organism in the tissues of cases of undulant fever, it next became necessary to investigate its pathogenic powers on the lower animals. The following inoculation experiments were made by Surgeon-Major Bruce in 1887, which he has kindly permitted me to include here :—

Experiment I.—A male monkey (Bonnet species) was inoculated in the left forearm with a pure growth obtained from the spleen of a case after death, by means of a perfectly clean Pravaz syringe, the growth having been grown on artificial media in a pure condition for a month previously. The temperature of this monkey for a fortnight before inoculation ranged between 99·8° F. and 100·5° F. He ate well, was very active, and to all appearances healthy. The virus was mixed with ten drops of sterilised water. On the day after inoculation the temperature began to rise (see Chart), and reaching 106°-107° F., he died 21 days after inoculation.

On post-mortem examination the lungs showed no signs of tuberculosis; the liver and spleen were enormously enlarged. On opening the intestine the mucous membrane was found to be free from ulceration.

Six tubes of agar-agar were inoculated from the spleen and two from

CHART I.

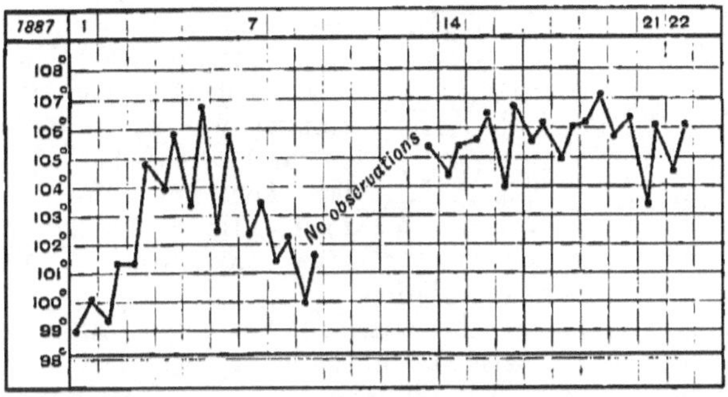

the liver, with full precautions. In all those from the spleen, and in one from the liver, the micrococcus Melitensis was isolated, the colonies appearing after 168 hours. In the remaining tube from the liver no growth appeared.

Experiment II.—Another male monkey (Bonnet species) was similarly inoculated. The temperature rose rapidly, and he died on the 13th day. Growths were obtained from the internal organs, making their appearance after four days.

Bruce found that rabbits and mice gave negative results. From one rabbit killed 23 days after inoculation, and from another after 26 days, the characteristic growth was obtained; but from many others no growth was obtained. Of nine mice inoculated but one died. The culture had been introduced beneath the root of the tail, and he died apparently from septicæmia, as in addition to the characteristic micrococcus other forms of bacteria were also present. From one only of the remaining eight mice could the micrococcus be recovered from the tissues.

In two guinea-pigs inoculated no change of symptoms appeared, though kept for two months under observation.

Since then the writer has had the opportunity of making the following confirmatory inoculation experiments:—

Experiment III.—A small male monkey, of the Bonnet species, was kept under observation for two months, during which period his appetite was good and his temperature stationary (average about 99°). He was inoculated on 1st November 1891 by the injection of a colony of micrococcus Melitensis, obtained from the spleen of Case No. 2, Chapter II., into the muscles of the forearm. The site of the inoculation had been previously shaved, cleaned with soap and water, and washed with a solution of perchloride of mercury. The syringe and all other apparatus had been carefully sterilised; while the colony had been mixed with 1 c.c. of sterilised bouillon, that had been under observation for one month previously. The colony had been visibly growing 14 days. Forty-eight hours afterwards the temperature began to rise, and daily increasing with a remitting curve, reached 106° F. on the 15th day. For the first 10 days the monkey was lively and continued to eat his food, but after that he lay about and refused almost all food. He was killed 362 hours after inoculation. No change took place at the seat of inoculation.

CHART II.

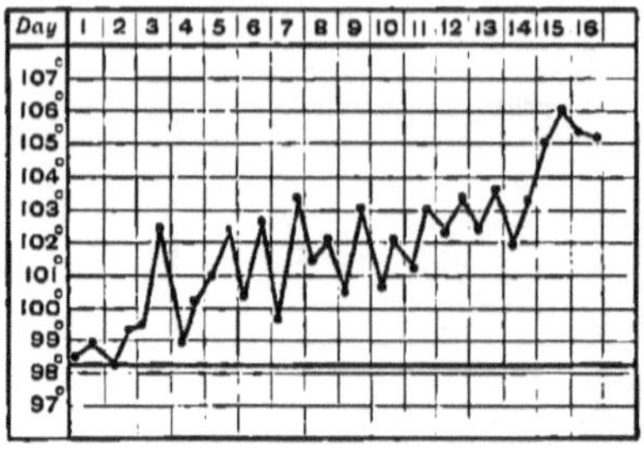

A post-mortem examination was made five minutes after death. The body was fairly well nourished, and the heart apparently normal. The lungs contained sero-purulent exudation in the bronchial tubes, but were otherwise normal. No tuberculosis, etc. The liver was congested, and the spleen was also congested, and very large in proportion to the total body-weight. The intestines were slightly congested at the ileo-cæcal valve, but Peyer's patches were unaffected, and no other pathological condition was noticeable.

Seven tubes of agar-agar were inoculated from the spleen in the usual manner. Two tubes were inoculated from the cardiac blood in the following manner :—

The pericardium was aseptically opened, and the large vessels ligatured with sterilised gut and divided above the ligature, the heart being removed entire together with its contained blood. A sterilised hollow needle fixed in a glass tube, guarded above by a sterilised cotton-wool pad, was thrust into the cavity of the ventricle, and the contained blood drawn into the tube by means of an attached syringe. The first and last drops were discarded and the remainder was at once passed into tubes of agar-agar.

All these tubes were at once placed in the incubator at a temperature of 37° C., and resulted as follows :—

Of seven splenic cultures: five showed numerous colonies of mic. Melitensis 168 hours after inoculation; two showed contamination with mic. albicans.

Of two from the cardiac blood: one showed numerous colonies of mic. Melitensis 168 hours from inoculation; one contained no growth of any kind.

These growths were identical with those obtained from human spleen, macroscopically and microscopically, and specimens forwarded to Bruce at Netley were identified by him. The growths were cultivated also in bouillon, and were carried through six generations of pure cultures on agar-agar, without change.

Experiment IV.—A small male African monkey was inoculated in the muscles of the left forearm, with the same precautions as were taken in the preceding experiment. The virus was taken from a growth obtained from the intra-cardiac blood of the monkey in Experiment III. The following day the temperature began to rise, and for eleven weeks he suffered from pyrexia of a distinctly remittent type (see Chart). He lost weight considerably, and at rare intervals

CHART III.

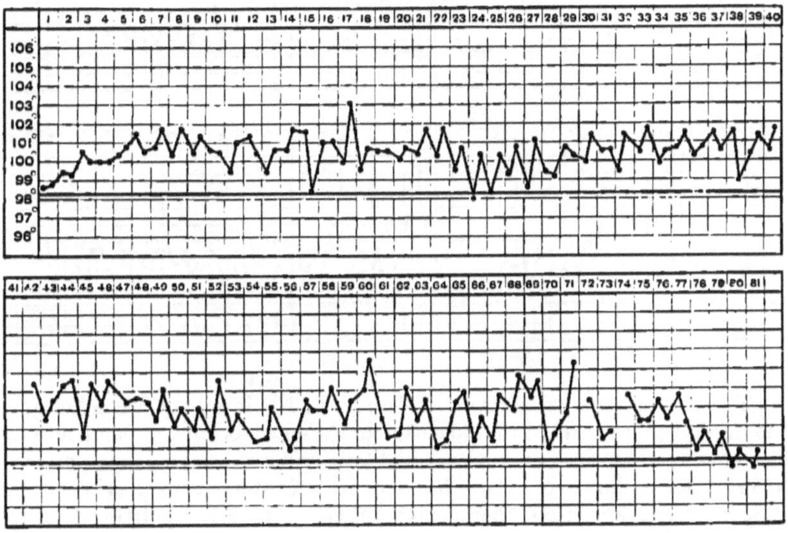

suffered from diarrhœa, but as a rule was rather constipated. No change took place at the seat of inoculation. The monkey completely recovered, and lived for a year in good health, when he died of acute poisoning from something he had eaten. The temperature was taken carefully three times a day in the axilla by the same two people from first to last.

Experiment V.—A female African monkey (Bonnet species), under observation and in good health for three months previously, was similarly inoculated in the muscles of the right thigh, with virus from a growth obtained from the spleen of the monkey in Experiment III. This, like the preceding growths used for inoculation purposes, was kept for a sufficiently long time in the incubator to ensure its purity. The monkey suffered from pyrexia, consisting of intermittent waves of remittent character, for over 94 days. She ultimately completely recovered, and lived in good health for three years until killed by a dog. No local symptoms appeared at the seat of inoculation. She lost weight and seemed to suffer from pain or rheumatism of the extremities at irregular intervals. The waves of temperature and the long duration of the pyrexia remind one forcibly of undulant fever occurring in man.

CHART IV.

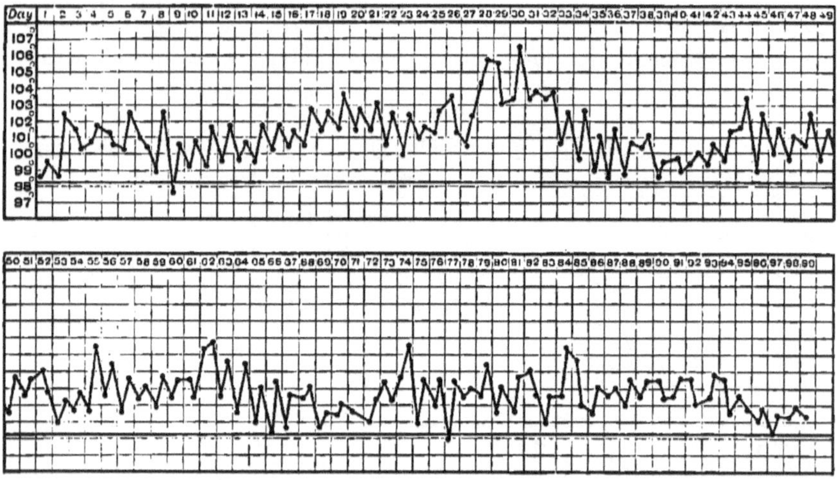

These monkeys were more or less tamed before they were bought, but needed a great deal of patience, and a considerable expenditure of thermometers at first, in order to obtain correct temperature records. After a time, however, they became so accustomed to having their temperature taken, that there came to be quite a competition for the accompanying petting and grape or other bribe. Their normal temperatures before inoculation were as nearly as possible 99° F.

Experiment VI.—A very savage and impatient monkey was also inoculated with virus obtained from the spleen of P.M. Case No. 3, and his temperature was taken at irregular intervals. It was elevated, while no local changes occurred at the seat of inoculation. He ultimately recovered, but little more can be said about the case.

Confirmatory experiments of a similar character have been carried out at Netley, with cultures obtained by the writer, in Malta, from human spleen after death, with conclusive results.

Summary.—Thus by direct experiment we have been able to produce in monkeys (though not so far in other animals), by inoculation with pure cultures of the micrococcus Melitensis vel Brucii, obtained from men suffering from undulant fever, a pyrexial condition analogous to that of undulant fever in man. We have, moreover, isolated pure cultures of this micrococcus from the tissues of monkeys (Bonnet species) so affected, which when inoculated into other similar monkeys have again produced a similar febrile condition.

As the micrococcus in question is morphologically distinct from other known pathogenic micro-organisms, and has completely fulfilled the postulates laid down by Professor Koch, we have strong evidence in favour of it being the proximate cause of undulant fever in man; moreover, it reacts to the serum test with blood obtained from those suffering from that fever.

The writer regrets that, owing to lack of spare time and money, he has been unable to carry these investigations further, but hopes that others will carry on the work, so that the question may be placed upon the firm and certain basis that more confirmatory inoculation experiments can only supply.

It is next necessary to endeavour to ascertain the manner in which this micro-organism enters the human body, and the circumstances which exert a direct or indirect influence on its life history.

Predisposing causes.—These are many and various; as is the case with other diseases, and especially with fevers, they are usually given the credit of being the actual cause.

As may be expected "chill" has had to bear the responsibility of most attacks in the past. This term is a convenient one, as it usually raises no outside responsibility beyond the carelessness of the patient himself. Most patients can remember a "chill" to which they attribute the disease, and the busy practitioner is bothered no more. The "chill" referred to is usually the effect of the fever, after the infection has taken place, and has probably less connection with exposure to actual cold, than many unremembered ones previous to the insidious onset of the fever. In these days it is unnecessary to discuss this subject, suffice it to say that the fever is most prevalent during the period of hot and equable temperature, and least prevalent when the weather is most cold, wet, and unequable. As a predisposing cause, to those exposed to the infection of this fever, chill may by its depressing effect upon the system aid the virus in its onslaught.

The same may be said of "exposure to sun," which the writer has often been given as a cause of this and even of enteric fever! He especially remembers a case of fatal enteric fever with extensive ulceration, attributed by a local doctor to playing polo in the sun, a few days before admission, in apparently the second week of the attack! The depressing effects of the climate, the sirocco winds and heat of the Mediterranean summer, may also be predisposing causes, without our being justified or satisfied in attributing this fever to climatic causes over which we mortals have no control. As our knowledge of disease causes increases we hear less and less of climatic diseases.

Unsuitable food, overwork, bodily fatigue, overcrowding, want of ventilation, damp rooms, and other unhygienic causes, all have their bearing on the case in aiding and abetting the poison where it is present. Again, in the subject attacked we may find such predisposing causes as tend towards an increased susceptibility, such as youth, extra-Mediterranean birth and origin, special idiosyncrasy, etc. Many others might be mentioned, but they are all matters bearing on the question of prophylaxis, which will be dealt with later.

The great point necessary, if we are to cope with the ravages of this fever successfully, is to remember that the essential factor which occasions its occurrence is the presence of a specific virus (requiring for its existence a certain degree of atmospheric temperature, etc.) within a measurable distance of a susceptible human being.

Mode of propagation and dissemination.—That the disease is not propagated by direct contagion from man to man is a fact that is agreed to by all observers (Marston, Bruce, Tomaselli, etc.) Patients suffering from other diseases, occupying beds next to cases of undulant fever, do not develop this fever, nor do the military sick attendants in fever wards suffer from this fever more than those working in other wards, or so much as the soldiers in many of the barracks in Malta, who have not entered the hospital previous to the onset of their attacks. When members of a family are attacked one after another it is due to the presence of a common infective cause, and not to contagion. It is difficult to say, in the present limited state of our knowledge, what is the exact mode by which the virus enters the human body, but by collecting all the pros and cons of circumstantial evidence at our disposal it will be possible to build up a theory which time alone can prove or disprove.

On the various theories which attribute its occurrence to chills, climate, exposure to sun, intemperance, etc., we need not waste our time, but refer readers back to the section on predisposing causes in which place these influences have been dealt with.

There does not appear to be any evidence in favour of entrance being by inoculation through the broken skin, as has been performed artificially in the case of monkeys. There is no connection, as is the case in tetanus, between attacks of this fever and accidents associated with broken skin. Those who suffer most from mosquito bites during their first summer in Malta are by no means specially subject to this fever, nor do patients or sick attendants bitten by these insects in the fever wards of the hospital develop this fever as a result; mosquitoes are said also to bite but once (Manson).

By a process of exclusion we have therefore to look to the substances which enter the body by way of the alimentary canal or air passages (*i.e.* drink, food, and air, and such accidental substances as they may contain) for the cause of this fever.

As regards drink, the soldiers in Malta are supplied with aqueduct water for drinking and cooking purposes, with mineral waters made from aqueduct water, and with milk obtained nominally under adequate supervision. They have also access in some cases to an inferior class of water used only for flushing and washing purposes, and in a very few instances to well water; but not only are they warned not to drink such water by notices on the taps or wells, but there are taps of good water at most of such places to prevent their using inferior water through laziness. Besides these they drink good English beer, tea, etc. and in many cases various wines and inferior drinks in the local grog shops. Though the distribution of enteric fever in Malta follows the distribution of water-supplies found accidentally polluted, this is not the case with undulant fever. Valetta Barracks have been almost entirely free from enteric fever, other than imported cases, during the past five years, and the same may be said for barracks situated in Floriana; but these barracks have been far from free from undulant fever. The immunity from enteric fever is due to the excellence of the drinking water, which comes through iron pipes from large covered settling tanks in the country, supplied from underground springs in the hills. These barracks have no wells, but have separate inferior aqueduct water-supply for washing and flushing purposes. Were this latter the cause of the fever, in spite of the absence of enteric fever, we should expect the inhabitants of private houses in the same area supplied only with the good water to be immune from undulant fever; but this is very far from being the case. Again, when a very large portion of another water-supply became polluted and enteric fever became general over that water-supply area, undulant fever remained localised, among the soldiers, to the same blocks of buildings and in the same quantity as before and after the pollution occurred. Again, epidemics of undulant fever occurring in any particular barracks have not been attended by an increased prevalence of the disease in other barracks on the same water-supply area.

The fact that well water in many of the Maltese houses, where cases of "remittent fever" occur, has been found polluted, has led some of the Maltese to the belief that polluted well water is the cause of the disease. There is a fallacy, however, in this theory, in that most cases of enteric fever which occur among Maltese are returned as "remittent fever," and an enormous part of the English garrison, and even of the Maltese, who suffer severely from this fever have no access to well water of any kind. Even, therefore, if such water causes certain cases, they are but a very small portion of those met with in Malta, and it is far from being the common cause. In Gibraltar, where the main supply is collected rain water from tanks, this fever is less prevalent than in Malta. Though it has been noticed in Malta that soldiers who are teetotalers (*i.e.* water drinkers) are especially liable to attacks of enteric fever, this is not the case with undulant fever. Also, the writer has found undulant fever occurring amongst families who drank nothing but the best aqueduct water which had been previously well boiled.

Again, at one period when all drinking water was ordered to be boiled on account of the prevalence of enteric fever at the time, though the effect of this proceeding on the prevalence of enteric fever was most noticeable, it did not appear to decrease the prevalence of undulant fever, even at an early date, when fear of infection led to the order being properly carried out.

Lastly, the localisation of attacks to individual barracks and buildings, and more particularly to individual rooms in those barracks or buildings, irrespective of the water-supply of these places, and the total want of connection between the prevalence of fever and the distribution of the various water-supplies general and local, is strongly against a water-borne cause in this disease.

The question of milk-supply is intimately connected with that of water, most infections carried by milk being communicated by means of contaminated water fraudulently or purposely added, or used for cleaning vessels, etc. Besides this the writer has known undulant fever attack families who used only Swiss condensed milk, regiments in which no other milk was allowed in barracks, and families whose milk-supply was always milked from goats on their own premises, into their own vessels, under reliable supervision. He has met with no fact that would favour a causal connection between milk-supply and this fever. In instances where milk contamination has undoubtedly caused localised outbreaks of enteric fever, undulant fever has not shown increased prevalence in the same area.

The question of mineral waters also depends upon the water-supply, and no causal connection has ever appeared, though the supplies are numerous enough to have made a distinct difference in prevalence among the different consumers, had there been any connection. Undulant fever also has attacked regiments which have made their own mineral waters under supervision, using only aqueduct water that has been previously boiled. The author has had the opportunity of visiting all the mineral water factories supplying the troops, and has ascertained their condition, and the fact that all had during his experience aqueduct water laid directly into their machines, there being no other supply of water on the premises available for use.

The local grog shop, evil and undesirable though it be, has been made responsible for nearly all the diseases that soldiers are subject to, as it is the easiest means of transferring sanitary responsibility from military to other shoulders. Though a very large number of those situated outside Valetta are still without a sound water-supply laid on to the premises, this is not the case with those in Valetta, and even at its worst, if this were a cause, it only brings us back to the same question of water-supply which we have already discussed. That actual alcoholic drinks, even of the most inferior kind, can cause fever other than from added pollutions, is a theory more worthy of discussion by rabid teetotalers than by scientific investigators. Moreover, a large number of officers, ladies, women, children, and even soldiers are attacked who have never entered a grog shop, so that any cause derived from these places can scarcely be of a peculiar nature, but common to other more respectable places.

On the whole there seems little reason to connect the cause of this fever with articles of drink, and, as the writer will show later, there is much to connect the cause with other factors.

That the disease is not usually propagated by food is fairly certain, as the soldiers' food is a well-known and definite quantity, bought and prepared under close supervision. It is most exceptional for soldiers to eat out of barracks, or to indulge in green uncooked vegetables, or other food liable to contamination.

Lastly, ice is but a form of water-supply, nor has its use in hospital or by the large numbers of individuals who use it habitually in their drinks during that hot period of the year when this fever is especially prevalent, appeared to be attended by fever prevalence.

By a process of exclusion we are brought to the discussion of polluted air as a cause of this fever. The writer has certain evidence to put forward in favour of such a cause, but as somewhat similar opinions have already been stated by others, it will be advisable first of all to briefly refer to their remarks. Unfortunately they have in most cases published their opinions only, without recording the facts or reasons which led to their conclusions.

Leaving out of the question the remarks of writers during what might be called the prehistoric age of this fever, we find the following remarks in the literature of the past thirty-five years:—

Marston in 1861 says: "I fancy that we may perceive the operation of two agencies: (1) The effects, whatever they may be, induced by residence in a hot, moist climate; (2) Certain localised conditions connected with drainage and dampness.

"If I were asked to indicate the cause of this disease, I would suggest the defective house-drainage."

Boileau in 1865 attributes four of his cases to fæcal emanations, giving no cause for the other cases.

Chartres in 1866 says: "The causes most active in the production of this fever were, I consider, the following, viz.: (1) Special peculiarities of locality; (2) Sanitary defects of barracks, more especially those of bad drainage and insufficient ventilation; (3) The effects of climate and a long residence in the Mediterranean; (4) Intemperance."

Donaldson in 1876 says: "I look upon enteric, fæco-malarial (*i.e.* undulant) fever and febrile dyspepsia (febricula) as but different expressions of a similar cause, viz., the breathing of an air or the drinking of a water polluted by sewage or its emanations, the former being due to the introduction of the poison through the drinking water, and the two latter to its entrance through the air." With regard to the latter, he gives his opinion on Verdala Barracks and the connection between undulant fever cases and sewer-gas emanations.

Oswald Wood in 1876 says: "I state my belief that one of the chief causes, if not the sole cause of Malta fever, is the *unsanitary condition of the island.*"

The italics are his own.

Prof. Notter, writing in 1876, says: "The drainage is extremely bad, the sewers are nothing but long cesspools, and from the porous nature of the stone the ground is in many places reeking with filth, and the ground saturated like a sponge with sewage filth, the rock disintegrated and foul to a degree. During my service in 1872, one of the worst outbreaks of this disease took place in Fort Ricasoli, where the system of drainage was known to be imperfect, and the smell pervading the place was at times sickening. This arose from the system adopted of hand-flushing of the water-closets, which was not properly carried out, the result being accumulation of soil in the sewer. . . . To sum up, this disease may be stated to be essentially a filth disease, intensified by the climate and moisture present in the air. . . . The cause essentially consists in defective drainage, in having to sleep in houses and breathe air impregnated with fœtid organic vapours given off from saturated subsoil or filthy water-closets, aided by climatic conditions."

The late Prof. de Chaumont (1884) regarded this disease as a blood poisoning due to defective sewerage and saturation of the soil with fæcal matter.

In Italy opinions are divided, except that those who discredit its fæcal origin give no other explanation of its cause.

Fazio, Capozzi, and Rummo have noticed in Naples that the disease developed itself more when the cleaning of cesspools was abandoned and the sewage drains were put in communication with the rain-water drains and the sinks. They also noticed its prevalence in the vicinity of latrines, and particularly where there was stagnation in the flow of sewage. Borelli and Dominicis also admit its fæcal origin in Naples, while De Renzi denies it. Galassi of Rome, Cardile and Guiffré of Palermo more or less deny it also.

Thus Fazio, in 1879, says: "Concludendo ripeto che la cosi detta *febbre napolitana* costituisca una entità nosologica distinta e che non debbe`confondersi con le ordinarie infezioni. Ch' essa trae movenza dal mefitismo delle fogne, e che, come nel caso da me riferito, può contenere elementi specifici sia della malaria, sia del tifo; è come si è svolta appo noi similmente potra manifestarsi anche in altri paesi, i quali si trovino in condizioni identiche."[1]

Tomaselli, in Catania, in the first edition of his monograph, considered that its cause and occurrence had some connection with local sanitary conditions, but in his later editions he seems less certain. Guiffré bases part of his argument against a fæcal origin on the fact that it occurs in places very healthy in all respects. From what the author has seen in one of the places mentioned, he can only say that whereas the hotels were clean and well drained, the houses of the lower classes were in anything but a sanitary condition.

Schrön and A. de Martini look upon it as a typho-malarial fever, Cantani as an atypical form of enteric fever.

[1] *Vide* Fazio, 1879 and 1893.

Duncan in 1888 writes: "I cannot help thinking that some form of fæcal poisoning is at the bottom of it. It is less common in Gibraltar than in Malta, for Gibraltar is better drained and on harder rock. Now, in both Malta and Gibraltar, but especially in Malta, there is danger of fæcal contamination of air and water, and Malta must be saturated with fæcal detritus. To me it seems that the constant breathing of a fæcally-polluted atmosphere—that is to say, in which the fæcal element exists widely diffused, and is so little concentrated as not to be perceptible by the senses—would result in such an affection."

Bruce, in 1889, says: "There is no mention anywhere of water contaminated by sewage being the vehicle."

Surgeon Moffet, at Gibraltar (*A.M.D. Rep.* 1889), says: "The disease is intimately related to enteric fever as regards etiology at least, which is apparent from the following facts:—Both diseases exist side by side, occurring as localised epidemics together or alternately with each other. Cases of both are furnished by the same barracks, often from the same rooms, the number of cases of one kind of fever bearing a marked proportion to those of the other, and while certain barracks in one year furnish a large number of cases of both diseases, the following year those remain tolerably healthy, whilst others, which during the previous year had been healthy, now become the foci of violent epidemics."

In 1886 the south wing of the Town Range Barracks, occupied by a company of the Royal Engineers, furnished forty-one cases of fever, twenty-one of which were returned as simple continued, the remainder, more severe in type, as enteric fever. All cases presented many symptoms in common, and it is probable that the number returned as enteric fever was over-estimated. Those who had an opportunity of watching the epidemic in all its details had no difficulty in assigning all the cases to a common origin. The following account of the sanitary defects in connection with this epidemic is taken from the report of the medical officer in charge of the station hospital:—"When the back yard, which was covered with asphalt, was opened up, a nine-inch earthenware sewer pipe leaked at every joint, saturating the soil with sewage, which also passed into a catch-pit, and thence into the tank containing rain water, which was used by the men. The drain from the men's ablution room also leaked, and allowed the escape of its contents into the drinking-water tank. The sewer gas which escaped found an exit up the rain-water pipe which opened just below the window of a room, from which the fatal case of enteric fever (? so returned) was admitted into hospital." The water of this tank was found to be polluted in an extreme degree, and condemned as quite unfit for use. The only fatal case was that of a man well known to be of intemperate habits, and who, according to his own account, never drank water, but he slept in a small room upstairs, the window of which opened immediately above the rain-water pipe, which had not been disconnected from the catch-pit of the tank, and which therefore acted as an escape pipe for the sewer gas generated in the catch-pit below. "This man's disease, at first returned as simple continued, was, as the symptoms became more serious, changed to enteric fever, but the post-mortem lesions did not bear out the latter diagnosis." He states that this was the only epidemic in which there was any suspicion of the disease having been conveyed by drinking water, while the bulk of evidence in this as well as in other epidemics strongly points to aërial contamination as the chief factor in the transmission of the disease poison. He adds that the defects were remedied, the tank cleaned out, and every precaution taken to prevent a recurrence of the disease. The following year this barrack furnished only fifteen cases of fever, two of which were severe, and returned as enteric.

He says "of its (*i.e.* undulant fever's) relation to certain localised sanitary defects there can be no doubt. In every barrack whence cases are furnished there existed grave defects, the remedying of which was invariably followed by a diminution or cessation of the disease."

We have therefore a number of opinions of men who have studied this fever, all more or less believing that the fever is due to an aërial fæcal poison. The writer has endeavoured during his service in Malta to follow up the cases which have occurred in the barracks under his sanitary care, and to group them with reference to locality and possible causation. With the exception of certain sporadic cases, they have all come from the same rooms, and have occupied beds in the same parts of those rooms in the barracks in question. At the same time certain other rooms have yielded no cases year after year. The rooms which have yielded cases have had one or more of three factors not common to the healthier ones. These have been: (*a*) Some insanitary condition connected either directly with drainage or with flooring of an absorbent nature which has had probabilities of contamination with human excrement (urine or fæces). (*b*) Dampness, especially of a varying nature. (*c*) Suitable climatic and topographical surroundings.

Even in the sporadic cases above excepted, items (*b*) and (*c*) have been present, while in rooms (with soft stone flooring) which were formerly used by the Knights and since used as barracks, the first item is not improbable, especially when one sees the filth which is to be found beneath the stone flags of such rooms on the ground floors of the buildings, and remembers the ambulatory nature of so many cases.

Where the disease has been epidemic these causes have been most pronounced. Moreover, the rectification of the insanitation has been invariably followed by a cessation of fever prevalence more or less complete according to the thoroughness or otherwise of the work done. Other factors seem to favour the dissemination of the poison, notably drying of the infected surface following the pollution, the presence of air currents, deficient ventilation, overcrowding, and the close proximity of the susceptible human subject. The flooding of the floors with sewage, a choked house-drain which has burst, an overflowing cesspit, an escape of sewer gas from an adjacent drain ventilator, a direct communication between sleeping-rooms and drains by means of untrapped sinks or cupboard latrines seem common causes of this fever.

Of numerous cases where such conditions seemed to be probable causes, the following are of a more certain character :—

EXAMPLES OF UNDULANT FEVER OUTBREAKS ASSOCIATED WITH INSANITATION

1. A row of houses was hired by Government for the use of married soldiers in Malta. These houses had cesspits, situated, as a very large number are in that country, under the rooms. The former Maltese occupants had allowed but little water to pass into the cesspits, in order to save frequent emptying. The English soldiers, used to a water drainage system, very soon filled these cesspits and caused them to overflow, soaking the flooring of the rooms with fæcal matter, etc. This was followed by an outbreak of undulant fever affecting every family exposed to this insanitation, and the houses had to be evacuated. The cesspits were removed and the floors cemented with marked result.

2. During the years 1892-3 only three cases of fever were admitted from an airy, well-built barrack in Valetta, holding 80 men. These three cases were admitted on 18th November 1892, 27th December 1892, and 5th January 1893 respectively. All three died, and post-mortem and bacteriological examinations were made, with the result that two proved to be suffering from undulant fever and the other from enteric fever (see Cases 7 and 8). The only apparent cause was that during November and December the barrack drain from the latrines, running through the yard to join the main drain in the street outside, had become choked and broken, and was discharging its sewage into the porous rock channel in which it ran, in an enclosed space under the windows of the canteen and close to the barrack-room door. The stench from this break and during its repair was very bad. The work was completed shortly after the admission of the last case, and no other case has occurred since. The milk and water supplies were excellent, and these men did not bathe in an insanitary place. These 80 men belonged to the same regiments that, while occupying other barracks close by, were by no means free from cases of this fever, though using similar milk and water supplies.

3. In a large building in Valetta, three bedrooms occupied by officers, and three only, had a reputation for producing undulant fever cases, which was put down to their insufficient ventilation. Further investigation in 1895 discovered a most insanitary water-closet in the dark and enclosed passage from which these bedrooms opened. On account of its faulty construction it had been locked up, and in its unused state it acted as a ventilator for sewer gas, which it discharged into the passage. This was rectified, and since then no further cases have occurred.

4. For three years, while stationed in Valetta, a staff officer resided

in a large official residence in one of the best parts of the town. The inmates (all English) consisted of four males, three adult and four young females. Two of the girls only were attacked with undulant fever in 1892, and both suffered from typical and severe attacks, the elder from 100, and the younger from 80 days' pyrexia, and both were a considerable time longer before convalescence became fully established. The elder had suffered from a severe attack of enteric fever in Brussels two years previously, complicated by a relapse. Both girls occupied the turret room, and were the only occupants of that room. On investigation it was found that the windows of this room were on a level with a neighbouring main drain ventilator, and that the smell from this not only entered the room in question, but affected the houses on the opposite side of the road, a much greater distance away. The house-drain ventilator also opened on to the roof of this room, and was very offensive at the time. Inquiry elicited the information that former occupants of the house, who had used this room as a bedroom, had suffered from the fever. The room was shut up, and no case has occurred since among the remaining occupants of a susceptible age, though four years have elapsed.

5. A certain house, hired as a Government quarter, had the following history :—First an officer, who occupied it, lost his wife and was himself invalided home on account of undulant fever. The next officer had both his children attacked—one died, while the other suffered severely from the fever and had to be taken to England. The next three officers were invalided home with the fever, though two of them had resided in the island in other houses for three years previously, during which time they had enjoyed good health.

Another medical officer moved in, when he found that his wife and children were suffering from frequent sore throats and slight febrile attacks, and had the drains examined. It was then found that, instead of the supposed modern connection with the main drainage system, the sewage of the house had for a long time been passing through house-drains made of porous stone. There was considerable fæcal extravasation under the flooring of the lower rooms. The house was evacuated for repairs, and has not yet been reoccupied.

6. In a new and well-constructed flat in Valetta the first occupant was invalided home with this fever. The next also suffered from the same fever, together with his wife and child; the child died and the man and wife were invalided home. The next occupant was a man, with a wife and sister. The sister suffered severely and the wife slightly from this fever. An inspection of the quarter disclosed a leaking pan-latrine on the verandah off the bedroom, and a leaking drain ventilator running in a circular turret staircase, communicating with the same room. The smell from both, neither of which was ten feet distant from the bed, entered the room and was most offensive. People of the same rank in life, occupying other portions of the block, were unaffected. The water-supply was excellent and common to the whole

of Valetta; the milk was obtained from goats milked at the door. The latrine was rectified, and the ventilator placed outside the building, with excellent results.

7. A regiment was quartered on a small island in one of the harbours of Valetta, from 2nd January 1892 until 10th October of the same year. During this period it suffered severely from "simple continued fever," 197 cases being admitted from a total strength of 760 men. The regiment had suffered severely from this fever elsewhere during its first year of service in Malta, had been seasoned by three years' residence, and was composed of men whose ages were not below the average of the station, yet their fever rate for 1892 far exceeded that of any other regiment. Of these men, 480 were quartered in wooden huts, and the remaining 280 in an old fort close by, which had been built by the Knights in 1775. A careful analysis of the fever admissions divides them into two classes—

(*a*) Cases of true Mediterranean or undulant fever.

(*b*) Relapses or slight cases of the same fever (?), cases of simple ardent fever (febricula), and other obscure but slight febrile ailments without localised symptoms.

The latter class were in hospital but a short time, and there is little to note, except that the numbers were greater than from any other barracks in the island, and that in proportion to strength the admissions from the fort were double those from the huts.

The admission-rate per mille for true undulant fever in Valetta district (strength 3511, including the island in question) in 1892 was 52·2, while those of the huts and fort in question were 46·3 and 178·6 respectively, showing that some special local cause of fever must exist within the fort. The men in the fort and huts, belonging to the same regiment, were of the same age and class, and under identical conditions as regards food, milk, and water supplies, the latter being common to a very large area of unaffected population, civil and military. In the fort 38 men, 2 women, and 5 children were affected; and of the men 1 died (see Case No. 11), 6 were invalided, of whom 1 was finally discharged from the service, 14 were sent to the sanitarium, and 17 returned to duty straight from hospital, but were in many cases readmitted with relapses after leaving Valetta district in October. The average stay in hospital was 109 days each for the men. The majority of the rooms in question were dark, close, and damp, and were never intended for barrack-rooms. Round the back of the rooms ran large channels, cut in the extremely porous rock, and passing on each side of the fort down to the sea. From 1870 these channels were used as sewers, until the substitution in 1885 of the present dry-earth system. Undulant fever occurred in the fort as an epidemic in 1870 and 1872, and though sporadic was not excessive from 1885 to 1891. During the latter period a quantity of sewage remained boxed up, with the result that the stone became soaked with sewage even through the walls and flooring to the adjacent rooms. Analysis of portions of the walls of the channels and rooms showed not only a larger percentage of chemical constituents of sewage, much organic matter, and a very large number of putrid and non-pathogenic organisms when compared with similar but unpolluted stone. Again, though unpolluted stone was highly alkaline, the stone of these walls was neutral or faintly alkaline, forming therefore a suitable nidus theoretically for the micrococcus of this fever. Between September and December 1891 a thorough overhauling of the drains took place, these channels being cleared and converted into surface-water drains, gratings being placed at intervals almost on a level with, adjacent to or even opposite the windows of the barrack-rooms. Owing to their situation and construction there was a varying yet constant current of air from the sea, travelling up these channels and passing out of the gratings into the fort, the porous walls at the same time being wet or dry according to the state of the atmosphere and the amount of rain. There was ample opportunity for miasmata to pass from the rock channels into the barrack-rooms, and it is a significant fact that these 45 cases slept in beds grouped in close and definite relation to the rock-channels and sewage-soaked walls, and in direct proportion to the amount of varying dampness present. The first case was admitted four days after the cessation of the heavy rain. There was no other apparent cause for the outbreak, and obvious sanitary measures have resulted in a cessation of this fever prevalence.

8. In a large modern and well-built hospital, built on one of the best sites in Malta, a number of cases of this fever (20-40) have for many years past been constantly treated in wards on the top floor, without the disease spreading to others in the same wards. The hospital had always been considered a very healthy one until recently, when a few cases of this fever began to occur among venereal patients on the middle floor, and the patients and sick attendants occupying the ground floor suffered severely and even fatally from this fever. In the kitchen behind the hospital two cooks died of its effects, and patients suffering from slight ailments such as sprains, etc., and who occupied tents immediately behind the building, also developed the fever. Many of the sufferers had been in hospital over a month, while others had resided in the building for many months previously. The water-supply was good and common to a large district, the milk-supply was above suspicion. On investigation it was found that the hospital drain-pipe, which ran along the back of the hospital, between the main building and the ground occupied by the kitchen and tents, had been blocked for some time, beyond the main building, and that the fæcal sewage, from the fever and other wards, had forced the joints of the pipe, and leaked in all directions under the hospital foundations and through the ground on which the kitchen and tents were situated.

At the same time, in three officers' quarters in the same grounds, but well detached and for many years considered to be among the healthiest in Malta, six cases of this fever occurred in one year. In this case the main and house drains were found blocked, and the backflow of sewage caused offensive odours of sewer gas to enter the back rooms from adjacent drain ventilators.

A similar condition existed at the other end of the same drain, in some adjacent barracks, with the result that of two occupants of a married quarter there, one died and the other suffered from a severe and prolonged attack of this fever. Many other cases were also admitted from the rooms near.

Though the details are not exactly laid down in this last instance, the writer has preferred it to many other smaller instances with exact details, on account of the large number of cases occurring in an English-built hospital, which had for a number of years been healthy.

9. In some married quarters in Valetta cases of true Mediterranean fever occurred from time to time; on investigation it was found that there was a large tunnel, built during the last century, running up under these quarters. Down the centre of this ran a leaking drain, which had sinks and ablution rooms from these quarters running straight into it. No one seemed to be aware of its existence, and certainly it had not been opened for twelve years. On opening, six cartloads of escaped house sewage were found. It was cleaned out, ventilated, redrained, and cut off, and no cases occurred during the following twelve months.

10. In the same barracks the schoolmaster suffered from a long attack of this fever. His room was over a drain-pipe that smelt whenever anything passed down it from the quarter above. The sink-pipe also passed straight into the drain without any intervening trap. This was remedied and the quarter became a healthy one.

11. In the same barracks cases had come continually from a certain end room. On investigation it was found to communicate by means of a wooden door (erroneously supposed to be nailed up) with a closed space under the staircase in which the ablution-room drain had burst. This drain was the upper end of the main latrine drain.

12. In a block containing officers' quarters, only the occupants of two rooms were attacked with this fever during the period 1892-95. In one room a drain-pipe passing down the wall had burst, at the time four cases occurred. In the other room nothing appeared wrong, though the only two officers occupying it were attacked; one died and the other was invalided home. It was, however, the only room which received all its air from the inner court, the surface drains of which were untrapped, and led straight into the main drain. These were trapped and no other case has occurred since.

13. Among the sick attendants in the Valetta Military Hospital, the annual daily sick-rate in proportion to strength had in 1890 been 1·83; in 1891, 0·93; in 1892, 1·07; in 1893, 1·37; in 1894, 1·52; or an average of 1·35 per cent.

In 1895 this rate rose to 4·48. The excessive sickness was due to an outbreak of S. C. fever, a disease which had but little affected these men previously, indeed they were considerably less often attacked than the soldiers in barracks, in spite of the fact that they were continuously nursing cases of this class of fever in the wards. With the exception of two slight cases of eleven and eight days' pyrexia, these cases were all cases of true undulant fever. This fever attacked a staff sergeant and his family (of whom more), and thirteen of the rank and file, but did not affect any others above the rank of corporal. The proportion of those attacked with undulant fever to strength (54) was over 25 per cent, an enormous rate when compared with that of the whole of Valetta district, which in spite of this being an unusually severe year, with an epidemic in a regiment in Floriana, only amounted to 7·3 per cent of strength (3522). The average stay in hospital of the rank and file, not counting the time spent in England by one invalid, was eighty days; two were invalided (of whom one died), seven were sent to the sanitarium at Citta Vecchia, only four returned straight to duty. The disease attacked those who slept in a certain room when on night duty, and its onset was contemporaneous with the opening of this room, which for many years before had been used as a drug store. With the exception of the staff sergeant it did not attack those who did not sleep in this room. There were no causes for fever present, other than this room, that had not been present in other years, nor that were not common to the other attendants above the rank of corporal, or indeed to all the patients in hospital, some 200 in number.

The room in question was very small, and the occupants slept on the floor or on bedsteads raised 2 feet above the floor, and was found to be damp from water which soaked through the wall and floor from an adjacent road at a higher level (2 feet)—at a place, too, where urine and house slops had been thrown. In the centre of the floor of the room was a circle of stone, closing an old porous drain, the remains of which, cut off at the outer wall, was found running through the damp portion under the flat porous stones which formed the flooring. Reliable records proved that for a very long time this room had been the dead-house of the hospital, where some years ago all post-mortem operations had been carried out. There is little doubt that a considerable amount of infective material must have passed on to the floor, and soaked through the porous drain under the flooring, in days gone by. The outbreak stopped on the use of this room being discontinued, nor have cases occurred since, though after the flooring was removed, and that and the walls covered with good cement, the room has again been used. The drain and central stone of the floor, pierced by a round hole connected with the drain, shows that the floor had not been renewed when the room ceased to be a dead-house.

The staff sergeant who was attacked at the same time occupied a two-room quarter a few rooms away. He was eighty-one days in hospital, after which he was invalided to England. His wife and child also suffered, and the previous occupant was invalided to England for the same disease, though up to that time the quarter had been healthy. On investigation, it was found that the wall of his bedroom was damp, and had been so for some time, and that this was due to the drain-pipe of a latrine next to his room having burst and allowed an extravasation of its contents to escape into the very porous wall of his room.

14. In a private house in Valetta where two previous occupants had been attacked with this fever, the writer was called in May 1896 to attend an officer and his wife who were suffering from this fever, and were sent to England. He found that their bedroom was built off a small passage (5 feet square) containing a latrine of an insanitary nature. The doors between had been kept open for coolness. There was no other cause apparent. The officer stated that he had had a new latrine pan put in on taking the house the winter before, and that its previous condition had been "most insanitary."

15. A doctor and his wife were attacked with undulant fever after the former had spent five and a half years in the Mediterranean, the latter one and a half years, all of which latter period they had spent in one flat. They were attacked within a fortnight of moving into a back bedroom (June 1896). Subsequent investigation discovered a disused and leaking latrine beneath their window (about 10 feet below), in a corner of a neighbouring yard, where on account of iron bars in the window, it had been invisible from the bedroom. A case had previously occurred in the flat immediately above. Their pyrexia lasted 310 and 31 days respectively. The smell from this latrine reached the room, and no other cause was apparent.

Numerous sporadic cases have occurred where either men slept in barracks under foul air outlets next main drain ventilators, or families were attacked in houses, the drains of which were subsequently found to be leaking into the flooring of certain rooms. In the latter cases, as the leaks were not noticed until some time after the outbreaks, they might be objected to as not having existed previously, but they occur so often that there would appear to be connection between the two. In large houses a few members only, often those sleeping together in the same room, are usually affected; but in small one or two-roomed quarters it is not uncommon for a number of members of the same family to be affected. This would appear to depend on the sleeping distance from the local infective cause.

Many naval medical officers have attributed its prevalence on board ship to the condition of the harbours of Malta.

Thus, 1. Burnett (1810) states: "To the influence of marsh miasma, aided by causes hereafter mentioned, has been assigned the appearance of this disease in most of the ships where it has occurred, and many circumstances induce me to believe that it has a very considerable share in producing an attack. . . .

"At Minorca and Malta, the two places where from the nature of my duty my principal observations have been made, there are at the head of each harbour marshes of this description which during the summer and autumn months emit very offensive exhalations. . . .

"The harbour of Mahon (Minorca) is divided by an island on which stands the Naval Hospital. Ships anchored during the summer or autumn above the hospital island for any length of time rarely escape without a number of men being attacked with fever, while the ships anchored below are commonly entirely free from it. Independent of the crews being within the influence of the marsh by lying above the hospital island, the common sewers of the town of Mahon, considerably elevated above the sea, pour their contents into the upper part of the harbour, and doubtless have an unsalutary effect on the atmosphere. The flux and reflux is solely influenced by the winds, and in summer there is always much calm weather, and water in the upper part of the harbour becomes perfectly black and stagnant, often continuing so for a week together. . . .

"In Malta it has always been remarked that ships fitting at the dockyard, situated at the upper part of one of the arms of the harbour, are more subject to attacks of fever than those lying out at their anchors, and on moving a ship where it was present, to Bighi Bay, the disease has uniformly ceased.[1] The reflux and flux of Mahon equally applied here." (Also the sewer outlets. Author.)

With regard to Malta, the marsh referred to has for many years been drained and converted into fields, and has ceased to affect the health of the garrison, whatever its influence may have been in years gone by. In the early part of the century (Hennen), and indeed during the last century (temp. Grand-Master Pinto), we find accounts of fevers caused by exhalations from this marsh, and Curmi was then said to be noted for its malarial fevers (?), while the Capuchin monks of St. Francis, Floriana, were granted dispensation from nightly devotions on this account. We do not find, however (see back), that the troops suffered from the malarial fevers, but from those of a continued type, and the occurrence of these malarial fevers has been much disproved by Davy (1833). Since 1885, when the sewage of the towns on either side of the Grand Harbour ceased to flow into its basin, and was diverted into the open sea, this harbour has vastly improved in its sanitary condition. Before 1885 it has been described as "one huge cesspool," and many references to its condition are to be found in the annual naval blue-books since 1840, and elsewhere.[2] Still, however, a large open sewer from Curmi enters its lower end, while the sewage of the many hundreds of sailors on the various naval and mercantile vessels in port is discharged daily into its confined and tideless basin, the presence of which is very evident in the enclosed creeks in rough weather. In the Quarantine Harbour a very large amount of sewage finds its way into its basin, at Misida, Marsamuscetto, and Lower St. Elmo, its discharge being very evident to the eye and nose. A scheme is under consideration for diverting this matter into the open sea.

[1] See also Surgeon Heastie, R.N., 1825-1828.

[2] See also *Il Barth. Gaz. di medicina*, No. 5 of 23rd Gennajo 1872, Malta; and Donaldson (1876).

2. Marston (1861) mentions the cases of two men who developed severe and fatal attacks of this fever ten days after bathing in a dirty part of the harbour.

3. Bruce (1889) mentions the case of an officer attacked with this fever, who attributed its occurrence to long exposure to the foul emanations in one of the filthiest parts of the Quarantine Harbour, nine days before.

4. Surgeon Gipps, R.N. (1890) states: "From my own observation I should unhesitatingly call it *dirt fever*, due to long-continued stagnation of sewage, both in the harbour from the shipping, and the fact that from days immemorial the whole porous stone of which the island is composed has been saturated with sewage, long previous to the introduction of the improvements in carrying the sewage out to sea. . . . The disease is not only much more frequent among naval officers and men than among the military, but the fever with the former is of a much more severe type. . . . Almost all cases occur either at or shortly after leaving Malta. . . . When away from Malta for any length of time there is almost a complete freedom from fever of any sort, except those cases which occur within some two or three weeks after leaving the island."

5. Fleet-Surgeon Ellis, R.N., in the *Naval Annual Blue-Book* for 1890, gives the following account of an outbreak:—

"All cases returned by H.M.S. *Orion* excepting one (strength 150 men) were cases of so-called 'Malta fever,' and occurred in the persons of thirty-two individuals between March 19th and May 20th, some of whom suffered from relapses. On March 14th the ship was placed in dock at the head of Dockyard Creek, to undergo repairs, and after the water had been pumped out of this dock a large quantity of very fœtid mud was exposed which had to be removed in buckets." The ship had arrived in Malta on March 7th, and the "proportion of cases far exceed those of any other ironclad at that time lying in Malta harbour."

Though there are similar polluted tideless harbours at Naples and elsewhere in the Mediterranean, this fever occurs in many inland villages and other places where no such polluted water exists. It was the fashion for some few non-professional persons to attribute the whole prevalence of this fever in the garrison of Malta to the condition of the harbours. This theory became widely disseminated in England. However much naval sickness it may be causally connected with, it cannot be the whole cause, nor even have much or any connection with a vast number of cases occurring among *soldiers* in Malta, Gibraltar, and elsewhere.

The evidence in favour of this pollution of harbour water as a cause of undulant fever is:—

(*a*) That cases on board ship occur mostly, if not altogether, while in Mediterranean ports, or when fitting in dock, and are not therefore due to causes inherent in the ships themselves. (Gipps and other naval surgeons.)

(*b*) That cases occur in ships whose only water-supply is distilled before use.

(*c*) That men who have not visited or slept in houses on shore have been said to be attacked.

(*d*) That the harbour water is undoubtedly polluted with human dejecta from persons infected with this fever.

(*e*) That the water of the creeks and round the ships in port contains a much larger number of germs than that in the open part of the harbour and in the open sea, and that the reaction of sea-water is suitable theoretically for the growth of the micrococcus Melitensis.

(*f*) That sailors bathe in the water of these creeks round their ships, and that soldiers bathe in many cases near sewer outlets, and take this polluted water into their mouths. This water is also used for washing down decks, where on drying it may give off poisonous exhalations.

That this is a plausible and convenient theory there is no doubt; and it is difficult to see where else the sailor catches his fever. The latter is, however, a question which the writer must leave to his naval colleagues, who are in a better position to judge, and confine his remarks to a theoretical examination of this theory. That it is not the whole cause goes without saying, when we reflect that the disease attacks soldiers who have neither bathed nor been in the harbour, and also inhabitants of inland villages who have not been near the sea for months or years before. We know from direct experiment, and indeed from practical experiènce, that micro-organisms do not rise from water or wet surfaces, unless "there is at the time a spurting up of the fluid by waves, or by violent agitation, or by the formation of bubbles, that particles of water and with them bacteria can be carried by currents of air over short distances" (Nageli quoted by Flügge), or after the moist surface has first dried. If the fever is therefore really contracted from polluted harbour water in certain cases, it is by reason of swallowing or absorbing it through accidental cuts or superficial abrasions when bathing, of breathing exhalations from decks washed with the water, or from eating oysters or insufficiently cooked fish caught in its waters, only too often round the mouths of the sewers. It is unlikely that any drying process at the water's edge can affect the inmates of ships in this tideless water at a time of year when there is an almost continuous calm, and it is a significant fact that the English inhabitants of houses on the borders of Dockyard Creek have not suffered from this fever, when those on ships at anchor close by have done so. There are at any rate ample means of avoiding the possibilities of infection mentioned, and of at the same time proving or disproving the theory in question by simple precautions.

The writer has failed experimentally to isolate the micrococcus Melitensis from the sea-water in question, or to grow it artificially in sterilised sea-water. Such experiments are, however, of little negative value on account of the difficulty of isolating so slow growing an organism from amongst other much more rapid growths, and from the changes which necessarily occur in sterilising sea-water.

This cause, if such it be, must therefore remain *sub judice*, and await further investigation, without, however, it is hoped, delaying in any way the good work of cleansing the harbours from their present objectionable pollution. The writer has not heard of cases arising among passengers on troopships or mail steamers, individuals from which weekly spend a few hours on shore when passing through Malta or Gibraltar, and who eat and drink on shore, and occasionally spend a night.

Its connection with the turning up of new clean soil, from which the human fæcal element is absent, has been mooted by those who hold that it is malarial in origin, but no such connection appears to exist. The countrymen who work all day in the fields are less subject to the fever than those who spend all their time in the towns and villages; and soldiers who are employed in the country do not suffer so much from this fever as those in barracks. Soldiers encamped on clean ground in the country do not suffer, but do so if on old and polluted ground near barracks, or on barrack squares. The Maltese of the large towns, from living in so small an island, have a peculiar habit of scarcely ever leaving their own town except to drive to certain country places, such as Notabile, Sliema, and St. Paul's Bay. The soldiers confine themselves to their recreation grounds and to the towns. These two classes of people are the ones which suffer most from the fever. The writer has not found that those officers and their friends and families who are in the habit of exploring the country valleys, and spending much of their time there, are in any way more subject to the effects of the disease. Officers and men at Gozo in tents and barracks seldom suffer (see p. 89). An outbreak is mentioned as occurring in 1844 during the excavation of a new dock at Cottonera; the works took place, however, in one of the most thickly populated, unhealthy, and dirty parts of Malta, and not in new ground. A medical officer, who was in Malta in 1884, has described to the writer an outbreak of most severe and fatal undulant fever which attacked some Royal Engineers employed in building fortifications in the country on the site of an old Roman (?) cemetery. No details are, however, available beyond three post-mortem reports, which were those of typical undulant fever. We can safely dismiss the subject, and feel justified in believing that the turning up of virgin or clean soil, clean from a human fæcal point of view, has no connection with the causation of this fever. Troops under canvas on cultivated or uncultivated fields in Malta have been most healthy and quite free from fever.

The influence of dust, polluted with human fæces, as a cause of enteric fever and other diseases in India, Egypt, and other dry and dusty places, has not in the writer's opinion been sufficiently investigated. We read of a French cavalry regiment[1] which contracted a number of cases of enteric fever (112 in 1600 men, 12 fatal) from manœuvring on a ploughed field recently manured with human fæces. Of course in well-kept roads the chances of human fæces containing the specific virus of any given disease must be small. Though in a fever of such an ambulatory type as the one under discussion the chances are increased, it is just as prevalent in those streets of Valetta that are paved as in other unpaved and dusty ones.

It is well, however, to bear this possible, if improbable, cause in mind, when dealing with excavations connected with old sewage drains, or the foundations of old houses, and not to allow fæcally polluted earth to lie about, where winds and breezes may carry it to the human mouth.

We have therefore, from an eminently practical point of view, reason to connect the occurrence of certain cases of this fever with fæcal pollution of air near the person affected. The bed in which the soldier sleeps is but 24 inches from the ground, so that when the pollution is in the floor of the room it has not far to go. In the cases where sewer gas has been thought to have caused the disease, the distance that the poison must have travelled downwards, or through the house in the direction of direct draughts, has varied from four to twenty or thirty feet. In all the instances mentioned there have been definite air currents to account for the carriage of the virus through the atmosphere. The deficient ventilation of certain rooms in which it has occurred has been most marked, tending to increase the strength of the dose of the poison inhaled, from absence of dilution with purer air. The influence of overcrowding and over-population has also been noted, increasing as it does the liability of the soil to pollution.

The organism is an exceedingly small one, even among its minute brother micrococci, and though spores and the miasmatic infection of paludism are often carried to considerable distances through the air, we know too little of at least the latter, to compare them with this disease germ. Flügge states: "Nothing certain is known as to the distances to which dry but living bacteria can be carried by the wind: from the extraordinary distances over which other particles of dust can be carried, we may conclude that when opportunity offers the bacteria may be carried over very considerable areas."

Now dust from the Mount Vesuvius eruption was found 400 miles off. Though as a rule the outside air contains but few micro-organisms, in the "air of dwelling-rooms they are found in very small numbers, even when all movement of the air has been avoided as much as possible for some time, while they are present in large numbers when the dust has been raised by movements and other disturbances. It is found that bacteria when once they have passed into the air float or are carried about by currents of air for a varying time" (Flügge).

[1] *Lancet*, vol. i. p. 307, 1896 (abstract from Dr. Henrot, *Revue d'Hygiene*).

From practical experiments in laboratories there is not much difficulty in accepting the passage of this disease virus through the atmosphere to the patient's mouth, throat, and possibly further, when once it has entered the air.

We have next to discuss the reasons for believing that it can rise from the polluted soil in which we believe it to exist. We know from experiment and from practical epidemiological experience, that germs do not rise spontaneously from moist surfaces, and that even strong currents of air are unable to detach them from such situations. Hoffmann (*Archiv für Hygiene*, vols. i. and ii. pt. ii.) has pointed out that there is in porous soils what he terms a superficial zone of evaporation, in which the moisture varies from saturation to zero. In hot weather the zone is considerable in extent, and when rain descends on it after a period of heat and drought, it is often capable of retaining the whole of the latter without its lower border becoming wet. In such there is always a dry layer, between the surface part which is temporarily wetted by the rain and the deeper strata in which the water lies. Under these conditions the impurities which reach the soil become deposited in the dry zone. Under this zone is situated a layer which is always wet. When the upper zone is filled with rain the amount of water in the second zone remains constant, for any excess which it may receive passes down into a third zone or that of the underground water. Any micro-organisms present in the first zone are alternately immersed in water or air. In the former case they remain in the soil, in the latter case they may be transferred to the atmosphere by air currents. The outermost layer of soil may be kept moist by slight and long-continued rain, in which case, however large the dry zone, its organisms would not easily escape into the air.[1]

The fact that the air[2] in well-flushed English sewers, in which decomposition and evolution of gases is not going on, does not contain an excessive number of micro-organisms (Frankland), when compared with outside air, does not invalidate the possible causal connection between sewer gas and this fever. It is not the quantity but the quality and pathogenic nature of the germs which are all important questions here. Enteric fever (Cameron, etc.),[3] diarrhœa, sore throats (tonsillitis), and other diseases have been traced to such a cause. Again, the number of germs found in cesspit air, and in air in the neighbourhood of sewage pollution of soil, has been found to largely exceed those of sewers or ordinary air. Arthur has shown that bacteria can undoubtedly grow up the sides or walls of the damp nutrient sewers, and if these latter become at all dry, air currents readily detach and disperse them. The temperature of sewers in the Mediterranean is higher than

[1] See also Cavendish Lecture in *Brit. Med. Journal*, June 11th, 1892.

[2] Arthur, "Bacteriology of Sewer Air," *Sanit. Record*, Nov. 10th, 1894. See also Robertson, "Study of the Micro-organisms in Air, especially in Sewer Air," *Brit. Med. Journal*, Dec. 15th, 1888, vol. ii. p. 1340.

[3] Tichbourne (R. Academy Med. Ireland), *Lancet*, vol. i. p. 1416, or *Brit. Med. Jour.* vol. i. p. 1285 (May 22nd, 1897). See also on p. 71.

that in England (average 55° F.),[1] and therefore more favourable to germ growth.

Now in Malta, besides the great influence of air temperature, from the point of view of actual heat, on the growth of the virus of this fever, we have clear evidence of the controlling power which rainfall has on the prevalence of the fever. While the surface of the ground is wet the fever lies dormant, ready to burst forth with dry weather, provided there is at the same time a suitable amount of warmth for its development. Dry summers have always been the most severe "fever years" with respect to undulant fever. The fever does not occur in any amount during spring or until the rains have ceased. The undulant fever prevalence curve follows the inverse ratio of the rainfall, month by month. In this respect a moderate but continued rainfall is better for prevention than an interrupted fall of similar amount. Moisture also seems to be necessary to the growth of the virus in the soil, but at the same time the virus does not leave the soil until the superficial layer has dried up. This would seem to explain how it is that rooms, the walls and floors of which are alternately wet and dry, give the greatest number of cases of this fever when infective causes are present, and how the question of dampness, so often connected with the occurrence of cases of this fever, comes in. It also explains the liability to fever on the part of those living in ground floor rooms with uncemented floors, and the undoubted efficacy of cementing floors in unhealthy ground floor tenements.

Until 1885 Valetta (one of the healthiest parts of Malta) was drained by means of large conduits, dug by the Knights in the porous stone, and running beneath the streets. These were directly connected with the houses by means of pipes made of porous stone. These covered ditches were in some cases as much as forty feet deep, and in all cases wide enough for a man to walk in. They were unflushed, and the sewage passed along them in a stagnant but constant stream which must have soaked into the porous foundations of the city in all directions. In 1885 new sewers were laid on modern principles along the bottoms of these conduits, the upper part of the gallery being utilised for storm water. The new main drains are well laid, but the means of flushing are insufficient. Moreover, the majority of the house closets, at any rate in Maltese houses, are hand flushed, and as water, in excess of a certain limited quantity, is charged for, the economical householder neglects to supply his share of flushing water. Owing to the enormous population crowded into a small space (Valetta is said to be one of the most thickly populated places in the world, 75,883 persons to the square mile), every available foot of ground is utilised for building purposes, and to arrange for a sufficient number of closets for so many people without having them unduly close to the living rooms, has proved an impossibility. Consequently bedroom cabinet

[1] See *Lancet*, vol. i. p. 131; 1897.

closets abound. To provide air and light to a small extent to the numerous small rooms found in the modern reconstructed buildings, small shafts are built varying from six to twenty feet square, while others are built round an enclosed yard. Many rooms have no external opening except into a passage or into such a shaft. In these shafts or yards, two, three, or more closets are placed one above another, on bracketed balconies. Room brick-ventilators often open from above a bed, straight into these closets, while in the majority the bedroom opens directly into the closet, or into a small passage and within a few feet of it. Each soil-pipe runs into a vertical pipe running up one side of the shaft, and opening as a ventilator on the roof at various heights above it. On calm days and when the sirocco wind is blowing, little air rises from these shafts, while exhalations from the ventilator appear to fall into them. The closets are rarely sewer-gas proof. Moreover, on account of the variability in altitude above the sea of the different portions of Valetta, main drain and house drain ventilators that may be carried well above the roof on which they are placed, are often on a level with the windows of adjacent houses. The same may be said of Gibraltar and many other Mediterranean towns. In some barracks also we find main drain ventilators and room louvred ventilators side by side. It is true that the latter are theoretically foul air outlets, but practically this depends greatly on the direction of air currents from time to time. The upper part of the old conduit, now used for surface and storm water, is wet in winter and dry in summer, and though trapped, the traps soon dry up in hot weather and cease to have any effect. The above remarks apply also to the Three Cities on the Cottonera side of the harbour.

That the writer does not attach any fever-producing power to smells, *per se*, goes without saying, for indeed in such case few dwellers in the Mediterranean would escape, but at the same time a smell is often an indication of sewer gas escape, and of the direction in which it travels. That enteric fever can arise from air pollution from sewers there seems little doubt,[1] but there we are dealing with a bacillus, and not with a micrococcus. In the case of this minute micrococcus we have much to make out before laying down anything definite on the question of its portability, but not only is it as minute as many aërial spores, but the writer has met with so many cases of this fever occurring next to such closets or drain ventilators, in otherwise healthy houses, as to believe firmly that their occurrence is more than accidental, and as much connected with sewer exhalations as many sore throats occurring in similar places.

It has been urged that direct experiment in England has proved that the air of sewers contains few micro-organisms; but it must be remembered that in these the wetted perimeter is a fairly constant factor,

[1] *Army Med. Report*, 1876 (Malta), p. 64; Ziemssen's *Encyclopedia of Medicine*, vol. i. p. 56; Uffelmann, *Indian Gazette*, Jan. 1, 1896; Tichbourne, *Brit. Med. Jour.* vol. i. p. 1285; 1897; etc.

owing to adequate general and individual flushing. In Malta, on the other hand, the flushing is very inadequate, and there is a condition of alternate wet and dry surfaces. The higher temperature in the Mediterranean also favours decomposition and germ life. It has also been said that sewage is too alkaline to allow of the growth of this micrococcus. This is not the case. Not only have a large number of undulant fever stools and specimens of sewerage effluent, which the author has tested, proved neutral or faintly alkaline in reaction, but also the walls and stone floors that have become soaked through with escaped sewage, in rooms where this fever has been especially prevalent, have proved of a faint and suitable alkalinity, whereas stone from clean walls and more especially newly-quarried stone of a similar nature have proved very strongly alkaline. The strongest argument in favour of the surmise that this fever is due to the effects of an aërial virus from infected soil (or drains), rests upon the basis of its localised and seasonable prevalence, and on the fact that there is, on the one hand, no other more strongly grounded theory of causation, nor, on the other side, any evidence to negative the theory. That it cannot be definitely proved until the almost insurmountable difficulties of obtaining plate cultivations of this slow-growing, heat-loving micro-organism are overcome, is granted; but the theory is one which will repay investigation, for its proof or disproof will equally lead to the path of truth, and towards the important goal of prevention.

In Sliema and other towns and villages, the cesspit system is still in vogue. The cesspits are, according to law, imperviously rendered, but this regulation is evaded by knocking holes in the cement after it has been passed by the Government inspector. That these cesspits drain into the porous foundations of the houses there is no doubt, a fact self-evident when their position and their capacity, with the infrequency with which they are emptied, is taken into account. They are placed in a large number of cases under the foot-path and front door, and their odour is most offensive to passers by. In this cesspit population undulant fever is most common, a condition to be expected if our former deductions are correct. In certain cases the house drain passes into natural clefts or caverns in the porous rocky foundations; a coveted condition on account of the saving of original expense in construction and subsequent emptying, which latter is never done. It need hardly be noted that these houses are the constant habitat of this fever. Fortunately, it has at last been decided, after years of discussion, to drain Sliema and neighbouring places, but it is a great pity that it was not done in the first instance, before the porous rock became infiltrated with filth, in which case this place might have been one of the pleasantest, most convenient, and healthiest of places to live, in Malta. Let us hope this will be realised in the future. The mistake that is made in overcrowded Malta, is to allow every new house outside Valetta and the Three Cities to build a cesspit under its foundations, instead of organising a general system of sewage removal. If such a plan was adopted in the early stages of suburban building the expense would be slight, gradual, and borne to a large extent by the builders. In the present case things are allowed to go on until the magnitude of the pollution and sickness calls for urgent and costly redress, at a time when the vested rights of the landlords make them averse to contributing towards the necessary outlay; without taking into account the financial loss entailed by attacks of this fever on individual bread-winners, a no small item.

The author has particularly noticed that the cases occurring when the fæcal soil pollution, to which an outbreak is attributed, is of long standing are the most severe. This may imply that the virus increases in virulence during a saprophytic assistance in soil. It is to be noted in connection with this fact that the monkeys inoculated with virus from man suffered more severely than those inoculated with virus obtained from monkeys. This is the case with certain other poisons.

The cases which the author has believed to arise from drain or sewer emanations have, as a general rule, been less severe than those from cess-pit exhalations, or more especially from fæcal pollution of soil. Outbreaks from the last cause have been more extended in their effects, have produced a greater number of cases in proportion to the number of persons exposed to the infection, and such cases have, on the whole, been mere severe in character. In houses where drain exhalations have been blamed, there has often been a marked interval between the onsets of the individual cases. In instances where soil pollution has been in question a number of cases have been admitted from one hut, room, or block of barracks within a short time of one another. In one flat containing two occupants one suffered severely from this fever in 1894, and went home to England; of the two succeeding occupants, one suffered severely during the following summer and also went to England. Of the next two occupants in the spring of 1896, the husband had a mild, though long attack, in the early part of May, the wife a similar attack commencing at the end of May. In this case the bedroom and dressing-room opened on to a small landing some five yards square containing a water-closet. The last occupants, who only were under the writer's medical charge, described this closet as being in a most insanitary condition when they entered the flat, and though they had replaced it by a modern one it was then far from satisfactory.

So far we have arrived at the conclusion that there are reasons for believing that undulant fever is caused, in the majority of instances, by a specific micrococcus emanating, during hot dry weather, from a saphrophytic existence in soil polluted with the fæces of those suffering from the same disease.

From the fact that the infection apparently travels through the air, and that the initial symptoms are, as has been recently noticed in certain other diseases, tightness in the throat, redness and tenderness of the tonsils with often a coating of translucent fur, a furred tongue, slight swelling of submaxillary and cervical lymphatic glands, epigastric tenderness, anorexia, nausea, and even vomiting, pain and stiffness of the muscles of the neck and back, it is not unlikely that the virus gains entrance to the human body by means of the inspired air. Though these local symptoms are, however, not strongly marked in many of the cases, we must remember that the virus does not usually produce strongly-marked local symptoms. In the case of inoculation, though a comparatively large amount of the virus was injected into the monkey's forearm, no local results were noticed. It has not produced local suppuration in any case that the writer has seen. Moreover, while there does not appear to be any other means of entrance which so fully fits in with the facts we have at our disposal, there is evidence against other usual modes of entrance.

That it enters the body tissues, and is not a toxic intestinal or bronchial parasite, is evident from the ineffectiveness of intestinal and respirative antiseptic remedies, and more particularly from the exceedingly varied and localised nature of many of the symptoms, implying a local action of the living virus rather than a general action of a circulating toxic agent.

It also seems probable that the living virus is excreted with the fæces and urine, and so returning to the soil is able to infect the air of a definite and circumscribed area and so re-enter the human subject.

Age and Sex.—All ages are liable to this fever. As in these short service days the majority of soldiers are under thirty years of age, we find this fever in the army in Malta between the ages of fifteen and thirty. Infants rarely suffer. The average age of 500 non-fatal cases collected by the author was twenty-three years and four months (sixteen to forty-seven); that of thirty fatal cases recorded in the books of the military hospital at Valetta was twenty-three years (nineteen to twenty-eight). Bruce states that of the cases treated by him in 1886, two were under twenty, seventy-six under thirty, and six under forty. Chartres states that in an epidemic in Malta in 1866, six were about thirty, forty-five over and fifty-seven under that age (nineteen to thirty-seven). Moffet, in Gibraltar, gives its military prevalence among men as 94 per cent under and 6 per cent over thirty years of age.

Among the inhabitants of Italy and Sicily, Guiffré gives between fifteen and forty years as the most susceptible ages, and states that children under six and adults over fifty are relatively exempt. Notification of this disease has only recently been instituted for the civil population of Malta, but the accounts given of its occurrence seem to agree with the above, except that as the disease in children is of a mild character and has few definite symptoms, it is probable that many such cases are missed. Native practitioners give from six to thirty as the most susceptible period. Marston, at Malta in 1860, stated "it affects *par excellence* young men under thirty-five, particularly those of rheumatic diathesis; next in frequency children; most unfrequently the aged." Tomaselli of Catania is of opinion that the greatest number of cases occur between the ages of six and thirty, less frequently from two to six, and from thirty to fifty; very rarely above fifty. Rummo of Naples is of the same opinion.

Sex appears to have little or no influence, any apparent difference being due to age, occupation, and surroundings. In a given number of married families in the army, the writer has for these reasons found the women if anything more subject than the men.

Incubation period.—In a fever whose onset is in many cases so markedly insidious, it is very difficult to collect evidence on this point. In the inoculation experiments upon monkeys the incubation period was about twenty-four hours. Here the poison being introduced directly into the tissues, had not to first overcome the resistance of the mucous membranes and other natural barriers to infection.

Chartres (1865) states that of forty-one cases occurring in one month, the first commenced six days after the regiment entered Verdala Barracks.

Marston (1861) mentions the cases of two men who were attacked ten days after bathing in a dirty part of the Grand Harbour.

Bruce (1889) gives the case of an officer who attributed his attack "to a long exposure to foul emanations in one of the filthiest parts of the Quarantine Harbour," nine days before. He also states that the disease has developed in England in persons who have been from fourteen to seventeen days away from Malta. He gives the probable duration as from a few days to twenty or thirty days, stating that there is no evidence that it exceeds two months.

Moffet (1889) gives reasons for believing it to be from six to forty-nine days.

Ellis (1890) states that the first case, in the outbreak on H.M.S. *Orion*, occurred five days after entering dock, and twelve days after arrival in Malta.

Guiffré (1893) gives six to ten days or more; Jaccoud (1886), who studied the disease in Paris, in persons who had come recently from Italy, makes the incubation not less than ten days.

Many persons are described as developing the fever at varying periods after arrival in England from Malta. All such cases that the author has personally met with have been reduced on investigation to within a fortnight, and many have appeared to have had the fever on them before leaving. There is no doubt that cases develop on board ship on the way to England, the author having met with cases of from one to five clear days, and one less certain of ten days. The two following are instances of cases said, but erroneously, to have developed after arrival in England, and are samples of a class of cases which have led to statements of long incubation periods. A colonel went on leave, and twelve days after leaving Malta consulted a doctor in England, who pronounced him to be suffering from this fever, from which he did not recover for nearly two years. He had, however, been feeling "seedy and liverish" all the voyage, and two days before embarking at Malta informed the writer, during a casual conversation, that he was "off his feed," had been suffering from headaches in the evening, and thought it was time he went on leave. This officer had doubtless been suffering from slight pyrexia even before leaving Malta. The other case was reported to have had an even longer incubation period (over fourteen days), but as he had been sick in his quarters for nearly a fortnight before leaving Malta (though not officially on the sick list), with a temperature every evening, the report must have been an erroneous one.

Where there is often a long latent period between the undulations or relapses, a variable onset, and a very large difference in the action of the virus (virulence or susceptibility) on different persons, there is doubtless a variable incubation period. The author has met with cases of fever commencing eight, ten, fourteen, and many within thirty days of their arrival in Malta. He is inclined to think that it may be as short as three days in some cases. Probably three to ten or fifteen days is near the mark, in cases where the first febrile onset is noted.

Seasonal prevalence.—In the military hospitals in Malta, where every case which occurs among the troops is necessarily admitted, the admission-rate is lowest during the first quarter of the year, rises rapidly in May to a maximum in July, August, and September, after which it soon falls until a low rate is again met with in December, January, and February.

The rate during the last quarter is higher than that of the first quarter for the following reasons:—(1) Certain relapses and ambulatory cases, which become infected earlier in the year, are admitted during this quarter; (2) the annual occurrence of enteric fever (which commences from two to three weeks after the first heavy rains) takes place at this time, and a few cases of this fever most probably are included among the undulant fever cases through error in diagnosis; (3) the average temperature during the last quarter is some 7·84° F. higher than that of the first quarter, and the average temperature of October and November is 10·6° F. higher than that of the succeeding four months (December to March inclusive), when the fever rate is lowest. This difference in temperature (reckoned from daily observations at 9 A.M. for ten years, taken in the official observatory) has been proved experimentally to have a distinct effect on the growth of the virus of the disease in question.

A similar mode of prevalence has been noted over and over again in the published Army Medical Reports since 1817 and in Naval Reports since 1840. Marston, writing in 1859, states: "The disease prevails particularly during the spring and summer months." A similar mode of prevalence is also met with in Gibraltar (Moffet), Palermo (Guiffré), Rome (Galassi), and Cyprus (Carageorgiades).

In the following table will be found the actual admissions for undulant fever into one hospital in Malta, from a body of men whose average strength for each year remained practically constant (compiled by Bruce and by the Author) contrasted with the mean monthly temperature (at 9 a.m.) for ten years (1881-1890):—

TABLE V.

Months of the Year.	Admissions. Bruce[1] 11 Years.	Admissions. Hughes 6 Years.	Total.	Ratio per cent.	Mean Monthly Temperature at 9 A.M. for 10 Years.	
January	12	40	52	4·1	56·74° F.	
February	13	30	43	3·4	57·06°	
March	20	44	64	5·0	59·64°	
April	23	55	78	5·2	62·76°	
May	75	77	152	11·5	66·94°	Max. prevalence.
June	80	83	163	12·3	72·81°	Max. prevalence.
July	102	118	220	16·5	79·43°	Max. prevalence.
August	52	119	171	12·8	80·17°	Max. prevalence.
September	42	116	158	11·8	78·96°	Max. prevalence.
October	38	73	111	8·4	72·73°	
November	32	46	68	5·2	64·88°	
December	12	37	49	3·8	59·35°	
Total	501	838	1339	100·0	67·82°	

Though the actual monthly variation in the admission-rate for this fever varies slightly from year to year, the above table gives the average of a number of years, and it moreover agrees with the experience of others in former years. The author is of opinion that a certain number of cases of undiagnosed enteric fever may have been included in his figures for the last three months of the year (October-December), as that fever was prevalent outside Valetta three times during those months, and to a less extent perhaps in January. It will be clearly seen, however, that undulant fever especially prevails from May to the middle of October, and is least prevalent from November to April inclusive—facts of import to those intending to visit Malta or other Mediterranean towns, and to residents able to spend a portion of the year away in England or elsewhere.

Climatic influences.—(*a*) *Rainfall.*—In Malta and Gibraltar the attack-rate of undulant fever has been found to increase in an inverse ratio to the amount and continuance of the rainfall from month to month. While the surface of the ground is kept constantly wet by rainfall, the attack-rate is low, but the cessation of rain in warm weather is at once followed by an increased activity on the part of the fever poison, and the attack-rate rises very rapidly, its fall being delayed until the commencement of the autumn rain, when it is well marked and often sudden.

This statement is based on the monthly admission-rate for undulant fever at Cottonera military hospital for the year 1891, and at Valetta military hospital for the years 1891, 1892, and 1895; collected in both

[1] *Vide British Medical Jour.* vol. i. p. 1101; 1889.

places by the writer, by excluding from the admissions for "Simple Continued Fever," as far as possible, all non-fatal cases in hospital for less than 20 days, and all cases subsequently proved to have been incorrectly diagnosed. The admission-rates so obtained have been compared with the rainfall collected daily on the roof of Valetta military hospital, at a spot not more than a mile and a half from the farthest barrack from which the cases were admitted, particulars of which are yearly published by Government in the *Army Medical Reports.*

This ratio is further confirmed by a comparison between the admission-rates to Valetta hospital for the years 1884 to 1887, kindly supplied to me in 1893 by Surgeon-Major Bruce, and the official monthly rainfall return for those years.

Tables VI. and VII. give some of these figures in detail, and Chart V. the same results in more graphic form for the years 1891 and 1892.

It is, moreover, interesting to note that in the past we find that recorded epidemic or excessive prevalence of this fever has, as a rule, occurred during unusually dry years;[1] and that the annual admission-rate for simple continued fever (which, as will be shown later on, has some bearing on the question), has during the last thirty-seven years varied inversely with the rainfall with but one exception. The exception occurred in the year 1876, when a comparatively low admission-rate was combined with a small amount of rainfall. Two factors were, however, at work that year, namely, a most unusually large number of rainy days occurring during the warm weather, and the fact that this year was midway between two periods of excessive prevalence, and should in the ordinary course of events have reached a much lower point on the scale than it actually did. It therefore appears that the rainfall was not without effect even during 1876.

[1] Chartres (*Army Medical Report* for 1866) describes an epidemic as occurring during that year in Malta, "after an unusually dry winter, so scanty a fall of rain not having been experienced in the island of Malta for many years," etc. See also *A.M.D. Reports* for 1837, 1840, 1841, 1865, 1867, 1872, 1885, and 1895.

[TABLES

TABLE VI.—*Admissions for Undulant Fever contrasted with Rainfall and Temperature*

Months.	1891.			1892.			1895.		
	Admissions.	Rainfall.	Average temp.	Admissions.	Rainfall.	Average temp.	Admissions.	Rainfall.	Average temp.
January . .	4	4·58	52·0°	7	2·84	60·8°	6[1]	1·85	55·3°
February .	6	4·72	51·0°	12	1·36	59·1°	1	1·01	56·9°
March . .	10	·11	57·6°	12	·11	61·9°	10	·39	58·2°
April . .	9	·55	61·5°	4	2·40	63·6°	30	·15	63·3°
May . .	11	·14	64·5°	16	3·21	66·5°	39	·65	66·2°
June . .	18	·01	72·7°	8	...	74·6°	37	...	72·1°
July . .	22	...	78·8°	21	·38	79·1°	46	...	80·6°
August . .	38	...	79·7°	33	...	80·2°	32	·15	80·0°
September .	20	·52	77·7°	28	3·61	75·8°	40	·37	77·8°
October . .	23	2·96	71·7°	16	1·62	73·7°	10	1·23	74·3°
November .	20	1·46	65·6°	5	7·16	65·7°	5	2·19	68·0°
December .	12	3·09	61·5°	16[1]	1·84	61·6°	1	3·63	59·5°
Total .	193	18·14	66·2°	178	24·53	68·6°	258	11·60	67·7°

[1] Enteric fever prevalent at this time.

TABLE VII.—*From Figures supplied by Surgeon-Major Bruce*

Month.	1884.		1885.		1886.		1887.	
	Admissions.	Rainfall.	Admissions.	Rainfall.	Admissions.	Rainfall.	Admissions.	Rainfall.
January .	4	10·87	...	4·07	6	4·93	6	2·92
February .	3	·64	...	·26	1	3·28	3	1·89
March . .	6	1·39	1	·10	5	·73	5	·23
April . .	...	·45	1	·55	2	·60	2	1·40
May . .	2	·48	38	...	30	...	7	·18
June . .	6	·16	28	...	16	·05	12	·15
July . .	8	...	19	·02	8	...	30	...
August .	3	·20	7	·08	11	...	19	·23
September	3	·24	8	·30	5	3·59	17	·35
October .	2	1·42	4	·68	9	·55	3	11·42
November	6	5·65	3	3·39	5	6·83	4	1·38
December	1	3·58	2	2·65	2	4·31	3	·97
Total. .	44	25·05	111	12·15	100	24·87	121	21·12

It is interesting also to note that while the fever prevailed in epidemic form in Naples and Catania in 1872, it also prevailed in most unusual quantity in Malta,[1] and with a severity that has not been exceeded since. This was an unusually hot and dry year (rainfall 13·5 in.). A similar state of affairs occurred again in 1885.

It is evident that meteorological conditions have a great deal to do with the amount of prevalence of the fever. In 1895 there was an unusual number of cases, whereas the rainfall (11·6 in.) was very small, and had the temperature been greater, doubtless the prevalence would have been greater. In the following spring of 1896 very few cases occurred, while there was unusually cold weather, and almost constant (though not heavy) rainfall; but in June, when it became dry and hot, the fever at once broke out.

CHART V.

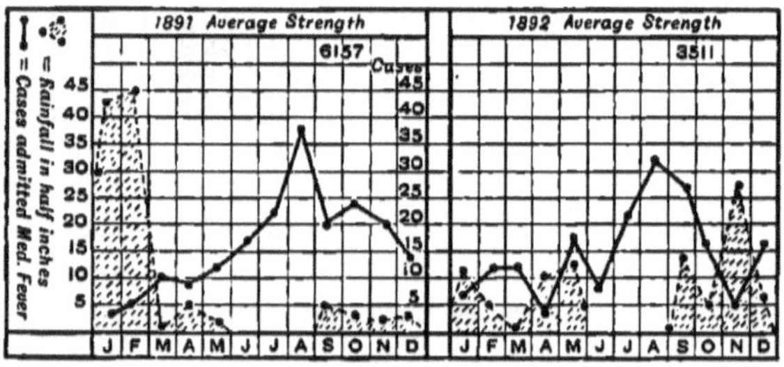

(b) *Temperature.*—That the virus of this fever requires a certain temperature for its artificial existence and growth has been already mentioned in the section on the bacteriology of this fever. That a similar factor is necessary for its saprophytic existence, and to enable it to produce effects upon the human body, is further proved by the relationship which exists between atmospheric temperature and the geographical prevalence of the disease.

Thus north of latitude 46° N., which roughly corresponds to the isotherm of 55° F. (average annual temperature), this fever does not appear to exist except as an imported disease. South of this line the fever is met with as an endemic disease, whose annual prevalence becomes of increasing importance as the average annual temperature rises above 60° F. It has usually been described as a subtropical disease, though experiments would lead us to believe that it may be able to exist in countries whose average daily temperature does not rise above 109° F., and according to some authors it would appear to exist as far south as Massowah in the Red Sea, which, being situated about latitude 15° N., is within the boundaries of the tropical isotherm of 80° F. This is said to be one of the hottest places in the world, with an actual average annual temperature of 90·5° F.[2]

[1] See Notter (1876) and *A.M.D. Reports.*
[2] *Manual of Hygiene,* Notter and Firth, 1896, p. 722.

In Malta but a few sporadic cases (and relapses) occur in the winter, and during January, February, and March they are rarely seen in the wards, but the number of admissions rapidly increases as the daily average temperature reaches 60° F. This usually occurs in May, but if this month be unusually cool (as in 1896) but few cases occur until June. The converse is also true. In the Navy we find the same state of things.[1] The limitations of its tropical existence must be left to future investigators.

Length of residence.—In Malta we do not find that residents acquire immunity from this fever, and whereas enteric fever specially favours newcomers, undulant fever attacks even those who have been in residence for six or more years. When a regiment is first placed in an unhealthy barrack the susceptible element is usually very great, and it suffers accordingly, nor does previous Mediterranean service confer an immunity. Moreover, though the younger soldiers (who usually have but short service in the locality) suffer a great deal on account of their youth, older soldiers with long local service also suffer, and to a much larger extent than is the case with enteric fever.

Thus the regiment mentioned in the epidemic of 1892 had been three years in Malta; and the majority of the men attacked had been all that time with the regiment. Again Chartres, in his account of an epidemic in Malta in 1866, says: "The men attacked (41) had all of them a continuous service of over seven years in the Mediterranean, two years and a half of which were spent in the island of Malta."

The average service in the Mediterranean of 270 cases in 1895 was 2·05 years (one month to 11 years). The writer has known this fever attack English residents after a stay of over twenty years in Malta. The apparent immunity enjoyed by many European residents is probably due to their having inhabited healthy houses during their stay in Malta, as those who are long in the place rarely change their houses; and to a certain survival of the insusceptible. There is no doubt that although the native Maltese suffer from this fever, they do not do so to anything like the extent to which European visitors suffer. This has been attributed to their having acquired an insusceptibility by having gone through an attack, mild or otherwise, during childhood, and to the fact that their parents have transmitted to them an hereditary power of resisting the encroaches of the poison. However this may be, they suffer most severely from non-endemic diseases (such as measles, etc.), whenever these are introduced from without, both of which facts are comparable with many instances of susceptibility of natives to endemic and non-endemic diseases all over the world.

The length of time previously spent in the Mediterranean (*i.e.* in Gibraltar and Malta) by 292 consecutive cases was as follows:—

[1] *Health of the Navy*, 1887, etc.; also *Trans. Epid. Soc.* vol. ix. p. 87 (Gipps).

TABLE VIII.

Previous Service.	Cases.
1 month	4
2 months	10
3-4 ,,	15
5-6 ,,	24
7-12 ,,	12
Total under one year	65
1 year but under two	19
2 years ,, ,, three	35
3 ,, ,, ,, four	88
4 ,, ,, ,, five	8
5 ,, ,, ,, six	8
6 ,, and over	4
	292

The large number attacked during their fourth year of residence is probably due to their having moved as a large-sized unit into an infective area at such a period in their service.

Acclimatisation, as applied to undulant fever, is therefore, in regiments or large bodies of men, simply a survival of the fittest (most insusceptible), or a weeding out of the susceptible; and is not acquired by those unattacked, by simple residence in countries where this fever prevails in healthy houses or barracks. The writer knows of three English residents who contracted this fever after twenty, seventeen, and twelve years' residence in Malta. He himself contracted the disease after five and a half years, and a brother officer after over six years' residence. Few of the regular English permanent residents appear to escape an attack at some period or other, but do not seem to have suffered twice from long attacks.

Immunity from subsequent attacks.—Though the writer and others have carefully examined the recorded medical histories of many thousands of soldiers serving in the Mediterranean, they have failed (with one exception) to find mention of a second attack of true undulant fever affecting one individual. This may, however, be owing to the fact that in these "short service" days, soldiers stay but a few years exposed to its influence; and that a large number of those who have suffered from this fever are invalided to England and do not return. The only exception was in the case of an officer, who, together with his wife, suffered from an attack of this fever in August 1895 in a small quarter in Malta, where the drain-pipe had burst and leaked into their room. Both individuals were about fifty years old, and the pyrexial and other symptoms were unmistakably those of undulant fever. In April 1871, when previously serving in Malta, this officer had (when in the ranks), suffered severely from fever when quartered in Isola Gate, for which he was invalided to England after ninety-three days' illness.

From his graphic description of his symptoms, both during the pyrexial period and during his subsequent convalescence in England, the writer is of opinion that he suffered at that time from a typical and severe attack of this fever. This would amount to two attacks in the same individual with an interval of twenty-four years.

It is not uncommon in Malta for cases, with every appearance of their being attacks of undulant fever, to be apparently cured in from one to four months, and to be discharged to duty, returning to the same barrack-room and bed from which they were originally admitted, only to again develop fever of an unmistakable, lengthy, or even fatal character, after a month or more of apparent good health. During their first admission these cases were certainly not suffering from mild enteric or other specific fever, nor from the common febricula of the place. In a disease whose duration is an unfixed quantity, it is not impossible that many of the cases of seven to fourteen days' fever, so often met with, may be abortive attacks of true undulant fever; but what is certain, is that these short attacks do not confer immunity from more severe ones occurring subsequently. Again, it is impossible to say in such cases (in which the apyrexial period does not much exceed a month in duration), whether the patient is suffering from a relapse from his original infection, or from the effects of a fresh dose of the poison. By the expression "true undulant fever," the writer in this work refers to cases whose pyrexia is typical and has lasted at least three weeks, or in which a post-mortem examination has been held.

Guilia (Malta, 1871) states that this fever has often been manifest more than once in the same individual, instancing a case in which an English lady had three separate attacks, but he does not give particulars of their length. Guiffré is of opinion that one attack does not confer immunity, and mentions that persons have suffered from it a second and third time in Naples, Palermo, and in Malta. Carageorgiades (Cyprus, 1891) states that as a rule one attack does confer immunity, and that he has "seen persons who had suffered from this fever ten or fifteen years ago protected from a second attack." Bruce says: "In my opinion one attack does confer immunity."

Many naval surgeons are of opinion that one attack rather predisposes to a second, and for this reason those invalided from the Mediterranean are not sent back until after a long period. Thus Gipps (1890) says: "I would here take the opportunity of calling in question the statement made by Surgeon Bruce as to one attack conferring immunity from a second. This is distinctly contradictory to the experience of naval medical and other officers; and so strongly is this held to be the case that officers and men who have once had this fever are not sent back to the station till after a long time has elapsed. In fact, in the naval service, exactly the opposite view is held to that just quoted, and so far from one attack granting immunity, it is looked on as predisposing very strongly to a second and third attack; and I have myself seen many men who have had more than two separate attacks."

The writer has often been told of cases of two or three separate attacks, which, on investigation, prove to be short febriculas, or relapses of one attack. The comparative immunity of the native adult population of Malta has been ascribed to individuals having suffered from the fever during youth (see death-rate tables), and though, in the writer's experience, many adult Maltese suffer from the fever, it cannot be denied that the native population have (as is the case with most endemic diseases) acquired a certain protective immunity. It is probable, from the facts at our disposal, that an attack of this fever does confer immunity, at any rate for a number of years; but that this immunity, like that of enteric fever, is by no means absolute in every individual; also it is impossible at present to lay down the period after which he becomes proof against relapses.

TABLE IX.—*Mortality Rates: Civilian population of Malta*, 1895, *per mille*

Place.	Infantile Mortality.	Under 5.	Over 5.	All Ages.	Population.
Malta . . .	267·35	100·05	14·43	25·41	153,399
Valetta . .	276·09	100·62	13·11	21·85	24,132
Floriana . .	210·81	68·31	14·41	23·37	6,076
Cottonera .	271·88	92·83	11·49	21·89	28,450
Villages . .	267·74	104·55	15·67	27·51	94,741
Gozo . . .	277·18	94·98	13·51	24·30	19,545
Victoria . .	338·16	102·53	20·88	31·56	6,337
Villages . .	258·89	91·31	10·22	21·12	13,208

The fact that a patient has suffered from enteric fever does not in any way protect him from a subsequent attack of undulant fever, nor does an attack of undulant fever confer immunity from subsequent enteric fever. On this point Guiffré, Bruce, Rummo, and Carageorgiades are very definite, and Maltese physicians are of the same opinion. Bruce states: "Several patients have come under my charge suffering from Malta fever who have previously had enteric fever."

Moreover, the serum of blood from patients suffering from (or who have recently suffered from) enteric fever has no agglomerative effect upon pure cultivations of the micrococcus Melitensis.

The writer has met with the following instances in his practice:—

Case 16.—*Enteric fever followed by undulant fever two years later.*

The writer's sister suffered from an attack of enteric fever with a relapse during the autumn of 1890, when at school in Brussels (aged seventeen years). In the autumn of 1892, together with a sister sleeping in the same room, she suffered from an unusually severe attack of undulant fever in Malta, the pyrexia of which lasted a hundred days. Between the attacks there was perfect convalescence, a year of which was spent in Malta, and a perfect convalescence was made from the second attack, the patient continuing to reside in Malta for two years afterwards.

Case 17.—*Mediterranean fever followed by fatal enteric fever four months later.*

An officer of the Royal Artillery suffered from unmistakable undulant fever from 26th November 1891 to 15th January 1892, when he was sent on leave to England and apparently recovered. He did not suffer from relapse, but returned to duty in Malta some two months after. On 5th May he was admitted to hospital suffering from acute enteric fever which proved fatal. At the post-mortem examination typical enteric ulcers were found, nor was there evidence of any previous Peyerian disease having existed. Eberth's bacillus was obtained and cultivated from the spleen.

Case 18.—*Enteric fever followed by Mediterranean fever four years later.*

A sergeant of the Welsh Regiment was stated in his medical history sheet to have suffered from enteric fever in Cairo in February 1889; duration of time in hospital, fifty-nine days. He assured me that there was no doubt at the time as to the nature of the disease he was then suffering from. In June 1893 he was under the writer's medical charge suffering from undoubted undulant fever, the pyrexia of which lasted for fifty-six days, after which he was invalided to the sanatorium at Citta Vecchia, where he completely recovered.

Case 19.—*Mediterranean fever followed by fatal enteric fever with an apparent interval of less than one month.*

A corporal of the Royal Scots Regiment was in hospital under the author's care from 10th April to 10th May 1891, suffering from irregular temperature and constipation. He returned to duty apparently cured, but was readmitted to hospital on 6th June. On this second occasion he suffered from a similar form of irregular pyrexia with obstinate constipation until the 6th July following. In both cases the clinical symptoms were like those of many cases of undulant fever, and quite unlike those of enteric fever. He was transferred to the sanatorium, and his temperature remained normal until the end of the month, when it began to rise daily, proving fatal on 12th August. At the post-mortem examination typical early enteric ulceration was found, but no signs of previous Peyerian disease. The interval between the two attacks is in this instance so short that it cannot be considered as conclusive, yet it is of value, as it has the appearance of a case in which the two poisons either coexisted, or followed one another very closely.

The writer has also met with a case which for the first month exhibited the intermittent pyrexia of undulant fever, and during the second month a continuous temperature in which he died. The latest symptoms and post-mortem appearances were those of acute enteric fever, but with no signs of previous (healing) ulcers.

Cases of apparent enteric fever becoming undulant fever after the primary wave will be dealt with later.

Many cases of this fever are at first erroneously diagnosed as enteric fever, and such cases must be clearly separated from the above examples. The following is such a case:—

Case 20.—Pte. W., K.R.R. Mediterranean Service one year. Admitted 20-12-92 for enteric fever, and discharged 7-2-93 (fifty days), but readmitted for undulant fever twenty days later (lasting 120 days). This was really a case of undulant fever incorrectly diagnosed at first.

A previous attack of malaria does not confer immunity from subsequent attacks of this fever, as has been thought by some. The writer has met with cases of this fever affecting men who have previously suffered from paludism in India or in Mauritius. Chartres, in his account of an epidemic in 1866 in Malta, says of 108 cases: "Thirty-two had previously suffered from ague and intermittents in Canada and elsewhere." Guiffré, Bruce, and Carageorgiades are of the same opinion, while Rummo considers that previous attacks of malaria predispose cases to the effects of this fever. The writer has met with one case where previously contracted paludism appeared to complicate undulant fever pyrexia.

The three to five day febricula (simple ardent fever), of such common occurrence in the summer in the Mediterranean, appears to have no bearing on this question, nor has syphilis. Attacks of undulant fever undoubtedly pave the way in many instances for tubercular sequelæ, while patients suffering from gonorrhœa have on many occasions developed concurrent undulant fever. Cases have contracted gonorrhœa and primary syphilis a fortnight after discharge from hospital after severe undulant fever; nor do these diseases protect. Patients who have previously suffered from rheumatic fever or rheumatism are exceptionally prone to the rheumatic symptoms of this fever, while some have gone so far as to say that such cases are specially predisposed to attacks of undulant fever in the first instance. Rheumatic fever, if it exists at all as an endemic disease in Malta, is most uncommon.

Marston (1859) has described a peculiar alternation in certain localities of undulant and enteric fevers in epidemic form. In Malta the writer has neither found this borne out by statistics nor by his personal experience. Such occurrences would appear to be a matter of coincidence.

Changes in type (quantitative and qualitative).—The question of changes in type with respect to the prevalence of this fever is a very difficult one, owing to the absence of reliable statistics, cases of this fever having been always included with other fevers, or under various symptomatic headings. These headings under which the fever has been returned during the past have, however, one and all decreased both as regards numbers and case mortality. But with this fact we must remember to consider the decrease which has also taken place in the prevalence of dysentery, enterica, and other (doubtless preventible) diseases. If we carefully study the accounts of continuous fevers in those places where endemic malarial fevers do not exist, we find a most notable disappearance of malignant and fatal cases of continued fever (other than enterica). One is, on the whole, led to believe, at any rate in Malta and Gibraltar, that on account of better treatment, more skilful diagnosis, increasing care as to sanitation and general hygiene, or it may be from some actual change in type for the better, undulant fever has decreased in its case severity with the growth of the present century.[1] We must not, however, be led away by accounts of these fevers written early in the century into thinking that there were not then a proportionate number of mild cases also, as such authors were apt to base their descriptions upon their most noticeable and severe cases, neglecting or failing to recognise their milder cases. There is a general impression in Malta at the present time among civilian practitioners that this undulant fever is increasing in prevalence in that place, a theory which reminds one of similar opinions held in Malta in the days of Marston and Notter.[2] The theory may be correct, and can only be disproved by actual statistics, covering a sufficient number of years. These cannot become available for some time to come. It must be carefully borne in mind that this fever varies in prevalence from year to year, appearing to follow some periodical cyclic influence. Hence it comes that the official reports and opinions of senior medical officers who have only spent from two to five years continuously in its endemic area, have varied greatly as to this point, being based on their personal experience, which in point of time is necessarily limited. Moreover, the majority of medical practitioners in Malta have only during the past seven or eight years begun to recognise and accept the existence of this endemic fever, and few are aware that it was well described before the year 1886. It is not surprising that such men are meeting with more and more cases every year, as it is only during the last ten years that the disease has been brought prominently forward in the medical journals. Many date its introduction from the year 1885-86, when a new drainage system was laid down. Thus Bruce says, when writing in 1889: "It is curious that the introduction of the system of removal of excreta by sewers has been looked upon, rightly or wrongly, as coinciding with an excessive development of this fever in Valetta, Naples, and Catania. Eugenio Fazio,[3] in writing of the Neapolitan fever, states that from the time the old-fashioned emptying of cesspools was suppressed and the house drains were carried into the main sewers, which had previously been used for the carrying off of rain water, the hygienic condition of Naples was changed. The fæcal materials being collected in a cloacal system which was not well constructed, being not only deficient in downfall, but also in water for flushing, there stagnate and infiltrate the sub-soil, especially as this is a porous rock, whence are poured into the atmosphere the products of putrid fermentations. Tomaselli[4] writes in

[1] The case mortality for S. C. fever in Malta has fallen from 3·08 per mille in the sixties to 2·60 in the seventies and 0·93 in the eighties. The majority of these fatal cases were probably undulant fever, as it has been more common to misdiagnose such cases enteric fever than the reverse, while diagnosis has become more accurate.

[2] See Chap. I. p. 16.

[3] Fazio (1879); also same author, *Il chima e la salubrità di Napoli*, 2nd ed. Naples, 1891, pp. 30-33.

[4] 1886, etc.

the same manner concerning the fever in Catania. He states that its occurrence and causation seemed to have some connection with local sanitary conditions, which had been modified by the introduction into the public streets of the sewer system, and the first outbreak corresponded in fact with the epoch of this reform. . . . He is certain that, under the existing circumstances, in which there is a scarcity of water for flushing purposes, the city of Catania lies under the malign influence of a poisonous miasma, which is continually given off from these subterranean sources. In like manner it was the fashion in 1886, in Valetta, Malta, to blame the introduction of a general system of drainage for the great increase in the number of cases of this fever during the two years in which the system had been in operation. Among soldiers this increase had certainly been very marked, and it appears that the sewers were in operation before an efficient method of flushing was introduced. Tomaselli's words in regard to Catania might have been applied to Valetta.

Tomaselli, in a later edition of his pamphlet, seems to place less stress upon this cause for an increase of prevalence.

Those who put forward the theory base it on the idea that a source of infection which in the cesspit days was confined to a single house, or to certain houses, became by means of a general, but insufficiently flushed, drainage system a more widespread cause of fever. This, as will be shown later on, does not altogether apply to Valetta, as a system of conduit drains was laid down in that place by the Knights. Again, the year in question (1885) was one in which the usual cycle of prevalence of S. C. fever was at its highest. It was a very hot and rainless one, similar to others in which there has been excessive prevalence of this fever. The same type of undulant fever was also very prevalent in Sicily at that time. Numerous cases of enteric fever were invalided to Malta from Egypt by the Army and Navy at that period. Moreover, while the new drainage was in progress, there were, we are told, heaps of sewage and other putrescent material from the old conduits lying on the roads beside the open drains. There is little wonder, therefore, that enteric, undulant, and other continued fevers were prevalent at the time, and that special attention was directed to their existence.

Dr. Pisani, chief Government medical officer at Malta, who had practised in that place since the Crimean War, states that the disease, in his opinion, was at first almost confined to the neighbourhood of military barracks, and that it spread at a later date to the civil population and villages. Very little information is to be gained from civil statistics upon this point, as notification has but recently come into force. The official death-rates are of little value, as not only is the death-rate of this fever exceedingly low, but the majority of the deaths from this cause have been returned under the heading of enteric fever, or under symptomatic headings. Moreover, few post-mortem examinations are held. It is a fact, however, that this and other continued fevers are and have always been more prevalent among the soldiers and other visitors than amongst the indigenous population which has had the opportunity of acquiring a certain immunity. We find that Dr. Hennen mentions that from 1821-23 fevers in the civil hospital accounted for over 14 per cent of the total deaths, and that from 1818-23 they accounted for 10·6 per cent of the deaths among the civil population (96,404). These fevers were of the continued type, were non-malarial in character, and were at that time the most prevalent diseases in the island.

At present, in Malta, we find this undulant fever prevailing in Valetta and the Three Cities, at those villages where the inhabitants of Valetta chiefly visit, *i.e.* Sliema, Notabile, Lia, Balsan, Attard, Birchicara, Nasciar, etc.; and also at Zabbar and Zeitun, which, besides being near the Three Cities, are inhabited by the men who coal the ships in harbour. In the other villages it is little prevalent, and enters but rarely into the official returns of such outlying villages as Melleha, Dingli, Gargur, etc. In Gozo it occurs in Victoria, the chief town, but scarcely ever in the villages, and with much less frequency among the troops than is the case in Malta. In fact, the greater number of cases of undulant fever which have occurred amongst the Gozo garrison have apparently been importations from Malta.

Surgeon-Major Robinson, A.M.S., who has been for four years in medical charge of troops in Gozo (average annual strength for that period, 540 men), says:—

"Attacks of this fever among men sent straight to Gozo (without previous residence elsewhere in the Mediterranean) are so rare, that, with the difficulty of being sure that even the few men attacked have not visited Malta since their arrival, I am inclined to doubt its endemic occurrence in the barracks of Gozo. I have made it a rule to ask all fever cases about their movements prior to admission, but unfortunately I have not recorded their answers, and cannot be certain of the movements of any individual case, as a number of men visit Malta from time to time on duty or pleasure.

"While attacks or relapses occur among bodies of men immediately after their transference from Malta, such attacks tend to become exceedingly rare, or cease entirely, after a certain time; as if these men had exhausted the stock of fever brought with them. Companies of men that have remained for a long time free from the fever in Gozo produce cases on their return from a course of musketry in Malta (duration two to three weeks).

"From 1892 to 1896, out of an average strength of about twenty women and thirty-four children occupying married quarters in barracks in Gozo, but one case of this fever occurred, and this in a child who was suffering from the disease when transferred from Malta. Amongst the officers' families for the same period (average strength three ladies and six children, all living out of barracks), three cases occurred. Of these two were transferred from Malta while suffering from the fever, and the remaining one had recently arrived from Egypt, where she had resided for some months. From November 1894 to November 1895 some twenty-six additional women and fourteen children arrived straight from England, and resided in the villages of Ghain Seilan and Migiaro, and in houses in the neighbourhood where sanitation is either absent or rudimentary. They inhabited with natives the small, badly-ventilated and overcrowded houses of the poorer classes. Though they suffered (especially the parturients) from ophthalmia, diarrhœa, sore throats, anæmia, etc., and were so heavily handicapped from a sanitary point of view, not a single case of this fever occurred amongst them. Other families have lived from three to six years in Gozo without suffering. Now the members of these families, unlike the soldiers, rarely, if ever, visit Malta. In barracks there are dry earth latrines, the urine and slops being carried off by water drainage to the sea. The water-supply is good, but excessively hard. Milk is obtained from goats, as in Malta. It would, therefore, appear that in Gozo during the last few years, situated only five miles from Malta, in similar barracks and houses, built upon similar porous rock, men and families of the same regiments, age, etc., living under similar climatic and domestic conditions as those met with in Malta, enjoy an enormously greater immunity from this particular fever, even though they in certain instances live under what might be considered most unfavourable sanitary conditions."

The places where it is at present most prevalent in Malta are those which for centuries have been the centres of the greatest mercantile activity. Those from which it is said to be absent, or in which it rarely occurs, are isolated agricultural villages, little or never visited by the inhabitants of the infected towns. Few of the houses in these villages have any sanitary arrangements, the native using an adjacent field for necessary purposes; while in those in which middens are built there is sufficient space to allow of their being away from the dwelling-rooms. The villagers also come but little to the towns, and then only for a few hours to sell their country produce; and as the distances are so short they can always return on the same day. It is possible, and indeed probable, that the outlying towns, and those villages in which the fever occurs, have received it from the mercantile cities around the Grand Harbour in the first instance. Although the troops have been massed about this harbour for many years, it scarcely justifies a belief that they are responsible for its occurrence, but rather they suffer from being strangers, obliged to live amid the closely-packed native population in the worst part of its Maltese endemic area.

There are many facts which might account for an *apparent* increase in prevalence, which might not at the same time be a *real* and actual increase of a permanent nature in the proportional amount of sickness from this cause. For instance, the civil population has nearly doubled itself in numbers since 1820, so that while a great many more persons exist within the infective area, there is also a proportional increase in the sources of infection. The garrison has also increased in numbers year by year, and at the same time, owing to the present short service system, and to the short period now spent by individual regiments in one place, the average age and service in the Mediterranean of individual soldiers has very considerably decreased. In these days, therefore, a much larger number of young susceptible British soldiers are annually exposed to the infection of this fever than was formerly the case.

Though the total admissions per thousand of strength for S. C. fever in Malta have been on the whole steadily decreasing during the past eighty years, the *actual* number of cases of undulant fever may have increased among the troops, and so any individual medical officer, by having more cases to treat, may have imagined that the disease was really more prevalent, unless he at the same time considered other attendant circumstances. More cases seem to have been admitted into the Valetta Military Hospital during the last six years (1891-1896) than were admitted during the thirteen years mentioned by Bruce (1876-1888) in his paper published in 1889.

The author is of opinion that the increase is more apparent than real, and that if the attack rates per thousand of susceptible people could be compared for sufficiently long periods, the increase would be absent from among the urban residents, and if present among the troops would prove to be due to the youth of the men and to the frequent arrival of new regiments in the command.

There is reason to believe that the statistics in the official military returns, referring to S. C. fever and remittent fever in Malta, since 1817, may throw some light upon the past prevalence of undulant fever. The reasons for so thinking are—

(1) That whenever undulant fever has been sufficiently prevalent to be remarked upon specially, the occurrence of S. C. fever and remittent fever has been proportionally great (1859, Marston; 1865-8, Boileau and Chartres; 1872, Notter; 1878-9,[1] Veale; 1885, Bruce; 1892, author. See also Army Medical Department Reports for these years).

(2) That whenever undulant fever has been epidemic in any special local area, it has been accompanied by an increase in the number of cases of febricula from the same area.

(3) That during the nine years in which statistics of undulant fever have been collected by Bruce and by the author, and the years in which its monthly prevalence happens to have been separately mentioned in the official reports, the seasonal prevalence and relation to climatic conditions have been roughly similar for both undulant and simple continued fevers.

(4) That from 1871 to 1885 cases returned as remittent fever were instances of attacks of this undulant fever.

(5) That the annual admission-rate for rheumatic affections, which in Malta are usually the sequelæ of undulant fever, has followed the same curve as that of simple continued fever.

Now, if we analyse the admissions to hospital among soldiers in

[1] See also *Health of the Navy.*

Malta which have been included under the name "Simple Continued Fever," we find that these consist of—

(*a*) Cases of a short specific febrile disease, often called simple ardent fever or febricula, whose pyrexial duration is from one to five days, which form the great bulk of these admissions. The prevalence of this fever seems to be governed a great deal by climatic conditions, of which temperature would appear to be an important factor, though not the only one. It is, and has been for very many years, an extremely common disease in Malta during the warmer months, occurring often in apparent waves of prevalence and attacking the same individual year after year, frequently affecting him about the same month in each year. Few of the garrison escape an attack of this fever, but in many cases it is so slight that but little notice is taken of it. Whatever form of poison is concerned in the production of this disease, there is every indication that it is separate and distinct from that of undulant fever. There is, however, a close resemblance between the seasonal prevalence of the two fevers, so that an increase in the activity of one is accompanied by a similar increase in the other.

(*b*) Cases of abortive or undiagnosed enteric fever, which previous to 1860 formed a larger proportion of these admissions than they do now. Enteric fever, however, in Malta occurs mostly during the autumn and winter months, when undulant fever is uncommon. We are, therefore, able to judge of the extent to which these cases may cause error in any individual year. Moreover, while the prevalence of enteric fever is very small when compared with that of simple continued or undulant fevers, its yearly prevalence since 1860 has been fairly steady, except during certain years when some known cause of infection has been at work. We find also, on comparing the admission-rates of enteric fever with those of simple continued fever, that there is no variation that would lead one to believe that undiagnosed enteric fever had caused an appreciable error in the curve of prevalence of the so-called simple continued fever.

(*c*) Cases of more or less remittent pyrexia of from six to twenty days' duration, which but for their extremely short duration have every appearance of being cases of undulant fever. These cases are particularly common when undulant fever is at all prevalent, and occur at the same time of year as that fever, and are admitted from the same barrack-rooms. That they are abortive undulant fever we are not at present justified in saying, but this class of case does not appear to interfere with the proportional admission-rates of simple continued and undulant fevers.

(*d*) Cases of slight pyrexia due to undiscovered local conditions, or to slight ailments, which form so small a proportion of these cases that they may be disregarded in a rough estimate.

(*e*) Cases of true undulant fever, which form about a third of the admissions for simple continued fever each year, and fresh admissions for relapses of undulant fever in men who have been discharged from hospital apparently cured, which latter form a large number of these cases.

Of the above we may disregard classes (*b*), (*c*), and (*d*), while class (*a*) appears to follow a similar annual prevalence curve to that of undulant fever (class *e*), the activity of its poison depending probably on somewhat similar factors. On these grounds it is possible that the annual prevalence curve of simple continued fever for Malta (and indeed there is reason to believe that the same may be said for Gibraltar), taken on the admission-rate per thousand of strength since 1860, may help us in estimating the behaviour of this fever year by year with regard to climatic conditions and changes in quantity. Subsequent observations, with the more accurate statistics which will become available when this fever is returned under a separate heading, can alone settle this point; and in the meanwhile the writer will merely state the facts as a guide for subsequent investigations.

TABLE X.—*Admission-Rate (Malta) per Mille of Strength for Simple Continued Fever (Military Garrison), compared with the Rainfall in Valetta,* 1859-1895.

Year.	Rate.	Rain.	Year.	Rate.	Rain.	Year.	Rate.	Rain.
1859 [1]	269·5	...	1872 [1]	233·4	13·5	1884	114·5	15·4
1860 [1]	208·6	16·2	1873	170·5	23·9	1885 [1 4]	181·9	12·1
1861	141·6	20·4	1874	197·0	23·6	1886 [3 4]	154·1	24·8
1862	141·7	15·5	1875	140·7	27·0	1887 [2]	103·6	21·1
1863	114·6	23·7	1876	136·1	14·2	1888	71·2	14·8
1864	186·9	21·0	1877	157·1	26·2	1889	83·6	26·0
1865 [1]	210·4	16·4	1878 [1]	189·2	17·9	1890	85·5	21·7
1866 [1]	198·1	10·0	1879 [1]	209·5	26·5	1891	109·1	18·1
1867 [1]	228·7	12·8	1880	173·4	19·3	1892 [1]	172·0	25·1
1868 [1]	205·7	24·0	1881	165·1	14·6	1893	130·8	23·6
1869	179·8	20·3	1882	111·7	28·3	1894	104·1	27·8
1870	131·9	16.0	1883	96·3	19·6	1895 [1]	168·9	11·6
1871	115·7	16·9						

[1] Epidemics of undulant fever noted.
[2] New water-supply to Valetta.
[3] New drainage in Burmola, Isola, and Ricasoli.
[4] New drainage in Valetta.

TABLE XI.—*Average Rates (from above) for Cyclical Periods.*[1]

Years.	Period in years.	Admission-rate average.	Decrease (periodic)
1859-1867	9	188·9	
1867-1872	6	182·5	6·4
1872-1879	8	179·2	3·3
1879-1885	7	150·3	28·9
1885-1892	8	120·1	30·2

[1] A cyclical period here extends from one maximum year of prevalence to the next maximum year, extending, therefore, from the summit of one wave of prevalence to the summit of the next.

CHAPTER III

Symptomatology.—(a) General remarks, with description of three types and irregular cases:—(1) Malignant type. (2) Undulatory type. (3) Intermittent type. (4) Irregular cases.—(*b*) *Physiognomy.*—(*c*) *Tegumentary system:* Non-exanthematous; Prickly heat, boils, purpuric spots, etc., may occur; Diaphoresis; Desquamation and loss of hair; Distinctive odour, etc.—(*d*) *Pyrexia:* Pyrexial waves; Nature and duration; Variations; Diurnal wave, nature and duration; Effects of external and internal influences.—(*e*) *Nervous system:* Fever pains, headache, general nervous irritability, impairment of mental functions and of special senses, cerebro-spinal symptoms, neuritic pains, paralysis and atrophy of certain muscles.—(*f*) *Arthritic symptoms:* Acute; Subacute.—(*g*) *Circulatory system:* Pulse, palpation, valvular disease, weak action, pericardial effusion.—(*h*) *Respiratory system:* Bronchitis, catarrhal pneumonia, hypostatic congestion at bases, cough, expectoration, Mediterranean phthisis.—(*k*) *Alimentary system:* Mouth, tongue, gastritis, constipation and diarrhœa.—(*l*) *Urinary and sexual system:* Epididymitis and orchitis, vesical irritability, retention, albuminuria, menstruation.—(*m*) *Complications and sequelæ.*

Symptomatology.—So variable are the symptoms and so uncertain is the duration and course of this fever, that it is impossible to give a description to which all cases can be referred. The various local symptoms would appear to be due to the action of a living virus upon the tissues, having a constant but comparatively mild irritative action. The more severe local and general symptoms met with in malignant cases appear to be due to the action of large quantities of the virus (with probably greater virulent power) in the tissues than are met with in mild cases. In the mildest intermittent cases, and in the later stages of other cases preceding convalescence, the disease appears to have a certain diurnal latency, which disappears in proportion as the disease increases in severity. In all cases there are periods of more or less abatement of symptoms, often marked by intervals of absolute but temporary latency between relapses. Where the virus rests during these latent periods we cannot say, though in many cases localised rheumatoid symptoms lead us to believe that a portion of the virus may remain in the locality of these symptoms. As a rule, however, when local symptoms are present pyrexia is also present. We can only compare this latency with that met with in syphilis, paludism, and tubercle; and with that lately observed in other fevers of more certain duration. Its irregular course and uncertain duration are somewhat like those of paludism, but unfortunately we have not a specific remedy like quinine with which to cut it short. In some of its clinical symptoms this disease has a connection with the effects on the body of the disease causes of typhoid and rheumatic fevers. Except that this virus never appears to cause suppuration in its local manifestations, it seems to have many of the general and local actions of that of pyæmia, falling short, however, of that disease in the severity of its action. Whatever its life action within the body proves to be, clinically the disease has every appearance of a blood infection, commencing in the mucous membranes of the mouth, throat, or possibly of the stomach and air passages; and from hence passing into the system and the various tissues, causing symptoms due to its general and local action on the body tissues and economy. Its chief and most constant clinical manifestation is pyrexia, and from this point of view must its clinical description and clinical variations be approached. Putting aside those short (abortive?) and indefinite cases of fever lasting from seven to twenty-one days, which are more severe than simple ardent fever and unlike enteric fever, we meet with three varieties to which all cases of this undulant fever seem to approximate clinically. These, however, are not necessarily distinct from one another, but must be looked upon as due to variations in the severity of the action of the virus, brought about by causes dependent upon the organism or the individual himself, or his surroundings. Any one variety or type may pass into any other.

As long as the patient is liable to pyrexia, so long is the virus still present in the body, and so long is it theoretically able, under suitable circumstances, to burst out at any time into an attack of any severity. When pyrexia has ceased entirely, the symptoms met with are those due to anæmia and debility of the various tissues, making them temporarily less able to carry out their usual functions, and to resist the action of any adverse surrounding circumstances.

As the various local symptoms are variable in constancy, writers of limited experience must necessarily vary in their accounts of the frequency of their symptoms.

The following descriptions are based upon notes of over a thousand cases which the writer has had the opportunity of seeing or treating in Malta and elsewhere in the Mediterranean, during six years of almost continuous hospital practice. These were selected, from the many hundreds of cases of continuous fever admitted to the military hospital "for simple continued fever," on account of their clinical or post-mortem appearances having left no doubt as to their nature.

1. *Malignant type.*—(*a*) The onset in many cases seems most sudden. The patient, often a strong, muscular man, is admitted to hospital suffering from severe pyrexia, stated to be of only one or two days' standing. He complains of severe headache, "pains all over him," distaste for food, thirst, nausea, and even vomiting. His face is flushed, his tongue thickly coated with whitish gray or yellow fur, pink at the tip and edges, moist, very swollen, and indented by the teeth laterally.

His temperature may be 104°-105° F. or more. There is epigastric, splenic, and perhaps hepatic tenderness on pressure, while the area of splenic dulness is increased. The patient's breath is unusually offensive. If left to take its course, after four or five days of constantly high temperature, signs of basal pneumonic congestion, with bronchial râles all over the chest, appear, and these may pass on to lobular consolidation. The pulse remains strong, or responds to stimulants, and the mind is unusually clear. The urine is decreased, dark in colour and loaded with lithates: the stools are most offensive. Diarrhœa may be present from implication of the great gut, a condition which adds materially to the gravity of the case. In such cases the stools are profuse and frequent, excessively offensive, usually brown in colour, and varying in consistency.

The temperature may abate slightly for a few days, but remains usually well under 103° F. After a varying number of days the pulse begins to flag and become intermittent, the breathing next becomes laboured, and obstinate vomiting may be present. The tongue becomes brown, dry, and cracked, the teeth are covered with sordes, and other symptoms of the so-called "typhoid state" set in. At this time there is a most offensive odour about the patient, more especially about his breath and skin; his whole appearance is that of a man saturated with the fever poison, as if it were attacking and rotting every tissue in his body. The respirations now become shallow and fast, with signs of increasing pulmonary congestion; delirium supervenes and passes into coma; the fæces are passed involuntarily; the temperature rises steadily; the heart gives way, and the patient dies of hyperpyrexia. At death the temperature in the mouth is about 110° F., but may continue to rise, so that 112°-115° F. have been registered in the internal organs shortly after death. Death in such cases occurs as a rule between the fifth and twenty-first days of the disease, but rapidly fatal cases are happily rare in these days of improved treatment.

(*b*) In a few cases the temperature may abate after the first few days, and remain between 102° and 103° F., but at the same time a condition of extreme nervous excitability sets in. This is soon followed by pronounced nervous exhaustion, resulting occasionally in death, due apparently to direct toxæmic poisoning of the higher nerve centres. These cases are uncommon, but need most careful management.

(*c*) In some instances the patient passes safely through the primary pyrexial undulation, the temperature abates at the end of two or three weeks for a few days, followed by the gradual rise of a second pyrexial undulation. This following the same course as the primary attack, but in a patient weakened by the previous fever, may cause a fatal result similar in every respect to those already mentioned.

(*d*) In two cases the writer has met with a temporary fall to normal combined with great exhaustion, lasting from six to eighteen hours, preceding death from hyperpyrexia (*vide* Cases 6 and 21).

(*e*) In cases which prove fatal at a later stage (70th-150th day) of the disease, death is usually due to sudden cardiac failure, pericardiac effusion, pleuritic or empyæmic mischief, to debility, exhaustion, or to the supervention of phthisis or some other intercurrent disease.

In 45 cases in which the day of the fatal result was noted, it occurred as follows :—

TABLE XII.

From 1- 7 days	6 cases or	13·33 per cent
,, 8-14 ,,	7 ,, ,,	15·56 per cent
,, 15-21 ,,	9 ,, ,,	20·00 per cent
,, 21-30 ,,	5 ,, ,,	11·11 per cent
During first month	27 cases or	60·00 per cent
,, second ,,	11 ,, ,,	24·44 per cent
,, third ,,	3 ,, ,,	6·67 per cent
,, fourth ,,	3 ,, ,,	6·67 per cent
,, fifth ,,	1 ,, ,,	2·22 per cent
Total	45	100·00

2. *Undulatory type.*—This may be considered to be the usual course of this fever, other types being but variations brought about by differences in severity of individual cases. The febrile course is marked by intermittent waves or undulations, of more or less remittent pyrexia, of variable length, separated from one another by periods of temporary abatement or absence of symptoms. In typical uncomplicated cases confined to bed there is usually a premonitory stage of low spirits, mental worry, sleeplessness, anorexia, with dyspeptic symptoms, with headache and slight pyrexia each evening. The temperature next rises gradually, remitting each morning about half the amount of the previous evening rise. With this are combined slight headache, pains in the neck, back, and limbs, moist furred tongue, swollen and indented laterally, a bad taste in the mouth, epigastric tenderness and constipation. Most patients do not at first report sick, trying to fight off the fever. The result is that all these symptoms become exaggerated, and on admission the temperature is high and the headache most severe.

The temperature having reached 103°-105° F. in the evening, accompanied by some bronchial catarrh or hypostatic congestion of the lungs in proportion to the severity of the case, after a variable period gradually falls to normal or thereabouts in the morning, and though it may rise higher in the evening, the patient feels much better and probably wishes to get up, a wish which, if gratified, is at once followed by a severe relapse. The primary wave of pyrexia may now be said to be over. For a few days the temperature may remain at or about normal, after which it again begins to rise and a relapse ensues similar to the primary attack, but usually less prolonged and less severe. This subsides only to be followed by other relapses forming the undulatory temperature charts so characteristic of this fever. Such pyrexia is almost always accompanied by obstinate constipation, though diarrhœa may occur temporarily in very severe cases, more especially during the primary attack. Each remission of temperature is accompanied by profuse sweating.

Anæmia and muscular wasting are progressive and often severe. At any stage, but usually late in the attack, or during convalescence, symptoms of localised interstitial neuritis may occur, leading to obstinate sciatica, intercostal neuralgia, etc. In other cases peripheral symptoms may point to irritation of the central nervous system, followed by more central symptoms, or by loss or impairment of function of the nerves of special sense. In many cases effusion into one or more joints may occur, often of a sudden, transitory and metastatic nature, but causing extreme tension and pain; or painful orchitis may appear.

Finally, the patient is reduced to an emaciated, anæmic, and bed-ridden condition; subject to attacks of bronchial catarrh, lobular pneumonia, cardiac palpitation, rheumatic or neuralgic complications on the slightest exposure to chill, excitement, or change in the weather. Disappointed at each relapse, his whole expression is the picture of despondent apathy, his only wish to get away to England. His emaciated appearance, his profuse night-sweats, often intermittent pyrexia, and cough, remind one forcibly of the last stage of phthisis. Gradually, however, his temperature, after showing more and more tendency to become intermittent towards the end of the second or third month, becomes normal or subnormal in the morning, and but slightly above normal in the evening. Next, the evening rise occurs only at increasingly long intervals, then ceases, and usually gives place to a few days of subnormal temperature, after which convalescence is established. This subnormal period is one of the surest signs of approaching convalescence, especially when it is accompanied by a clean tongue and other signs of mitigation of symptoms. The strength now slowly returns, the cheeks fill out, and the patient gets up for an increasing period every day. After a few weeks, if not invalided home, he is sent to a sanitorium, or perhaps may be strong enough to return to duty, but for months he is liable to attacks of neuralgic pain, to swollen joints or testicles, combined often with a return of mild pyrexia. Final recovery cannot be said to take place for many months, and until the anæmia has disappeared, and the mucous membranes have regained their complete functions. When, however, the patient is completely free from the disease, it does not, like paludism, recur. The pyrexial duration, which averages some 60 days, varies within such wide limits as from 20 to 300 days or more; while the total stay in hospital, which averages some 90 days, may extend to two years, where sciatica or other sequelæ are present.

3. *Intermittent type.*—In these cases the onset is generally extremely insidious, the general course mild, and the duration less than in the previous types mentioned. There is usually a premonitory stage, during which the patient suffers from a sense of weariness and lassitude in the

evening, a feeling of worry and irritability about the details of his daily occupations, and possibly slight headache in the evening. At the same time his appetite is diminished—he wakes each morning with a "nasty taste" in his mouth and a slightly coated tongue. If his temperature is taken at this stage, it is found to be normal or subnormal in the morning, about 99° F. in the afternoon, and normal again about ten or eleven at night. Usually he thinks it is "liver or biliousness," takes an aperient, and often, urged on by his friends, attempts to work it off by hard exercise. After a game of polo, a stiff walk or other exercise, he returns with a racking headache and retires early to bed, where he spends a somewhat restless night. Next morning, feeling better, he returns to work, but sooner or later seeks medical advice, generally in the evening. He now complains of bad headache in the evening, sleeplessness, pains in the muscles of the neck and back, loss of appetite and night-sweats. His tongue is furred, swollen and marked laterally by the teeth, he has epigastric tenderness and possibly pain, there may be slight redness and relaxation of the tonsils, uvula, and pharyngeal pillars, and the submaxillary, cervical or sublingual lymphatic glands may be slightly tender and enlarged. His temperature will be found to vary between normal and 100° F. in the morning and 99°-101° F. or more in the evening, its height depending a great deal on the extent to which he has endeavoured to fight off the fever. Possibly, but not necessarily, he may complain of effusion into a joint or of an attack of sciatica or neuralgia. After a good night's rest following a sleeping draught, an absence for some hours of mental worry and unsuitable food, with the warmth of bed, he feels much better. If he does not suffer from arthritic or neuralgic complications or high pyrexia, he will complain of little or nothing on the first or second morning following his retirement to bed. About 2 P.M. each afternoon, or possibly earlier, he will complain of a creepy feeling in the back, a sensation of general irritability and malaise. His temperature will be found to be rising to a maximum of 99° to 105° F. slowly and steadily until between 2 and 5 P.M., but without rigor or paroxysm. During the night it will again fall gradually to normal or thereabouts, at which time the patient will be subject to a perspiration proportional in amount to the diurnal variation of temperature and the debility present.

This daily intermitting temperature has a close resemblance to hectic fever, and may continue for months without other symptoms than daily afternoon malaise, nightly perspirations, constipation, increasing anæmia and debility. On the other hand, it may at any time, especially if the patient is not well looked after, and endeavours to continue at work, develop into the remittent or continuously high type of pyrexia of the undulatory or malignant varieties already described. It may also be accompanied by any of the complications or sequelæ met with in those types, or those types may by a mitigation of severity pass into this intermittent type, a not uncommon ending of many undulatory cases.

The remarkable point about this pyrexia is the curious way in which it often goes on day after day without any serious complications. Except in the afternoon and evening, when his temperature is highest, the patient eats well, and complains of little, while drugs have little or no effect upon its course or duration. At any moment, however, the slumbering fever may, so to speak, burst into flame.

If the temperature be accurately taken, so as to register the true daily maximum and minimum, these are found to form waves or undulations of pyrexial intensity similar to those already described, the daily remittence being exaggerated into an intermittence. On the ordinary chart, where the temperature is taken at fixed times, without reference to the times of maximum or minimum, these undulations are not necessarily clearly marked, and as there are rarely absolute apyrexial periods other than the daily intermissions, there is less despondency than with the well-marked and disappointing relapses of the undulatory type. The amount of pyrexia may vary within wide limits, but however high the evening temperature rises, this elevation is of a distinctly non-paroxysmal nature, shivering being confined usually to children or persons of marked nervous excitability. Its duration is most variable, but usually the pyrexia is seldom prolonged beyond the sixth week in purely intermittent cases, though in exceptional cases it has been known to continue for as long as six months.

It is always well in the Mediterranean to take the temperature of every case reporting sick with symptoms of dyspepsia, debility, etc., as a preliminary measure, and if there is any doubt to take it during the afternoon or evening. Fever is often overlooked for want of such precaution, and cases treated for slight symptoms for some time before the real condition is discovered, to the detriment of the patient's health and the doctor's reputation.

Irregular and mixed types.—Between the undulatory type with its continuous or remittent temperature, and the intermittent type, we meet with every variety of curve that can be said to approximate to the descriptions given, or to any mixture of both. There is always, however, that tendency to the formation of waves or undulations of pyrexial intensity if the curve is accurately registered, a feature not common to other types of fever. The differences are of a pyrexial nature, and will be dealt with in detail under that heading.

Intermittence is a not infrequent mode of ending in cases of an undulant type, while an intermittent case may pass into the undulant type, this latter being, however, a much less common occurrence.

Certain cases, in which diarrhœa has been present during the primary wave, have been thought to have been enteric fever passing on to undulant fever, and due to a double infection. So many severe cases have a resemblance at times to enteric fever, that it is impossible to state definitely whether such a double infection can take place.

In such cases in which the writer has been able to make a post-mortem examination no signs of previous enteric fever have been present.

In one case already mentioned, a month of intermittent pyrexia similar to that of undulant fever, was followed by a continuously high temperature, diarrhœa, and considerable hæmorrhage. The case proved fatal, and at the post-mortem the typical ulceration of the third week of enteric fever was present, but no signs of previous Peyerian ulceration that could be referred back to the first month of the attack. It would seem possible that both poisons existed in the body at the same time, as has been observed with other fevers.[1]

Tomaselli (1886-95) describes four types of undulant fever:—(1) Forma gastrica; (2) Forma indeterminata; (3) Forma nervosa; (4) Forma letale o paralitica.

Symptoms in Detail

Physiognomy.—The ordinary case, in which the onset is insidious, and the patient does not report sick until the fourth or fifth day, when he has a languid air and a washed-out and somewhat pale countenance, and on the malar eminences an almost hectic flush.

In the more severe onset, with high temperature, the face, the mucous membranes of the gums, the mouth and fauces, and the conjunctivæ, are at first somewhat congested, while in rapidly fatal cases they are often extremely cyanosed before death. The dull, heavy expression of enteric fever is rarely present. Later on in the attack the skin and exposed mucous surfaces become anæmic, and the former occasionally somewhat bronzed, the expression dull and apathetic. This listless resignation is replaced by an expression of extreme pain and anxiety when a large joint becomes suddenly inflamed, such as the hip, vertebral joints, or the sacro-iliac synchondroses; or by an unmistakable expression of mental worry and irritation, when there is pronounced cerebro-spinal irritation. As the anæmia increases the skin becomes gradually of a dull clay colour, and becomes tightly drawn over the face, the limbs shrink, and the muscles of the neck stand out like cords, and an expression of extreme listless apathy comes over the patient, who has suffered perhaps for three or four months from this protracted and disappointing form of fever. The outward appearance of many patients at this stage of the attack may be compared to that often seen in cases of phthisis with pyrexia.

During convalescence, if there are no rheumatic or neuralgic sequelæ, the body weight is gradually if not rapidly increased, but the anæmia, breathlessness, and debility take a considerable time to disappear, so that there is often for a long time an unhealthy-looking fatness of face, combined with a puffy, anæmic look. The eyelids and ankles often remain swollen and puffy for months during convalescence,

[1] *Vide* Chap. I. p. 10, Chap. IV. p. 160, and *Brit. Med. Jour.* vol. i. pp. 129, 148; 1897.

though there be no albumin in the urine. When rheumatic or neuralgic sequelæ occur during convalescence, the patient drags himself about, and looks a most miserable individual, an appearance heightened in the extreme by the loss of hair which occurs in this disease. Patients suffering severely from this fever appear to age very rapidly during the attack, an appearance which does not entirely disappear on recovery. The sallow, anæmic complexion, the gray hairs, and new wrinkles, cause the patient of from twenty to twenty-five to appear over thirty-five years of age.

The decubitus is lateral, except in exceptional and very severe cases, or when the vertebral joints are affected, when it may be dorsal.

Tegumentary system.—This fever is not an exanthematous disease.

In a very few severe cases pimples have been met with on the anterior surface of the abdomen, which have been at first sight mistaken for the rose spots of enteric fever. Though their appearance may have been deceptive, they did not come out in crops, nor was their duration in any way typical. Their extreme rarity, and their similarity to pimples which occur in those who are in otherwise good health, point to their occurrence being accidental in this disease. In England the typical rose rash is said by Murchison and other authorities to occur in from 70 to 80 per cent of cases of enteric fever; but in Malta it is more often absent or slightly marked, than clearly present, in cases of undoubted enteric fever of all varieties of severity. The writer has rarely in Malta met with those decided crops of copious spots that he has frequently met with in more temperate climates. Not only does the exanthem of enteric fever become a very small factor in diagnosis in Malta, but it is well to be cautious when declaring spots occurring with pyrexia to be enteric in origin, and to watch them for a day or two before giving a decided opinion as to their nature.

Case 21.—*Illustrating pimples which were mistaken for the rose-rash of enteric fever.*—Pte. K., Connaught Rangers, aged 21, previous medical history very good, except that he had suffered from pneumonia two and a half years previously. Onset sudden on the 1st of August 1891, pyrexia not severe until the 8th day, when it rose from 102° F. in the morning to 104° in the evening, and remained high, with the exception of those periods when it was brought down by cold pack or sponging, until the 19th. About the 13th day he developed diarrhœa of a light yellow colour and very loose in character, combined with general abdominal tenderness, and a few rose spots on the anterior surface of the abdomen. This diarrhœa lasted until the 23rd day, when he became somewhat better. The condition had been very similar to that met with in enteric fever, where perforation was threatening, and this opinion was strengthened by the remarkable way in which the patient improved under large doses of opium. The rose spots were few in number and soon disappeared, and they were not at all typical in appearance after the first day. They were probably sudamina. On the 26th day signs of severe congestion, and, later on, consolidation of the right lung were apparent, and the temperature rose from 102° on the 26th to 104° on the 29th; and on the 32nd day, though the right lung was clearing, a similar condition was present in the left. On the 34th day the temperature fell, reaching normal on the 35th, and he seemed much better but extremely exhausted, and the writer handed the case over to another medical officer. He was subsequently informed that his temperature began to rise suddenly and steadily on the evening of the next day, and he died of hyperpyrexia at 3 A.M. on the 38th day of the disease. The post-mortem appearances were those of undulant fever, and there were no changes visible in Peyer's patches, the writer being present at the examination.

Sudamina are not uncommon during and after the third week, occurring on the back and chest, especially when the perspiration has been profuse and the skin not sufficiently well attended to nor kept clean.

In summer a common and most distressing symptom is prickly heat, which, however, occurs at the same time among healthy persons and among those suffering from other diseases. In a few instances it may become pustular, and resembling in that stage the pustular rash met with beneath strong mercurial dressings. This condition must be carefully looked after, especially when it occurs upon the back, as otherwise, and more particularly when scratched, boils or ulcers may complicate matters and lead to tiresome bed-sores.

In spring and autumn boils may occur in various parts of the body, either singly or in crops. They are not especially connected with this disease in any way, but are a fertile source of bed-sore in neglected patients, as they often appear on the backs or gluteal regions of debilitated cases at a late stage in the disease. The great point to be remembered is that they are apt to spread along the skin by direct transference of infective matter, and must therefore be dressed carefully, the surrounding skin being disinfected with some mild antiseptic at each dressing. The author has seen, for instance, boils occur on the inner side of one thigh by inoculation from a burst boil on a similar position on the opposite thigh.

Subcutaneous abscesses occasionally occur in debilitated cases during the progress of the fever. They cause a slight increase in the pyrexia, but are apparently accidental and unconnected with the virus of the fever, and heal readily when evacuated and suitably dressed. Small temporary subcutaneous nodules are very occasionally met with on the face and extremities, such as the anterior surface of the leg. They last about a week and then disappear spontaneously, never exceeding an orange pip in size.

Subcutaneous hæmorrhages, with or without scorbutic symptoms, occasionally occur in debilitated subjects late in the disease. The author has only met with this condition twice, and in neither case were the subcutaneous hæmorrhages severe or connected with scorbutic symptoms.

Case 22.—*Illustrating purpuric symptoms.*—Pte. J., King's R. Rifles, aged 22, was admitted to hospital on May 26th 1895, suffering from a severe attack of undulant fever. He was sent to the sanitarium from August 5th to September 27th, when he returned to hospital in Valetta. During the whole of this time he had been subject to intermittent attacks of remittent pyrexia. He continued to suffer from nocturnal pyrexia, varying from 99° to 102° F., with usually a normal temperature in the morning, until November, when pyrexia was limited to occasional slight nocturnal rises every three or four days, without, however, any regular periodicity. On the 22nd of December, while still subject to occasional rise of temperature at night, and seven months after the onset of the disease and his admission to hospital, numerous spots of hæmorrhagic extravasation appeared on his legs below the knee. They varied in size, but did not exceed a quarter of an inch in diameter. They were scattered about the skin from an eighth to half an inch apart, being very closely arranged on the front of the leg and instep, but less so at the back. They were less numerous on the right than on the left side, and appeared to come out in crops for three days. In colour they were dark red, which did not disappear on pressure. There was no increase in pyrexia. About the same time his nose bled whenever it was picked. About the 26th of December the spots began to fade from dark to light red; next a slightly yellow spot appeared in the centre of each patch, after which they passed through the various shades of yellow and gray common to these conditions, and most familiar to us in the ordinary bruise. No further symptoms appeared, and he lost all signs of pyrexia soon afterwards. The condition appeared to depend upon anæmia, hydræmia, and debility, following long-continued fever (seven months).

About the fourth week desquamation occurs, being most noticeable on the soles of the feet, where the skin peels off in large flakes, leaving the skin of the feet soft and tender for a considerable time, so that boots are irksome during early convalescence. As is the case in enteric fever, a certain amount of bronzing takes place as the anæmia progresses; but there is never any approach to the excessive pigmentation met with in paludism.

A distinctive and disagreeable odour, emanating apparently from the skin and breath, is present in nearly all cases, and is best marked in severe cases, when it may be almost offensive. This odour is most noticeable at post-mortem examinations, and the same smell is not met with in enteric fever cases, though such cases are said to have a peculiar odour of their own. The distinctive odour referred to in undulant fever does not depend upon dyspepsia or uncleanliness, as it is present in cases where these conditions are absent, in hospital patients and gentlefolk who receive every attention, in as great a degree as in those who are under reverse conditions. It is comparable to the odours emanating from cases of typhus or rheumatic fever, and though quite distinct from these, is more disagreeable, and perhaps from its nature less easily recognisable in the sick-room. It is one of the points which often unconsciously aid the experienced physician and nurse in distinguishing between cases of this and other febrile conditions, while its presence in marked degree in a doubtful and severe case has often been the only clinical sign of difference from enteric fever during the first day or two after admission to hospital.

During the fourth month, towards the end of long attacks, or even during early convalescence, the hair falls out extensively. Though this also occurs after other fevers, it is much more the rule than the exception in severe or prolonged attacks of this fever. Though the shedding of the hair is extensive, it is gradually and completely replaced during convalescence, unless the general condition of the patient remains below par. It is well, therefore, to warn patients of this fact when their attack is prolonged, while there need be no hesitation about cutting the hair, or even shaving the head, in the case of female patients if it conduces to their comfort, as they are not only cooler without it, but besides doing away with the necessity of brushing, it appears to tend towards strengthening the new hair when it comes. Dark hair frequently becomes mixed with numerous gray hairs even in young men of twenty-three, a condition which may not completely disappear with recovery.

In long cases the nails often have a grooved or longitudinally striated appearance.

While the temperature remains continuously high the skin is hot and dry. Each remission is, however, followed by diaphoresis, which tends to be most profuse in cases in which there is an intermittence or a very marked remission. The more moderate diaphoresis following moderate remissions at the beginning of severe attacks with high temperature, is refreshing and to be encouraged as a sign of a temporary or permanent amelioration of the disease; but this is a very different condition from that following greater intermittent variations in the height of the temperature curve.

So profuse is the latter diaphoresis in most cases, that following no paroyxsm, it comes to be one of the peculiar characteristics of the disease; and in fact the fever has been named in Italy "febbris sudoralis" (Tomaselli) on account of this symptom. It may be compared with the night-sweats of phthisis, and those accompanying the hectic fever of other suppurating conditions, but it is much more profuse. The condition is most debilitating and depressing, and seems to increase in severity as the disease progresses and the patient becomes weaker.

These profuse perspirations follow the diurnal fall of the temperature, their time of onset being governed, therefore, by the pyrexial curve of each individual case. In the greater number of cases it occurs between 11 P.M. at night and 2 or 3 A.M. the next morning. At the time the sweat literally rolls off the patient's face in large drops, soaking through the pillow; while at the same time that coming from the surface of the body soaks through his clothes, the sheets, and even the blankets. This may go on for an hour or two, necessitating two, three, or more changes of clothes and sheets. The sweat is acid in reaction.

Besides these profuse perspirations, smaller ones may occur at any time during the day or night, owing to slight variations in the temperature curve, or they may be brought on by any emotion, excitement, or exertion. In fact, as the case progresses, the nervous element of the thermogenic apparatus appears to become more and more susceptible to excitation, and to react disproportionally to any stimulation. This characteristic of undulant fever seems to depend to so large an extent upon the action of the poison on the nervous system, and to vary so much with the individual nervous excitability of each patient, that it would appear to be more in its proper place among the nervous symptoms than here. It is the custom, however, to deal with it more as a local tegumentary symptom, and it comes very well before the consideration of the pyrexia, with which it is closely connected.

In a few cases diaphoresis appears to be temporarily localised to certain portions of the body, such as the face, or it may be more profuse on one side of the body than on the other. One arm may be covered with perspiration and the other quite dry.

Pyrexia.—This is the chief and often the only clinical manifestation of the disease, while many of the common symptoms and post-mortem appearances are but due to functional derangements, the result of the febrile condition present. Other characteristic clinical symptoms there are, but none of these are so uniformly present as pyrexia of a characteristic nature, while many of them are due to local manifestations of the action of the virus closely connected with the direct production of this pyrexia.

In all the acute diseases termed fevers, the phenomenon of excessive production or elevation of the body temperature is met with. Moreover, in each of these fevers this elevation of temperature follows a somewhat different course, due to causes dependent upon the action of the virus or to products elaborated by the virus of the particular disease in question, the exact nature and mode of action of these causes being at present a matter of doubt. We believe, however, that two factors are concerned in this excessive body temperature: (1) A disturbance in the process of oxidation and nutrition within the tissues of the body; and (2) An alteration in the normal relations between the (restraining?) action of the nervous system and these last-mentioned processes, and an interference with the nervous mechanism of heat regulation. The exact quantity and quality of the action of these processes of the virus of each individual disease marks to a great extent the character of the resulting pyrexia.

Speaking generally, we find in undulant fever that the action of the poison on the nervous mechanism of body heat regulation has a marked effect on the character of the pyrexia present in very many, if not all of the cases. This is on a par with other symptoms due to the action of the poison on other portions of the nervous system. We find in many mild (intermittent) cases that the temperature rises in the afternoon to 104° or 105° without any great constitutional disturbance; that while some cases may be seriously and even dangerously ill at a constant temperature of 103°, others may be but little affected by a continued temperature of 104°-105°; that paroxysms are absent, and rigors rare; that the temperature is highest in children and nervous and excitable patients; that it is affected by anything that affects the nervous system, such as emotion, fatigue, excitement, worry, etc., the presence of the depressing sirocco wind, and indeed anything of a mentally depressing nature; and that these manifestations are in excess of those met with in the case of other fevers.

Again we find in those cases in which the central nervous system appears especially affected, characterised by symptoms referable to cerebro-spinal irritation, that the temperature may remain continuously high (103°-104°) even for a month, without there being the usual and proportional accompanying symptoms of dry or brown tongue, congestion of internal organs, derangement of function of these organs, etc.

Speaking generally, there is some relation between the height of the temperature and the activity of the disease causes, but to a different degree in each individual case, so that the exact pyrexial severity is not necessarily an index of the urgency of the symptoms, nor of the prognosis in any abstract case. In each individual case, however, there is a relationship between the temperature curve and the satisfactory progress or otherwise of that particular case which it is necessary for the medical officer who treats the case to accurately realise.

The chief characteristics of the pyrexia of this fever when compared with that of others are—(1) The variability which exists in the amount and duration of the pyrexia of different cases. The duration is quite indefinite, and follows no rule applicable to even a majority of cases. The daily pyrexial curve may vary between a continuously high temperature and an intermittent one in different cases, or even in the same attack. (2) The tendency of the daily maximum and minimum temperatures to form waves or undulations of intensity, of varying character and length in different cases, but with a tendency in individual cases to resemble the primary wave, while generally decreasing in length and severity as the case progresses.

The most regular and, so to speak, typical wave of pyrexial intensity, in uncomplicated cases confined to bed, rises like the ideal curve of enteric fever, and subsides in an equally regular manner. The daily temperature is usually remittent in character, the evening temperature being about two degrees higher than that of the same morning. The average length of 300 waves was about ten days, the primary wave being usually longer (average 18 to 23 days), while in a few cases it even lasted almost the whole pyrexial period. The duration of 300 well-marked waves occurring in 95 cases was :—

TABLE XIII.

One week and under . . .	70 waves.
Between one and two weeks .	97 ,,
Between two and three ,, . .	60 ,,
Between three and four ,, . .	23 ,,
Between four and five ,, . .	42 ,,
Between five and six ,, . .	3 ,,
Between six and seven ,, . .	3 ,,
Between seven and eight ,, . .	2 ,,
	300 ,,

The average number of these waves in an attack was three (1-7).

The interval between waves is marked by a period of apyrexia and absence of morbid symptoms, lasting from one to ten days or more (average 3-4 days); or simply by a period of comparative remission of pyrexial and other symptoms of variable degree.

CHART VI.

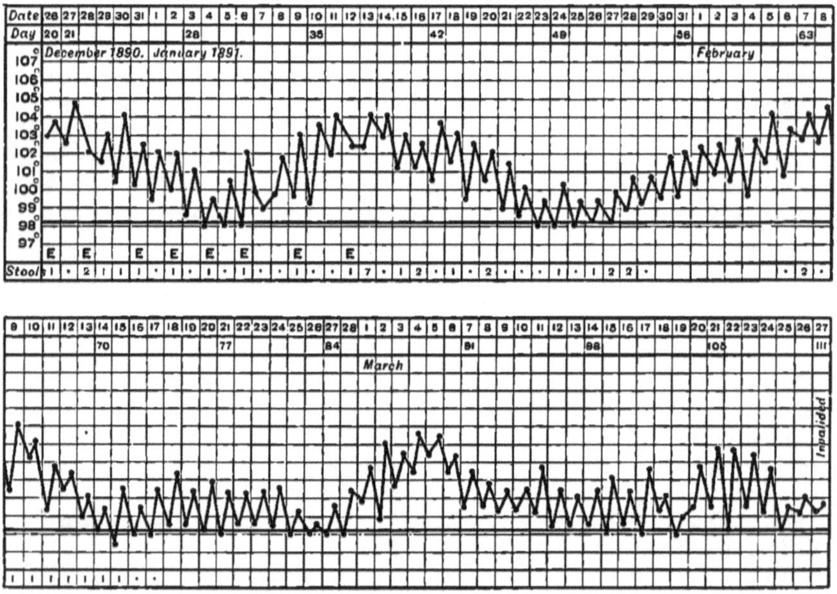

Note.—E = Enema administered.
Typical undulations of remittent pyrexia in undulant fever.

The typical temperature curve of this fever, for the sake of description, may be said to be a series of intermittent waves or undulations of remittent pyrexia.

Case 23.—*Illustrating such a curve.*—Capt. P., admitted to hospital with undulant fever of 20 days' standing on the 26th of December 1890, after having been under treatment in private lodgings in Vittoriosa, Malta. He suffered from obstinate constipation, progressive anæmia and debility,

CHART VII.

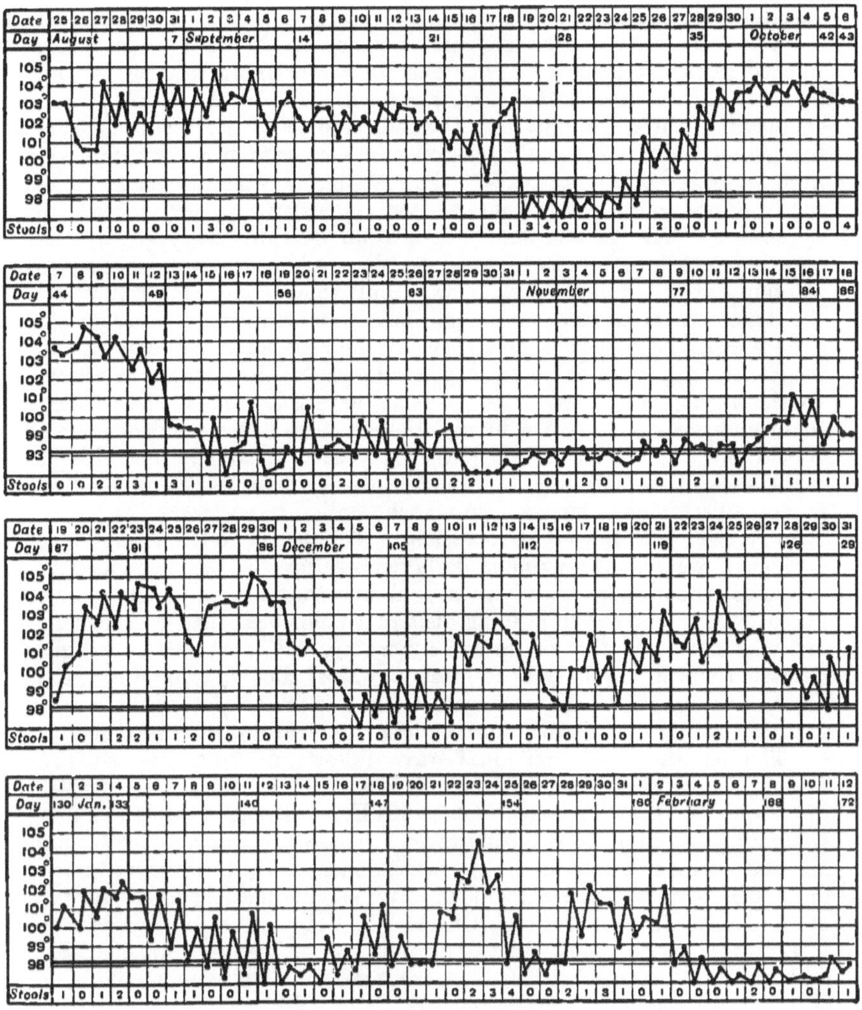

Undulations of somewhat continuous pyrexia.

Unusually long case, with somewhat continuous temperature, marked apyrexial periods, and falls to normal at the endings of waves, treated by the expectant method. This was thought at first to be a case of enteric fever.

dyspeptic troubles, loss of weight, and pyrexia (see Chart VI.). He was never dangerously ill, but became much debilitated, and was invalided to England on March 28th, 1891, where he continued for three months to be subject to occasional rises of temperature and the rheumatic complications of this fever. He ultimately recovered and returned to duty with his regiment in Malta in January of 1892. Since then, except for a slight attack of febricula in July 1892, lasting three days, he has remained in good health.

This regularity in pyrexial undulations, which has by some been likened to enteric fever with from one to five or more relapses, is not, however, by any means the rule, every variation in the duration and character of the waves, apyrexial periods, and daily temperature curves being met with. The daily temperature may vary from continuously high pyrexia to intermittence. The attack may consist entirely of pyrexial undulations or of intermittent pyrexia; may commence with pyrexial undulations, and pass later into an intermittent type; or commencing with intermittence, pass into the undulatory type with waves of remittent or continuous pyrexia. In all these cases, however, where the true maximum and minimum daily temperatures are accurately ascertained, these show a tendency, by their increase and decrease in height, to form more or less marked undulations of pyrexial intensity. At the beginning of a wave the pyrexial curve may steadily rise without remittence, or it may rise suddenly, though this latter is not common. At the end of a wave a fall to normal may occur gradually but without remittance, or the fall may be a sudden one, by crisis. This last ending is most uncommon, while as a permanent ending to an attack the writer has only met with it on two occasions. In such recorded risings and fallings, however, the maximum daily temperature (which occurs usually in the afternoon) may have been missed, and the temperature may have fallen by the time of the evening visit to a point near that of the next morning and below that of the same morning, and so masked any slight remission which may have been present. Most commonly, however, the ascent and descent of the temperature curve in these pyrexial waves is gradual and associated with more or less remittence or intermittence.

The length of an individual wave follows no rule, so that the primary wave may last the whole attack, or the attack may consist of a series of short waves (*vide* Chart XVII.), in some instances almost simulating the curve of relapsing fever. These two extreme conditions are not common, nearly all cases conforming roughly to three types:—(1) Cases with well-marked moderately long undulations of remittent or continuous temperature (*vide* Charts VI., VII., and X.); (2) Cases of intermittent or extremely remittent pyrexia, with waves only marked, and then not always clearly, by the maximum and minimum daily temperature records (*vide* Charts VIII. and IX.); (3) Cases in which these two preceding types succeed one another, the intermittent usually (though not invariably) following the undulatory type, and indeed being a not uncommon ending to all varieties of attacks of this fever (*vide* Charts VIII. and XIX. and Case 42).

As has been said, most cases end with a longer or shorter period of intermittence, which, in a large number of cases, may be drawn out by a period during which the only symptom is an occasional rise of temperature in the afternoon or evening of a slight nature (99°-101°) at irregular intervals. As long, however, as a patient is subject to these slight

CHART VIII.

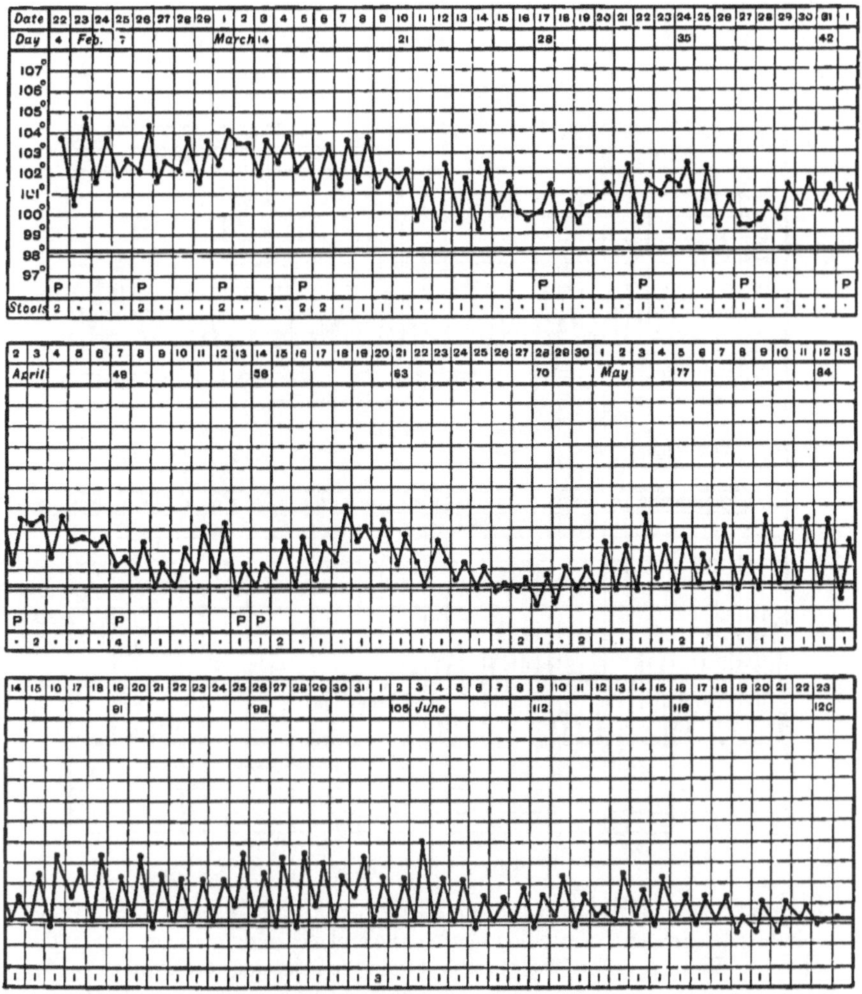

Note.—P = Purgative administered.
Undulatory passing to intermittent type.

noctural rises, he is liable to a relapse of any severity, even fatal in character. In such cases the virus seems to be lying hidden somewhere, ready at any indiscretion to burst forth and produce more serious effects.

In cases where relapses occur after long intervals (one to three months) of apparent convalescence, it is generally found that the patient has at times felt seedy, or suffered from headache, shivering, or diaphoresis on certain days, when, if his temperature had been taken in the evening, it would have been found to be slightly elevated. There is no periodicity about these slight irregular rises. Other relapses occur after periods of apparently complete recovery in men who, after their discharge from

CHART IX.

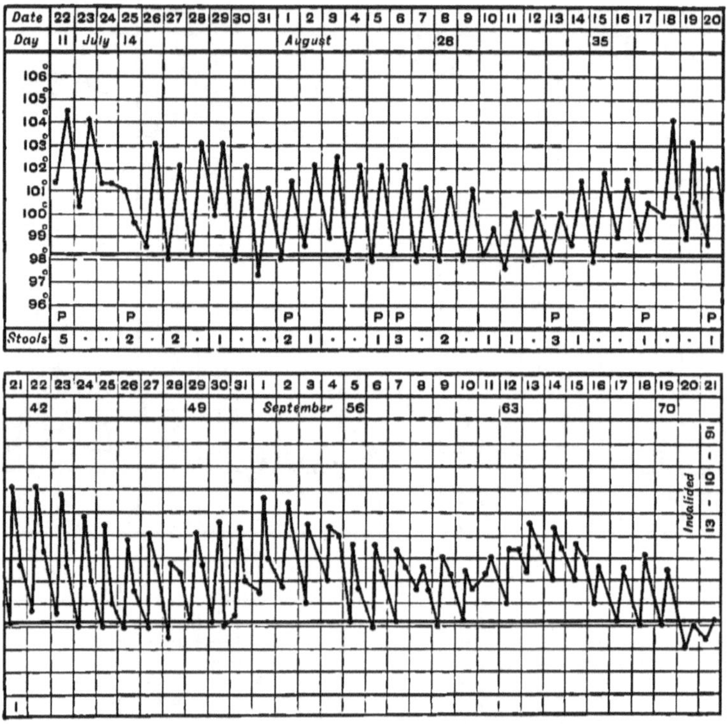

Intermittent type showing waves.

hospital, have returned to the same bed in the same barrack-room they inhabited when the original infection took place, and to the same mode of life. In such cases is it possible that a re-infection took place? In cases that have quite recovered, and have been a year free from fever, or who have left the infective area after recovery, we do not meet with recurrences of pyrexia such as are met with in paludism. Once, therefore, completely free from the fever the patient may consider himself cured. A not uncommon ending in acute attacks is a wave of a short but unusually severe nature immediately preceding permanent cessation of the pyrexia. The slumbering fever appears to suddenly flare up into a strong flame and, as it were, burn itself out (see Charts XII. and XIX.).

One of the surest signs of permanent cessation of pyrexia is a period of *subnormal temperature* lasting from one to six or more days *with a clean tongue.* Without this subnormal period an apyrexial interval can never be trusted to remain permanent, while in those cases where, on

CHART X.

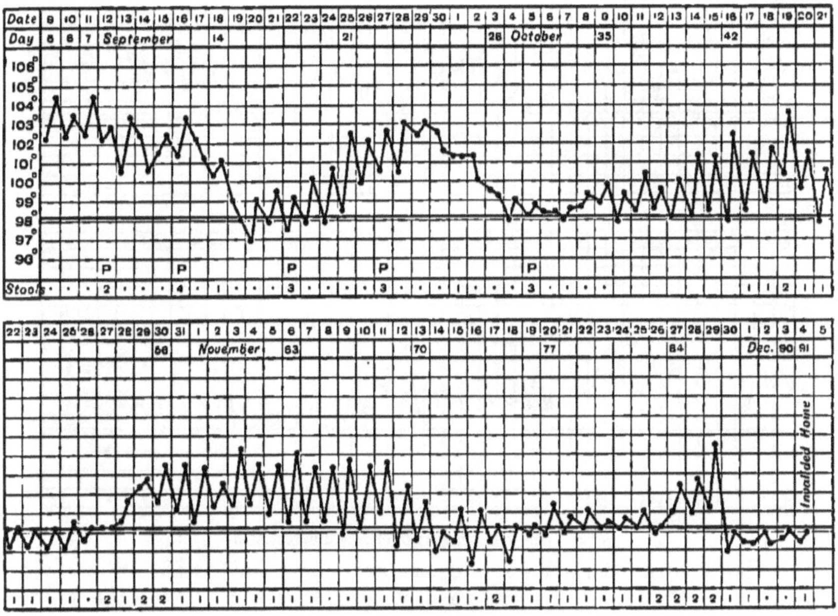

Undulatory type with well-marked waves.

account of debility or other cause the temporary apyrexial periods between waves are subnormal in character, it is found that the permanent cessation of pyrexia is marked by a still lower point or longer period below the normal line.

The apyrexial periods between waves (taking pyrexia to mean excessive temperature above normal) vary in length as much as the waves of pyrexia, though they are considerably shorter as a general rule. In some cases they are most clearly marked (Charts VII. and X.), while in others they are only replaced by a comparative abatement in the severity of the symptoms (Charts VI. and XI.). Or one wave may seem to overlap the next with only a slightly marked abatement.

A sudden fall of temperature (or accidental intermission) during a wave, and lasting only a few hours, is often met with. When occurring during the first few days after admission during the primary wave, it is comparable with the fall accompanying hæmorrhage in enteric fever.

At this period, in the absence of hæmorrhage or other accountable symptom, it is a most valuable diagnostic sign in favour of a doubtful case being one of undulant fever (*vide* Chart XIII.).

CHART XI.

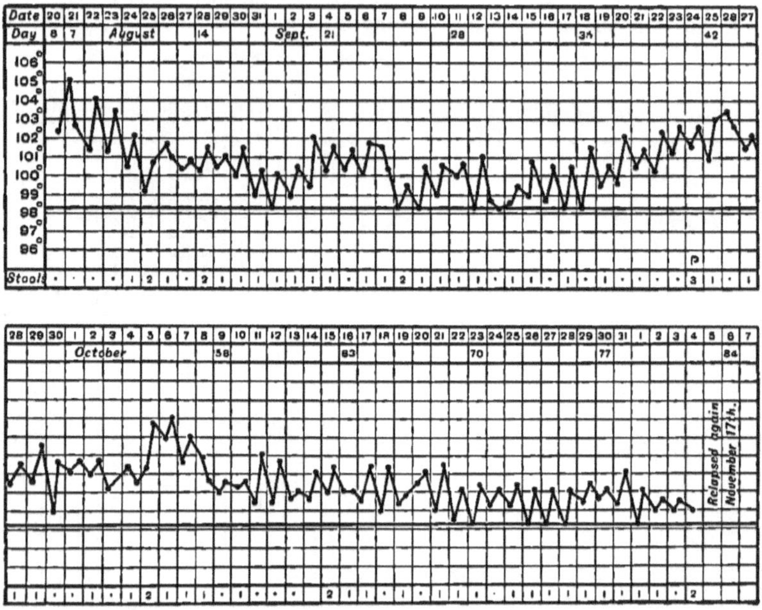

Chart with undulations not clearly differentiated.

The continuously high temperature curve met with in certain malignant and fatal types has already been described. Also the tend-

CHART XII.

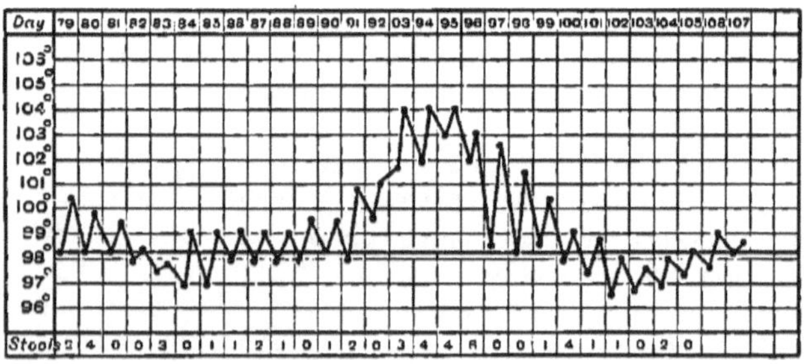

Severe wave at end of an attack. See also Chart XIX.

ency to extreme hyperpyrexia in such cases, the temperature continuing to rise after death, so that 112° and 115° F. have been registered in the internal organs.

The following is a specimen case, for the notes of which I am indebted to Surgeon-Major Bruce :—

Case 24.—*Illustrating extreme and rapidly fatal pyrexia.*—Pte. G., admitted to hospital 28th August 1888, on the third day of severe pyrexia; previous history good; age 23. On admission his face was dusky, his hands tremulous, his tongue dry and brown, his pulse weak, and there was a tendency to delirium. His condition became gradually worse, and he died of hyperpyrexia on the tenth day of the disease. He was on milk diet with a suitable amount of brandy, combined with stimulating drugs (see Chart XIV.).

At the post-mortem examination the lungs were found to be congested at the bases, the liver congested, and the spleen (weight 19

CHART XIII.

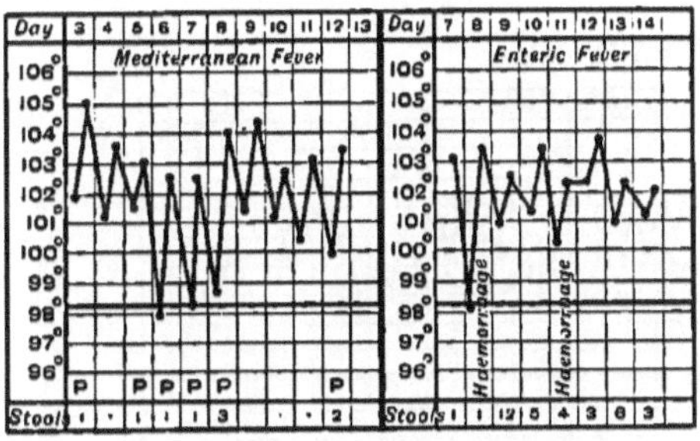

Note.—P = Purgative administered.

Early temporary falls of temperature in undulant and enteric fevers.

CHART XIV.

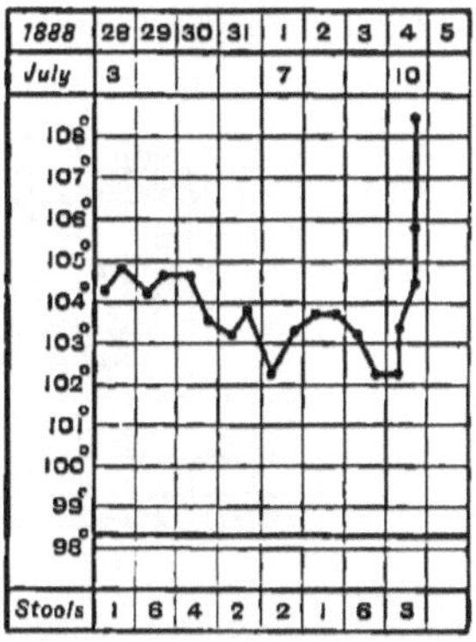

Malignant rapidly fatal case.

ounces) deeply congested. Peyer's patches were quite normal throughout, and but for a few patches of congestion the intestines were also normal in appearance. Colonies of the micrococcus Melitensis were obtained from the spleen after death.

In a few fatal cases, after a period of high pyrexia, the temperature may fall gradually to normal in an apparently satisfactory manner, but the patients show most unsatisfactory signs of exhaustion, possibly with muttering delirium, and after a few hours this temperature may begin to rise and attain to fatal hyperpyrexia. Even if attempts be made to check this final and fatal rise by external cold it is found to be of no avail, the nervous pyrexia-restraining mechanism appearing to have completely lost its power of responding even to external stimulation. These cases are always those in which the temperature has been allowed to remain high for a long time previously without artificial interference. Such an end is met with occasionally in other acute fevers, notably in cases of enteric fever.

Case 7.—*Illustrating decline of temperature with extreme exhaustion, followed by uncontrollable hyperpyrexia.*—Pte. C., R. Berkshire Regt., aged 22, admitted to hospital in Valetta, 11th January 1893, on the sixth day of the disease. He was a quite temperate man, who had been serving in Malta for nearly two years. Previous health good, but for attacks of slight febricula in July 1891 and December 1892. This and Case No. 8 occurred near burst drain, as has been mentioned in the chapter on etiology. Accompanying the extremely high pyrexia were diarrhœa, dry brown tongue, catarrhal pneumonic symptoms, extreme nervous prostration, and a tendency to pass into the so-called "typhoid state." The case was thought by many to be one of enteric fever. There was general abdominal tenderness at times, and towards the end persistent vomiting of every form of nourishment. When his temperature fell to normal on the 35th day he was extremely debilitated, exhausted, and collapsed, and the next day uncontrollable hyperpyrexia of a fatal character set in. Had the temperature been treated by external application of cold from the

CHART XV.

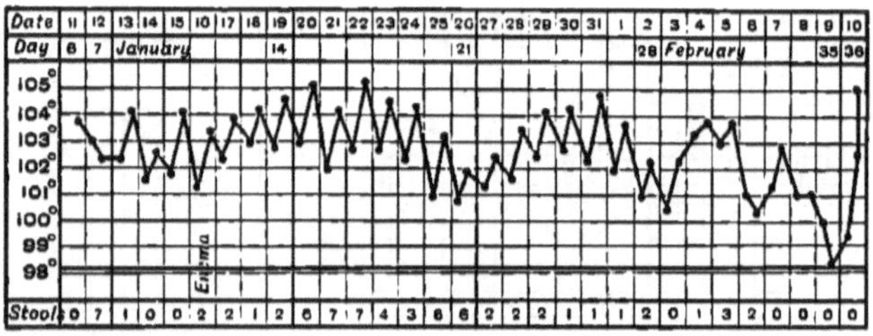

Fall of temperature followed by fatal hyperpyrexia.

beginning it is probable that a different result would have been attained (see Chart XV.).

At the post-mortem the lungs were found to be extremely congested and consolidated in patches at the bases. The spleen weighed 18 ounces, and was excessively congested. The intestines were congested in patches, but were not ulcerated, while Peyer's patches were all normal in appearance. The mesenteric glands were somewhat enlarged.

The micrococcus Melitensis was isolated from the spleen in pure cultivations on agar after death. See also Case 21.

Case 3.—Illustrating a fatal result during a relapse.—Case 3 similar to No. 2 in character. Admitted July 10th, 1892. Age 20; service six years, two of which had been in Malta. This man slept in a bed from which a comrade in his room said that other cases had been admitted to hospital. The bed in question was under a roof ventilator, placed next a main drain ventilator, the smell from which was complained of in the room.

Previous history.—Had suffered from slight attacks of febricula and bronchial catarrh in Cairo in 1887; from gonorrhœa four times in Malta between October 1891 and June 1892. Habits latterly intemperate, physique on admittance fairly good.

Clinical history.—Onset somewhat sudden, admitted on the third day of the attack with pains in the back and limbs, epigastric tenderness and some vomiting, the latter relieved by bismuth. Primary attack lasted 24 days, during which time there was a tendency to diarrhœa, but no other symptom of an enteric nature. After an apyrexial period of about five days the second wave began on the 25th day of the disease, the temperature ranged high and the patient became daily worse. On the 49th day he suffered from subcutaneous hæmorrhages over the sacrum and buttocks, but no bed-sores appeared. There was tenderness on pressure in the epigastric, splenic, and left iliac regions; a tendency to diarrhœa with loose yellow stools throughout the relapse; while during the last four days the stools were passed involuntarily. Death occurred on the 54th day at 7.15 P.M., from heart failure and exhaustion (see Chart XVI.).

CHART XVI.

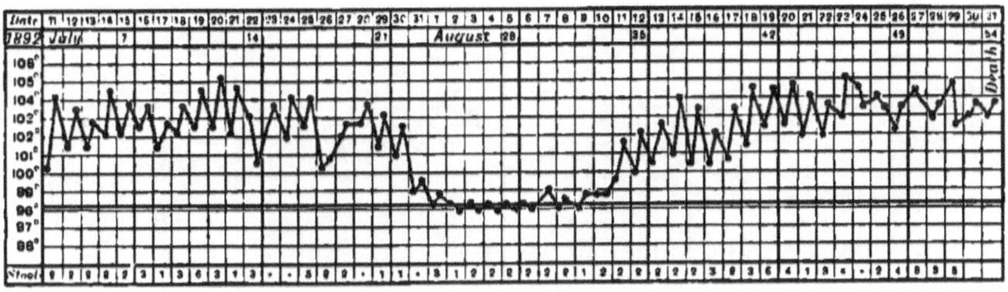

Death during a relapse.

Treatment.—Careful dietary and free use of stimulants. Gastric sedatives and antipyrin. Lead and opium internally, and opium and starch enemata for diarrhœa.

Examination one hour after death.—Body emaciated. Heart normal. Lungs showed hypostatic congestion of both bases. Spleen weighed 14 ounces, was very dark in colour and soft in consistency. Liver weighed 59 ounces, was slightly congested. Stomach distended with gas and fluid food, but was otherwise normal. Duodenum normal. Small intestine contracted and shrunken, and about 2½ feet from the cæcum it was hyperæmic with arborescent congestion, in the course of the vessels. Peyer's patches and the mesenteric glands were all normal. The large intestine, for two feet from the ileo-cæcal valve, was intensely congested and offensive, which explained the presence of diarrhœa during life.

Case 10.—*Illustrating short irregular waves and death during a relapse.*—Admitted April 18th, 1892. Age 26; service five years.

Previous history very good; no previous illness during army service.

Clinical history.—Onset sudden on day before admission. Severe pyrexial symptoms for 18 days, after which they became of an adynamic character, combined with delirium, a dry brown tongue, tendency to diarrhœa, splenic tenderness, and much sleeplessness. On the 21st day there were symptoms of impending death, with involuntary passage of fæces; but the patient rallied. On the 23rd day there were symptoms of lobular consolidation of the right lung, which became extreme about the 38th day and endangered life. There were extreme dyspnœa, cyanosis of skin, and symptoms of œdema of the right lung, from which, however, he again rallied on the 45th day. On the 50th day he was much better, but on the 56th day the temperature began to rise again. On the 57th day he became very exhausted, with laboured breathing, and died on the morning of the 58th day (see Chart XVII.).

Treatment.—Careful dietary and free use of stimulants. Dry cupping, poultices and turpentine to chest. Expectorants, astringents, etc.

Examination one hour after death.—Body emaciated. Heart normal. Lungs œdematous, congested, and with lobular consolidation of both

CHART XVII.

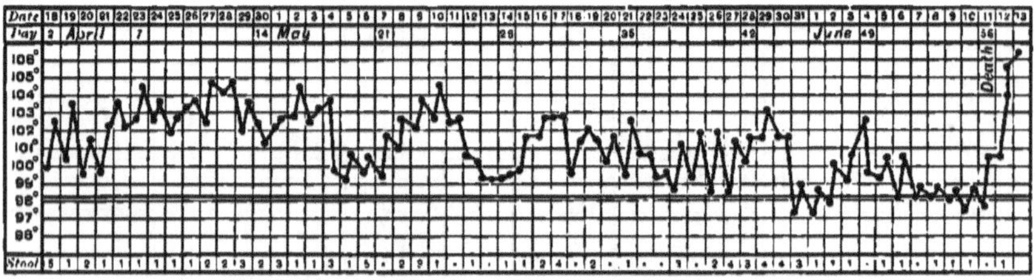

Short irregular pyrexial waves, with death during a relapse.

bases. Intestines normal except for slight duodenal hyperæmia, Peyer's patches and mesenteric glands normal. Liver weighed 80 ounces and was extremely congested. Kidneys, 8 ounces, and also congested. Spleen, 12 ounces, congested, but firm in texture.

Experiment.—Cover-glass preparations of fresh splenic substance showed many micrococci. Pure cultures of characteristic micro-organism obtained from the spleen as in former cases.

Another, but uncommon form of temperature curve in fatal cases, is one in which an originally high temperature falls gradually and satisfactorily to within what is usually considered a safe limit, by the second week; but the fall is accompanied by symptoms of extreme nervous exhaustion of increasing severity. The condition appears to be one of acute poisoning from toxic substances distinct from those causing the pyrexia. One might almost consider that there was present in the alimentary canal some toxic alkaloid similar to those met with in acute ptomaine poisonings, over and above the fever virus. Such cases, happily not of frequent occurrence, complicated as they are by serious nervous and adynamic symptoms, are most difficult to treat successfully, and are of a most fatal character.

Of cases which die at a later date there is little to be said, as they either die during a relapse under circumstances comparable with death during the primary attack; or at a late stage in the disease from some complication, or intercurrent or succeeding disease, when there is little to be said of special nature about the temperature curve.

The *daily* temperature curve is usually remittent in character, *i.e.* the morning temperature is as a rule one or two degrees lower than that in the evening, without actually touching the normal line or thereabouts except during the apyrexial intervals. As has been mentioned, this curve may, however, in difficult cases assume any type between intermittence and a continuously high temperature; or pass from one to another type in one and the same attack.

To understand the course of the daily pyrexial curve, it is best to first take the intermittent temperature of mild cases. In these it is usually at or near normal during the morning visit (8 A.M.), and begins

CHART XVIII.

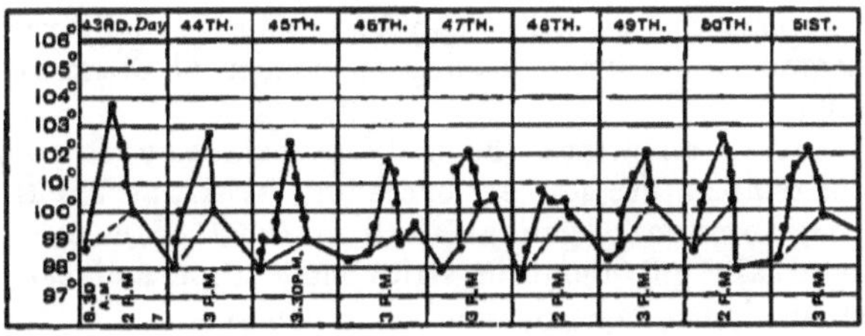

Diurnal curve (43rd to 51st day) of Chart 9.

to rise steadily a little before 11 A.M. to a maximum between 2 and 3 P.M. From this it gradually falls to half-way about 6 P.M. (the time of the evening visit), and reaches normal again about 10 or 11 P.M., or later; after which profuse diaphoresis occurs. Occasionally slight supernumerary rises of temperature are added to this curve, a common one being just after the evening visit and bedmaking. This diurnal curve is accentuated by any mental emotion or excitement, by exertion, injudicious dietary or medicine, excessive constipation or the reverse, by the damp, enervating sirocco wind, or by the appearance of any special localised symptom. It is not an uncommon occurrence to find all the temperatures of a ward unusually high on the evening following a bad sirocco wind, or the afternoon on which friends are allowed to visit patients. Though a similar rise is met with in enteric and other fevers, it is rarely so constant or well marked as in the undulant fever cases in hospital. The relief of constipation, or a change in the weather, often prove to be excellent antipyretics. This daily curve is quite non-paroxysmal in nature, resembling more the hectic fever of phthisis than the paroxysms of ague. The rise of temperature is associated with the feeling of chilliness in the hands or feet and malaise, a creeping, crawling feeling in the back. Rigors are most rare, and confined to children and patients with a specially nervous temperament.

The maximum and minimum may be postponed (or less often anticipated), so that in a few extreme cases the morning temperature becomes the high one and the evening the reverse. In all these mild cases the temperature is apt to reach a far higher point than the general condition and other symptoms would usually warrant, and this fact is accentuated in children, and those of nervous and excitable temperament.

From the above mild type the daily temperature curve may be increased in duration so as to postpone the fall well into the night and the diaphoresis to the early morning, while at the same time the morning rise is anticipated. Thus though the height may not increase very much, the amount or duration of pyrexia is increased considerably. With this increase in the duration of pyrexia, there comes an increase in those symptoms due to interference with the oxidation, nutrition, metabolism, and excretion in the body. These materially increase the severity of the case. In more severe cases one day's curve appears to run into and overlap that of the next, until with less and less remittence the temperature comes to be continuously high, and the daily variation less than one degree—a condition leading to danger of death from sudden hyperpyrexia.

At the end of an attack the daily pyrexia may be confined to a slight rise of temperature scarcely exceeding 99° F., at 2 P.M. or thereabouts, falling to normal again about 5 or 6 P.M. In these cases the patient can usually get about in strict moderation and eat his meals, except that his lunch must be limited to soup or milk, and he must lie down during the early part of the afternoon. During such time, however, he is liable to a relapse on any indiscretion.

Nervous System.—The action of the virus on the nervous system, as evinced by the common clinical phenomena of the disease, is next to pyrexia one of the most constant and characteristic features in this fever.

Speaking generally, the disease poison seems to have an irritative action on the cerebro-spinal system, evinced by exaggerated reflexes, if not by more evident symptoms. We cannot say whether this is due to the action of the virus or of its products on the central and peripheral nervous tissues or on the fibrous sheaths of these structures, but are inclined to attribute it to a mixture of both. Whether it produces a neuritis, a perineuritis, or some other pathological condition, the results are of a typical neuralgic character, whether the exciting cause be central or peripheral.

While many local symptoms may be referred to its direct action on special parts of the nervous mechanism, many other constant but more general symptoms doubtless have their origin in a similar action. The action of the virus would appear to be of two kinds, direct and indirect. The virus (or its products) in certain cases appear to directly attack the central and peripheral cerebro-spinal nerve tissue. By means of certain toxic substances formed during the life cycle of the virus within the human body, an indirect action is brought to bear upon the higher nerve centres, notably those regulating the thermic mechanism (including the perspiration), the heart and lungs, etc. By its action upon the fibrous structures of the body, including apparently the fibrous coverings of the various nerve structures, it appears to have also local effect upon certain parts of the cerebro-spinal and peripheral nervous system. This latter action would seem to be closely analogous to its action upon other fibrous structures, such as the aponeuroses, the joints, the pericardium, pleura, etc. These latter are localised and variable in distribution, and though common in occurrence are by no means essential symptoms, though a tendency to nerve irritation appears to be always present in some degree. Their localised and metastatic nature, the fact that they occasionally leave their effects behind after the actual fever has disappeared, and that they usually occur during the later and less severe stages of the fever, lead one to the belief that they are due to the direct action of the virus on local structures.

"Fever pains," headache, general malaise and weakness, are the initial symptoms that most patients complain of when first seeking medical advice.

(*a*) The so-called "fever pains," though not specially characteristic of this particular fever, are rarely absent. The patient usually complains of "pains all over him," and when pressed to particularise, lays special stress on his neck and the middle of his back and behind his eyeballs. The muscles of the neck and back are the seat of slight but numerous darting pains when stretched or moved; and these pains seem to radiate round the abdomen, and along the upper and lower extremities, or into the face or scalp, following the course of the nerves, and giving rise to slight tingling, localised and varying hyperæsthesia of the skin and much stiffness in the muscles. These pains are most severe in those who have been trying to work off their "stiffness" by exercise. They are greatly relieved by warmth and rest in bed, being rarely complained of after the patient has been twenty-four hours in a comfortable bed in hospital. In intermittent cases they may recur to a slight extent when the temperature is rising in the afternoon, causing that peculiar "creepy feeling" in the back which, combined with a feeling of dryness of the skin, are to the patient infallible indications of the onset of his daily non-paroxysmal rise. The pain behind the eyeballs is felt whenever the eyes are quickly turned in any new direction.

(*b*) The headache is usually present in direct proportion to the severity of the pyrexia and the amount of muscular and mental work that the patient has undergone since the onset of the pyrexia. Thus it usually disappears after a day or two of rest and quiet in bed or after a good natural or artificial sleep. In malignant cases it may be most severe, while in mild, intermittent ones, who have refrained from exertion, mentally and physically, it may be absent or confined to the onset of the afternoon rise of temperature. It is cerebral in nature, usually frontal, less often occipital. When it returns during treatment in hospital it is usually associated with a sudden rise of temperature, or with constipation.

(*c*) Wakefulness and sleeplessness are common early symptoms. The mental faculties are usually clearer at first than in enteric fever cases of equal pyrexial severity, the general muscular and nervous prostration being much less marked at the commencement of the disease. Rigors are very rarely met with. In some few cases general nervous irritability referable to the cerebro-spinal system is present. In such cases mental irritability and sleeplessness are combined with cutaneous hyperæsthesia of variable or varying extent, girdle pains, hemianæsthesia, alteration in the function of the nerves of special sense, etc., though these symptoms are rarely constant or severe. Delusions and delirium are uncommon except in severe cases, or occasionally in cases when the temperature, which has maintained a high level for some days, begins to fall permanently. In these latter instances they rarely last more than a few days. They are more marked when the fall is rapid or great. Thus, a sergeant who, during a very severe primary attack, had retained his mental faculties, about the 27th day became subject to delusions for four days at the beginning of an amelioration of his condition, of a marked and permanent nature. During these four days he believed that he had received a commission as an officer, and tried to get up and perform the duties appertaining to his new rank in life. Another sergeant of equal standing in his own regiment had lately received such a commission, hence the delusion in his case. After four days he recovered his mental equilibrium.

Nearly all patients become low spirited when their temperature returns to normal at all quickly, after remaining high for any time. A lady who kept up her spirits most cheerfully through a severe attack lasting ninety days, was reduced almost to despair, passing into floods of tears on the slightest provocation, after a somewhat sudden and permanent fall of temperature before convalescence. This latter is a most common condition, the pyrexia seeming to act as a false stimulant to the nervous system, its removal being followed by an absence of nervous excitation, necessitating stimulating and sympathetic treatment until the nervous equilibrium has been re-established. It is a somewhat favourable symptom in many cases. It should be borne in mind though, as it often alarms the patient and his friends, who think he is worse instead of better. It must not, however, be mistaken for that nervous prostration occasionally present with a moderate temperature in a few very serious and even fatal cases, where a condition somewhat similar to that met with in cases of ptomaine poisoning is met with.

With reference to this depression, it has been shown that, though as a rule, when the body-weight falls 40 per cent the patient dies of inanition, life may be sustained under greater loss when pyrexia is present, the body heat being sustained (Chossat), the pyrexia acting as a kind of stimulant.

In very severe cases with high temperature delirium may be present and pass on to coma before a fatal issue from hyperpyrexia, if suitable and energetic treatment be not adopted.

Nervous prostration is very marked at the end of prolonged attacks, and even for some time during convalescence. In such cases the power of concentration of ideas or of following out a train of thought, the remembrance of names or figures, and similar fine mental actions, are often temporarily impaired, and only very slowly return.

Common sensation sometimes remains impaired for a long time; deafness, not due to quinine, is often met with but ultimately gets all right, though it takes time. Hyperæsthesia with acute pain on pressure or even exaggerated reflexes may occur, so that even the weight of the bedclothes may become unendurable. These pains and neuralgic symptoms when present often disappear when the temperature rises at all high. Aberrations of sensations to touch may occur, and taste become deficient. General cutaneous hyperæsthesia or hemianæsthesia may occur.

The memory may become impaired for some length of time, especially with respect to dates, names, and the chronological order of events. A clergyman found difficulty in preaching for some months after an attack, a doctor in remembering doses, etc.

Tremulous condition of the hands may persist. Some weakness of vision may occur, but this disappears with recovery. Retention of urine may occur during the acute stages. Slight weakness of the sphincter urinæ has followed attacks and remained permanently. Involuntary passage of fæces only occurs in the last stages of most severe cases, usually before death.

The writer has not met with actual mania or imbecility following attacks of this fever; but hysterical symptoms may occur.

The decubitus is lateral until the patient becomes very seriously or dangerously ill.

There is in all cases a certain irritability of the nervous system characterised by increased reflexes, more particularly of the patella and plantar reflexes, and in one case ankle clonus was present. Periosteal reflexes do not appear to be increased. In a large percentage of cases there are neuralgic pains which will be described later. In other cases mental irritability and sleeplessness are combined with actual signs of cerebro-spinal irritation, such as cutaneous hyperæsthesia, anæsthesia, alteration in function of certain nerves of special sense, girdle pains, optic neuritis, etc. The chief and most constant characteristic about these symptoms is their variability in the same individual from hour to hour, or from day to day. Whereas some of these symptoms appear to be due to the direct action of the virus on the nervous tissues, others seem also due to serous effusion into the ventricles of the brain and beneath the cerebro-spinal meninges, comparable to the effusions into the joints, tendons, pleuræ, pericardium, etc., and like these usually late symptoms. Intense burning pain in the soles of the feet is not an uncommon symptom in such cases, while it also occurs in other cases during desquamation of these parts.

Case 25.—*With cerebro-spinal irritation early in the attack.*—Ptc. H., admitted to hospital July 31st, 1895, on the fourth day of the attack. The usual symptoms of headache, fever pains, furred tongue, and epigastric tenderness were present. Morning temperature 101°, evening 102° F. On the evening of the 6th day temperature fell to 98·4°, and remained beneath 100° until the evening of the 10th day, when a long but remittent wave began, lasting until the 65th day, during which period the temperature varied between 100°-104·4° F. The temperature varied between 98° to 101° until he was invalided on the 90th day. After this there was no return of the pyrexia, and he made a good and uninterrupted recovery.

During this long wave lasting 56 days, he suffered at times from hyperæsthesia of the lower part of the abdomen and of the extremities, varying in locality and degree. Towards the end of the wave he suffered from most severe hyperæsthesia of the soles of the feet, relieved by soaking them in cold water; desquamation also occurred at this period. He also complained from time to time of girdle pains, and of pains shooting down the nerves of the legs. He suffered from frequent headaches, at times of a continuous character. From being of a bright and lively disposition, he changed at this time to an extremely irritable and often sulky nature, and was continually arguing or quarrelling with the hospital attendants. His sight at one time became somewhat affected and reading made his head ache. Bromide of potassium, rest, and quiet gave great relief to these symptoms, which all passed away with the cessation of the pyrexia. When the writer met him some two months later he had entirely recovered his original lively disposition and gave no trouble whatever.

Case 15.—*Of cerebro-spinal irritation with fatal intercranial pressure.*—Sergt. R., age 23, army service five years, arrived in Malta Feb. 2nd, 1895. Previous medical history good, only one entry in medical history sheet for a mild attack of measles in 1891 at Aldershot. No other foreign service.

Admitted to hospital Jan. 16th, 1896, on the third day of an attack of undulant fever, temperature 105·4° F. at 6 P.M. Tongue thickly coated, bowels constipated. The bowels were relieved by five grains of calomel with powdered jalap, followed next morning by an enema. He complained of intense frontal headache and the usual pains in the back and limbs. The temperature remained high until the 10th day, necessitating frequent artificial reduction by means of cold water sponging; after which it fell a degree a day (the difference between morning and evening being about 2°) until the 13th day, when it again rose above 103°, necessitating similar treatment. The temporary fall was accompanied by diarrhœa, easily controlled by a lead and opium pill. Until the 25th day the temperature remained high, the tongue became dry and brown, the breath foul, and only beef juice, peptonised milk, albumin water, and champagne, could be digested. After this his temperature became more remittent, varying between 99° in the morning and 102° in the evening until the 45th day.

The amelioration of pyrexial symptoms on the 27th day was accompanied by delusions lasting for four days, though he had retained his mental faculties previously. On the 33rd day he complained of "rheumatic pains" following the course of the nerves of the legs, dull and aching with occasional shooting pains. With flannel drawers and hot applications these began to disappear on the 36th day, and were completely gone by the 39th day. Throughout the whole of the remainder of the attack he suffered from obstinate constipation, requiring frequent doses of liquorice powder, calomel and jalap, compound senna mixture, or enemas.

On the 45th day the temperature reached normal, and continued a mild intermittent character until the 102nd day, with no other symptoms except constipation, nocturnal diaphoresis, and, for three days about the 55th day, some neuritic pains in the shoulders and arms.

On the 102nd day his temperature rose, and the intermittent character changed to a more continuous type between 100° and 103° until the 111th day. At this time also he began to complain of pains shooting down the legs, and some dull aching pain in the anterior portion of the legs. From a quiet, uncomplaining man, he changed to an irritable one, complaining that his "nerves had all gone wrong." He talked a great deal at this period, and on the 107th day complained of a pain shooting through his head when he tried to think of an answer to any question put to him. He suffered from sleeplessness. He had during the previous months various antiseptic and other drugs, none of which cut short the attack, and on account of his anæmia and debility he had passed an invaliding board, and was awaiting passage to England. His hair was falling out, and his feet peeling in large flakes, and he suffered from intense burning pain at times in the soles of his feet. On the 112th day the headache became very severe, his reflexes were found to be enormously exaggerated, and he began to make many purposeless and nonsensical remarks, while there was hyperæsthesia of varying amount on the left side and girdle pains. On the 113th and 114th days he became unconscious, but could still be roused into semi-consciousness at times. Constipation was marked, and only slightly relieved by strong measures. His pulse remained good. On the 115th day he was found to be blind of the left eye, the pupil of the same side was slightly enlarged, there were slight ptosis and divergent strabismus of the same side of varying amount, slight facial paralysis (left), some rigidity and stiffness of the muscles of the back of the neck, with pain when the head was moved. These symptoms varied in amount during the 115th and 116th days, becoming most marked about 7.30 P.M. on the latter, when he became comatose, while retention replaced an involuntary passage of urine which had existed for the two previous days, his breathing became stertorous, his pulse for the first time weak and soft, mucus collected in his throat and lungs, and death seemed imminent, his temperature having risen from 100·6° at 2 P.M. to 104·4°.

During the last few days, besides ordinary treatment, he had had strong aperients without much effect, blisters to the neck and head, and full doses of bromide and iodide of potash. He was now treated with mercury ointment inunction over the abdomen, groin, and thighs, which was followed by marked but temporary improvement. The temperature fell to 100·8°, at 9.30 P.M. the breathing became deeper, the pulse slightly fuller, the "death rattle" disappeared, power of swallowing returned, and the skin became moist. He suffered, however, from occasional convulsive spasms, his hands were passed frequently over the abdomen and pubis; he moaned a good deal. Signs of facial paralysis had disappeared the next morning, but the amaurosis and divergent strabismus and ptosis remained, though the pupils were equal. On the morning of the 117th day his temperature was 101·8°, and he appeared better, except that his pulse was weak and thready, and he remained quite unconscious. About 10.30 A.M. the difficulty in swallowing returned, the breathing became stertorous, the pulse weaker and weaker, until, with failure of circulation and respiration, he died quietly at 1 P.M., his temperature steadily rising before death.

Post-mortem.—The spleen was removed two hours after death, and inoculations were made in the usual way in the laboratory on nutrient agar-agar, from which numerous pure cultivations of the micrococcus Melitensis were obtained subsequently. Cover-glass smear preparations were made and portions preserved in alcohol for further investigation. The organ weighed 12 ounces, was fairly firm in consistence, and not markedly congested. Twenty hours after:—Heart muscle flabby, weighed 10·5 ounces, otherwise normal; ante-mortem clot in both ventricles. Right lung (32 ounces), left lung (29 ounces), both bases in a state of hypostatic congestion. Liver (68 ounces) congested and nutmeg. Kidneys congested, capsules peeled easily. Alimentary tract normal except for a few patches of arborescent or dendritic venous congestion. Peyer's patches and the mesenteric glands normal. Brain, both membranes and cerebral tissue much congested. On section the "puncta vasculosa" were very marked, the cerebral tissues were extremely soft, especially at the base, where they also appeared to be œdematous. There was a considerable excess of cerebro-spinal fluid beneath the membranes and in the lateral ventricles, while in the latter and on the choroid plexus were small flocculi of exudation (lymph). Specimens of the liver, kidney, cerebrum (optic thalamus, cortex, and decussation), cerebellum and anterior crural nerve were also kept for investigation. Cover-glass smear preparations and inoculations of the brain were made on to agar-agar, cultivations of the micrococcus Melitensis being obtained. (See section on "Morbid Anatomy.")

(*d*) *Neuralgic and neuritic pains.*—These are met with in some form, as symptoms or sequelæ, in some 75 per cent of cases. They may occur at any stage of the attack, but are rarely present during the primary acute pyrexia of severe cases. Like the arthritic effusions these symptoms are most commonly met with at a late stage in the attack, when the pyrexia has, so to speak, become chronic and mild in character, or in cases whose pyrexia has been mild from the beginning. They often disappear on the onset of high pyrexia. For these reasons they are considered by some persons as a favourable sign, indicating an abatement in the severity of the attack or a step on the road to recovery. They are, however, the most painful symptoms met with in the disease. In all cases the nerves appear to be in a state in which the slightest exposure to chill is followed by an attack of neuralgic pain and tenderness; and they remain in this state during convalescence, so that attacks of neuralgic pain are not uncommon after the pyrexial condition has entirely ceased. As a rule a definite nerve or a set of nerves is attacked. The pain may take the form of severe facial, frontal, or occipital neuralgia; of lumbago, sciatica, or of pain following the course of any nerve, or cutaneous hyperæsthesia may be present. The pain may be acute or chronic in nature, may follow a definite exposure to chill very rapidly, or may arise apparently without cause.

(1) When acute, their course is accompanied by slight increase in the quantity of the temperature, amplifying slightly its daily length and elevation. They last from one to ten or more days, and are usually amenable to treatment. There is acute intermittent shooting pain down the branches of the nerve affected, more especially on moving the limb, constant dull pain and marked tenderness in the trunk of the nerve itself, and often slight localised cutaneous hyperæsthesia. These symptoms would seem to depend upon acute invòlvement (inflammatory congestion?) of the fibrous sheath of the affected nerve. Pain of a similar character may be referred to the aponeuroses, muscle or tendon sheaths, joints, etc.; all appearing to be dependent upon a similar pathological action on fibrous structures. They usually occur during or just after the decline of a pyrexial wave, during the late chronic stages of the pyrexia, or as the chief symptom of an otherwise mild attack.

(2) When chronic or subacute in nature these pains are less amenable to treatment. They occur in some form or other in about 60 per cent of cases, nearly always late in the attack or during convalescence, and even after return to duty following apparent recovery. They are extremely common during the late relapses of severe and prolonged attacks. When occurring during convalescence or during a slight relapse, after apparent recovery, their presence is usually marked by an elevation of temperature, varying from 99° to 100° F., or this may be absent or confined to the onset of the pains. When they occur during pyrexia, a similar amount appears to be added to the previous amount of temperature. Clinically, their appearance is that of a localised action of the

virus, with slight secondary pyrexia, occurring after the phenomena of the general infection have passed away. Possibly there is some subacute inflammatory action going on in the fibrous nerve sheath, leading to exudation and pressure on the nerve tissue proper. The condition may last from a week to many months, but recovery is the rule. There is generally in this fever a slight hyperæsthesia of the peripheral nervous system, and an undue susceptibility of the sensory nerves to the effects of heat, cold, pressure, and other stimuli. This may become exaggerated in the case of any particular nerve, in which case localised symptoms of neuritis arise.[1] The nerve the writer has found most often affected has been the sciatic. In such cases the onset has usually been sudden and accompanied by pyrexia, however slight, its first appearance being while the poison is still present in the tissues of the body. The cases may be relieved in a fortnight, or may continue for months after all pyrexia has ceased, or recovery may be followed by relapses of sciatica following any exposure to cold, fatigue, etc., the susceptibility, however, decreasing with time.

The symptoms consist of varying tenderness over the course of the nerve, pains of a shooting, tingling, and variable nature over the branches of distribution, and aching pain in the region of the sciatic nerve itself. These pains are decreased by rest and equable warmth, increased by movement and variations in atmospheric temperature. Occasionally there is localised hyperæsthesia of certain parts of the thigh or leg, contact with the bedclothes being even intolerable. In a few cases there is temporary atrophy or paralysis of certain muscles of the leg, but this is rarely associated with sciatica directly, being more often a separate symptom confined to the pedal extensors or deltoid. The left sciatic is not more often affected than the right; and its occurrence is not due to constipation. Both sides may be affected simultaneously or successively. Any other nerve or nerves may become similarly affected.

The writer has not met with intercurrent herpes, though that condition occurs in Malta apart from this fever.

It is a very common thing to find entries for "rheumatism" in a soldier's medical history sheet following an attack of undulant fever, even months after apparent recovery from that fever. Such entries usually refer to neuritic symptoms, with or without pyrexia, and are strictly speaking sequelæ of and directly connected with the attack of undulant fever.

Thus we find in looking through the medical history records of any regiment such cases as the following:—

Cases 26-36.—Pte. E., admitted to hospital in Gibraltar, Dec. 1st 1893, suffering from Mediterranean fever, for which he was discharged to duty 107 days after. Five days later he was readmitted for "rheumatism" which lasted 13 days.

[1] For symptoms of neuritis during typhoid fever see Dr. Osler, *Johns Hopkins Hospital Reports*, vii., vol. v. p. 397.

Pte. T., admitted to hospital in Malta for Mediterranean fever on August 2nd, 1895, and discharged to duty 88 days after. Seven days later he was readmitted for "rheumatism" lasting 15 days.

Pte. B., admitted to hospital, Nov. 6th, 1895, with Mediterranean fever lasting 69 days. Readmitted 7 days after being discharged, for "rheumatism" lasting 55 days.

Pte. H., admitted to hospital, June 14th, 1895, for Mediterranean fever lasting 123 days. Readmitted 10 days after discharge to duty, for "rheumatism" lasting 83 days.

Pte. L., admitted to hospital in Gibraltar for Mediterranean fever lasting 149 days, June 14th, 1894. Readmitted 15 days after discharge from hospital, for "rheumatism" lasting 10 days.

Pte. N., admitted to hospital in Malta, July 13th, 1895, for Mediterranean fever, and discharged to duty 94 days after. Readmitted for "rheumatism" 24 days later, which lasted 19 days.

Pte. R., admitted to hospital, May 20th, 1895, suffering from Mediterranean fever, and discharged to duty 169 days later. Readmitted for "rheumatism" 35 days after, for which he remained in hospital for 61 days longer.

Pte. R., admitted to hospital, June 10th, 1895, with Mediterranean fever, and discharged to duty 106 days after. Readmitted with a relapse, Dec. 10th, for 36 days. Readmitted 22 days later for "rheumatism," which lasted 29 days.

Pte. L., admitted to hospital, May 20th, 1895, for 71 days with very severe Mediterranean fever. Readmitted, 41 days after discharge from hospital, for 10 days with "rheumatism" and sciatica.

Pte. R., admitted to hospital, May 31st, 1895, for Mediterranean fever, and discharged to duty 69 days later. 140 days later, readmitted with "rheumatism" for 23 days.

Pte. M., admitted to hospital, July 6th, 1895, for 108 days suffering from Mediterranean fever. Readmitted, after being at duty for 118 days, for "rheumatism," and was in hospital for 39 days with sciatica, pains in the legs following the course of the nerves, and slight œdema of the ankles. No albuminuria.

Less commonly we find swollen joints and neuritic pains at the beginning of an attack, in which case the pyrexia is usually mild and intermittent in type. Thus we find in a few medical history sheets, such entries as these :—

Cases 37-40.—Pte. C., admitted to hospital in Malta with "rheumatism" and pyrexia on June 6th, 1895, and discharged to duty 19 days later. Readmitted with Mediterranean fever of a pronounced type 10 days later, for which he remained in hospital for 89 days.

Pte. W., admitted August 2nd with "rheumatism" and pyrexia for 36 days, ultimately proving to be Mediterranean fever. Readmitted 43 days later for a febrile relapse lasting 21 days.

Pte. H., admitted to hospital, July 24th, 1895, with "rheumatism," which proved to be Mediterranean fever, lasting 52 days. Readmitted for 12 days in November, and for 22 days in December and January, with the characteristic "rheumatic" symptoms.

Case 41.—*Illustrating the later neuritic and arthritic symptoms of the fever.*—Pte. B., King's R. Rifles, aged 22; service abroad, three years at Gibraltar and ten months in Malta; was admitted to hospital in Malta on June 2nd, 1895, on about 14th day of an attack of Mediterranean fever. His temperature, which was high on admission, fell steadily until it reached normal on the 21st day of the disease. After an apyrexial period of five days it again rose, and from the 26th to the 39th day was irregularly intermittent. After this he suffered from three well-marked pyrexial undulations of remittent temperature from the 40th to the 49th, from the 58th to the 66th, and from the 72nd to the 87th days. His temperature was normal or subnormal for the next 14 days, and he was sent to the sanitarium on August 26th on the 99th day of the attack.

During this period he had no neuritic or arthritic symptoms, but while at the sanitorium he suffered for a fortnight from rheumatic pains in the right hip and knee. On the 7th of October he was discharged to duty apparently cured, but five days later he was again admitted to hospital suffering from slight nocturnal pyrexia and rheumatic pains in the right hip and knee. After 17 days he returned to duty apparently cured.

Twenty-eight days later he was again admitted to hospital with pyrexia lasting 12 days, and varying between 100° in the morning and 102° F. in the evening. He also suffered pain and tenderness along the right sciatic nerve, pain in the right hip and knee, great anæmia, debility and swelling of the ankles after exertion. These symptoms disappeared about the 7th of December, and he began to convalesce steadily, and was invalided to England.

Case 42.—*Intermittent type passing into undulant type with neuritic symptoms.*—Dr. M. L. H., aged 29 years. Previous Mediterranean service (in Malta) five and a half years. Previous health very good; since 1877 only suffered from tonsillitis in 1887, mild influenza in 1893, and slight attacks of febricula (two or three days in duration) annually during service in Malta. During the first week of June 1896 the patient felt irritable and worried during the afternoon, and was told by others "that he was not looking well." He had moved with his wife for the first time, a fortnight before, into a back bedroom where insanitary surroundings were subsequently found to be present (*vide* outbreak 15, Chapter II.). On June 3rd his wife developed undulant fever (*vide* Case 45). On June 7th the patient returned from a five-mile bicycle ride with a bad headache and a temperature of 100° F. in the evening. On the morning of the 8th after sleeping in a direct draught on duty, patient awoke with severe neuralgia of the left or exposed side of the head which passed off about midday. The onset was most insidious, and during the first week of pyrexia he suffered from soreness and stiffness of the throat, redness of the tonsils, and increase in size of the cervical and submaxillary glands. The patient was removed to an airy house overlooking the sea. At this time his tongue was coated, and his evening temperature 99·8° F. During the night of June 9th a high wind arose after the patient had gone to sleep, and came directly on his head. On the morning of the 10th he awoke with very severe neuralgia of the frontal and occipital nerves of both sides of the head, and "fever pains" in the muscles of the back. The latter lasted only one day, but the former for three days, while the pain was very severe, each hair seemed painfully fixed to the scalp, and the patient vomited all food. During this time the temperature had varied between 99°-101° F. By June 13th the neuralgia had disappeared, having been greatly relieved by warm applications and by wearing a cap. From June 13th

CHART XIX.—*First Part.*

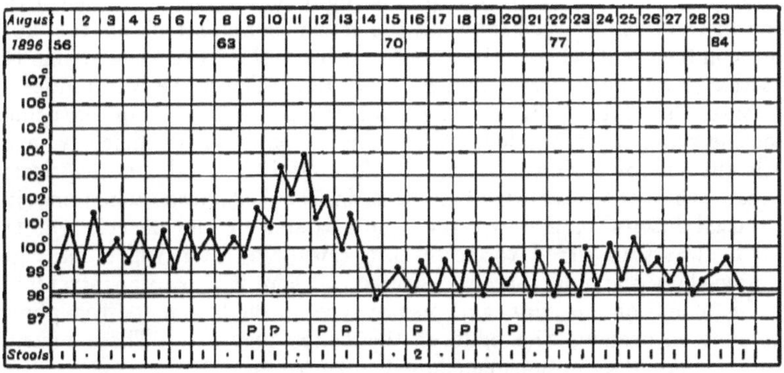

Note.—P = Purgative administered.
Chart of third month of pyrexia of Case 42.

to the 28th the temperature in the afternoon varied between 99°-100° F., while in the morning it was normal or slightly under normal, and but for occasional and rather vague pains about the hips, and a somewhat coated tongue, no other symptoms were present. On July 2nd he returned to light duty, and from that date until July the 12th, though at work, his temperature was always about 99° F. in the afternoon, and he suffered from pain on lateral movement of the left maxillary articulation. On July 13th he suffered from stiffness of the elbow joints with slight pain on movement; while the maxillary pain began to disappear. On the 14th he returned at 8 P.M. from a short bicycle ride, with pains in the lumbar region, a great sense of fatigue, and a temperature of 100° F. The lumbar pain passed off during the night, but returned most severely next evening, the temperature being 101° F., and he was again placed upon the sick-list. From this date until the 19th he suffered from very severe neuralgia of the lumbar portion of the spinal cord, with shooting pains down the nerves of the legs (anterior crural and sciatic), round the abdomen, and on one occasion into the left testicle.

These were treated with rest, warm applications locally, and with salicylate of quinine and morphia internally. The tongue was furred, and the temperature continued the mild intermittent character it had exhibited from the beginning of the attack but was somewhat higher (99°-100·2° in the morning and 100·2°-100·8° in the evening). Each night the patient sweated profusely. The condition appeared to have commenced in the intervertebral joint ligaments, and to have extended later to the spinal cord or its membranes, the pain being always severe but most intense upon the slightest movement. The spinal pain passed off on the 19th and 20th. From the 20th to the 26th there was only pain on movement and tenderness on pressure in the left anterior crural and to a less extent in the right sciatic nerves. The bowels were kept open, and had been so during the whole period of the neuritic symptoms. The temperature varied between 99° and 100·2° F., and he began to be up and about and to take light solid food. On the afternoon of the 28th the patient took too much exercise, and on the 29th was confined entirely to bed again with very severe pain in the anterior crural nerve (left) and its branches. The nerve was tender to pressure, the seat of dull aching pain at all times, and of occasional shooting pains down the leg. The patient found great difficulty, even with the aid of cushions, in placing his leg in a comfortable position of rest, while the catching of the toes in the bedclothes when moving it caused intense pain down the whole course of the nerve. On the 31st he was transferred to hospital, a few days after which his right acromio-clavicular joint became affected. There was pain on stretching the ligaments of the joint, and on pressure on the ligaments from above, but none on pressing the ends of the bones together. These neuritic and rheumatoid symptoms continued until August 10th, together with constipation, night sweating, and intermittent temperature between 99°-101·4°. On August 10th the temperature began to rise, and formed a wave of six days' duration (immediately following the administration of liq. arsenicalis, which drug was discontinued upon August 12th), reaching normal on the evening of the 15th, and then continuing an intermittent course until the end of the month (between 98°-100·2° F.) With the rise of temperature on the 10th the neuritic and arthritic symptoms disappeared entirely. On the night of the 18th of August the patient slept with the right knee uncovered, and exposed to the wind blowing in at an open window. In the morning there was much œdema and swelling round the inner and outer hamstring tendons, pain on pressure and movement. This gradually subsided, but did not finally disappear until the 31st. On August the 26th an acute inflammatory swelling appeared upon the posterior surface of the left olecranon, which in three days had all the appearances and sensations of an acute tense bursal abscess. With hot applications and rest in a sling the pain and tension subsided, and the redness, peri-bursal swelling, and tenderness slowly disappeared in about fourteen days from the onset. A few days after the worst period of this swelling a similar one appeared upon the right olecranon, and ran a similar course. On September 3rd another similar but less severe swelling appeared on the tendons and fascia of the extensor brevis digitorum of the right foot, lasting about five days.

During July and the first half of the month of August the patient suffered from excessive pulsation of the abdominal aorta, giving the sensation and appearance of an aneurysm, except that no tumour was present. The pulsation was easily felt on the surface of the abdomen, between the ensiform cartilage and the umbilicus, especially on deep pressure, while the bedclothes were visibly moved by it. The condition entirely disappeared towards the end of August.

On the 30th of August the patient left Malta for England by sea. His health and strength improved daily during the voyage, and he was able to be on deck from 11 A.M. to 5 P.M. There was a slight rise of temperature each afternoon about 2 P.M., which subsided again by 6 P.M., and he was able to take his usual food without ill effect, excepting lunch and tea, for which soup and milk were substituted. On arrival in England on September 8th all acute symptoms, including pyrexia, had disappeared.

For three weeks the temperature remained normal, and the patient was able to eat and take exercise as usual, and appeared to have quite recovered from the effects of the fever, except for muscular debility and shortness of breath on exertion. At the end of September he suffered from slight sore throat, and a temperature of 99°-101° of an evening, which ended in a heavy cold in the head. He had been in Guildford, and at this stage went to Leamington. By the 12th of October, 128 days from the onset of the fever, the cold subsided, but the temperature began to rise in a typical relapse of undulant fever, and followed a course of well-marked undulations of distinctly remittent pyrexia (*vide* Chart XIX.).

The pyrexial undulations were at first short and well marked, being associated with few local symptoms beyond constipation and diaphoresis. About the 150th day he suffered from paroxysms of coughing, without expectoration, especially in the early morning. This dry irritable cough continued until the beginning of January, or the 217th day. Added to this was a morning expectoration, which was proportionate in amount to the height of the temperature. The sputum was soft, semi-transparent, and, when the temperature was high, slightly blood-stained. This blood-staining was bright in colour, and limited to a small fleck of blood in each lump of sputum. At the same time, and again in February and March, he suffered from palpitation on the slightest exertion, even when turning at all quickly in bed. From the 218th to the 243rd day he was much better, and gained strength and weight. He was able to get up during the afternoon, take gentle exercise in the garden, and eat solid food for breakfast and dinner. He spent December and January at Frodsham in Cheshire. On the 3rd of February he was carefully moved by train to Colwyn Bay, in North Wales. This move was followed by a severe relapse (*vide* Chart). The temperature had to be frequently reduced by means of cold water towels and sponging,

CHART XIX.—*Second Part.*

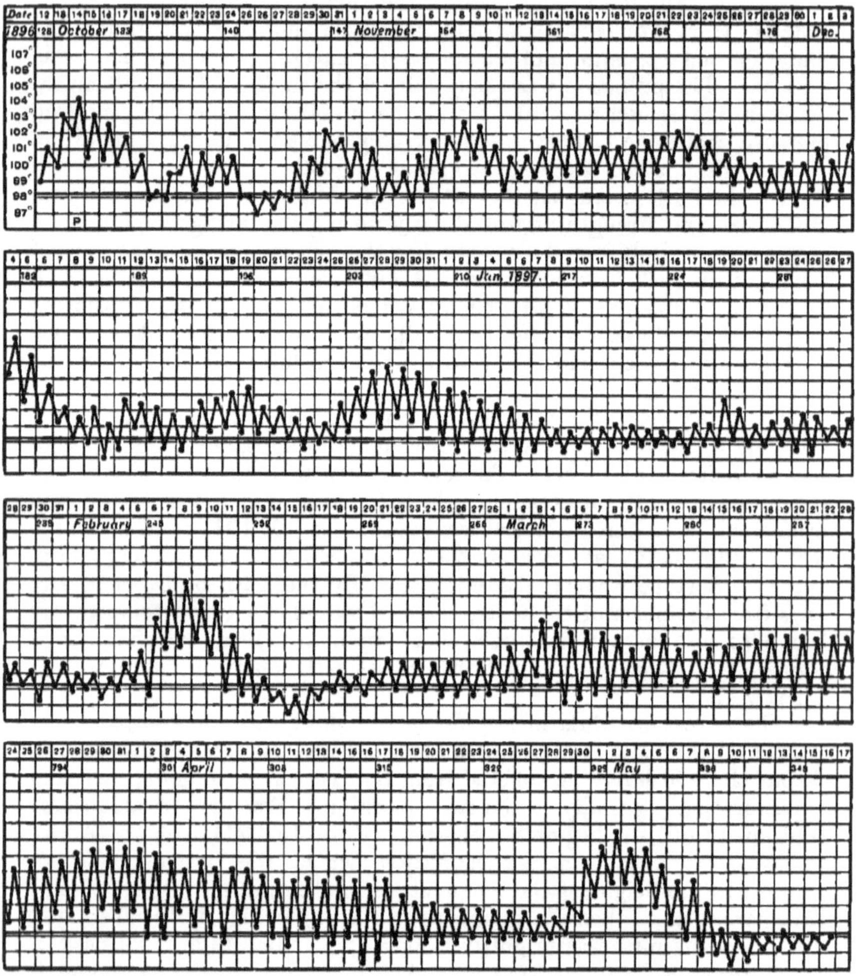

Undulations of pyrexia following four months of intermittence, passing into intermittence and ending with a final severe pyrexial wave.

—a course which had been adopted whenever the temperature exceeded 103° F. After this he suffered from intermittent pyrexia until the 326th day. From the 256th to the 266th day he suffered from very severe sciatica of the left side. This was treated with salicylate of quinine, internally and externally, with belladonna and menthol plasters. The disappearance of neuritic symptoms occurred synchronously with the increase of pyrexia following the 266th day. From the 276th to the 283rd day he complained of most severe pain in the left side on the slightest movement of the chest wall. Breathing was painful and coughing very painful when lying on that side; while in a sitting position breathing was insupportable agony for the first three days. The pain was referred to the diaphragm, on the left side under the margin of the ribs, along the upper margin of the anterior portion of the spleen. The spleen was not noticeably enlarged at this stage, though it had been at an earlier stage in the attack. The pain was considerably relieved by morphia, and after three days began to gradually disappear, so that he was able to sit at stool. At this time (284th day) a large round worm was seen in a stool, and a dose of santonin was given, followed by a second on the 289th day, but without bringing away any more worms. The second dose, given at 9 P.M., was followed at 2 A.M. by a very severe shivering fit, lasting for half an hour. This was the only approach to a rigor during the whole attack. The breath, which had been offensive at times, improved from this period. From the 316th to the 326th day he suffered from neuritis in the left arm and forearm, which disappeared with the rise of temperature on the 327th day. About the 316th day the tongue began to clean, and steadily improved until the cessation of pyrexia on the 337th day. This final burst of pyrexia was restrained by five-grain doses of phenacetin whenever the temperature exceeded 103° F., the patient having previously gained in strength enough to justify its use. Each dose was followed by profuse perspiration, a fall of temperature of from 2° to 3° F. and an amelioration of cerebral symptoms due to the pyrexia. Its use was not, however, followed by any strengthening in force or decrease in rapidity of the heart's action, while the temperature usually rose again to nearly its former height a few hours after the administration, necessitating a second dose. With cold water towels and cold sponging, on former occasions, the pulse-rate was always decreased, even as much as from 120 to 84 beats a minute. After the final burst of pyrexia the temperature remained subnormal in the mornings and for most of the day for nearly two months, rising, however, a few points above normal after long walks or bicycle rides, but not exceeding 99° F.

During early convalescence he suffered considerably from tenderness of the soles of the feet, pain and stiffness in the muscles of the legs and in the tendons round the knees and ankles, and pain in the hips, knees, and ankles on movement, more especially after periods of rest. At the end of a month of more or less subnormal temperature he was moved to Guildford. Though he suffered from palpitation on the slightest exertion at first, this together with the stiffness and pain in the joints gradually disappeared towards the end of the second month of convalescence. His appetite was good, and he soon reached and then exceeded his normal weight. Anæmia was not very marked. During the first two months of convalescence he was given Blaud's pills and small doses of quinine daily. During the attack he was variously treated with numerous drugs, including quinine, arsenic, and mercury. These, far from improving the condition, appeared if anything to do harm. The final cessation of pryexia was synchronous with a period of three weeks, during which all medication had been stopped, but during which the weather had improved considerably. During the attack he was given as much variety in diet as possible, solid diet of a light nature being given whenever the temperature was normal and the tongue fairly clean. This, combined with bismuth and pepsin, did much to keep up the patient's strength and weight, so that he was not unduly handicapped when convalescence was finally established. During convalescence he spent as much time as possible in the open air, but was not able to take much exercise or do much mental work for the first two months, though the daily improvement was marked. He returned to work on 20th August 1897.

Paralysis and atrophy of certain muscles.—This is distinctly a late symptom of long attacks, and for this reason it is less commonly met with in Malta than among invalids after their arrival at Netley (England). The writer has met with it once affecting the extensor muscles of the leg, simulating the foot-drop of alcoholic neuritis, and three times in the deltoid muscle. Unlike the paralysis of lead and alcohol poisoning the reflexes are not lost. When affecting the leg, the big toe drops in a most characteristic manner from paralysis of the extensor proprius pollicis, and the patient is unable to lift his toes from the ground when standing with his heels together. When affecting the deltoid he is unable to raise his arm above a right angle. The affected muscle slowly atrophies, and as slowly regains, first its function and then its proportions. Recovery appears to be complete, though it may take two or more months to become established. Surgeon-Captain Westcott, who has specially investigated the condition of these muscles, states: "This symptom is a late manifestation, seldom appearing within four months, but in one case it occurred as early as the end of the second week of the disease. The alterations in the electrical reactions are both quantitative and qualitative. Diminution in the muscular response is the only quantitative alteration that I have noticed. The qualitative alterations are both nodal and serial; the former consists in a sluggish contraction with marked duration of tetanus; in some cases this is the only change, but in those of long duration there is an overtaking of the cathodal closing contraction by the anodal closing contraction."[1]

Patients experience much pain and tenderness in the muscles of the calves of the legs after walking, etc., for some time, after being long in bed in a recumbent position.

[1] *Brit. Med. Jour.* vol. ii. p. 60, 1893.

Arthritic symptoms.—Effusion into one or more joints occurs in some 40 per cent of cases, and may be acute or subacute in nature. In either instance the onset is usually sudden, and in the greater number of cases there appears to be no ostensible cause for its occurrence. Acute attacks may arise during a wave of pyrexia, or more often during its decline. Subacute attacks occur generally later on in an attack, during a relapse, or at the beginning of certain mild and intermittent cases, in which the slight pyrexia appears to be secondary to the arthritic condition. Thus cases have been admitted to hospital in the morning suffering from effusion into the knee-joint, without traumatic history, and with a normal temperature, but with a furred tongue. In the evening the temperature has been found to be from 99° to 101° F. This may persist for a few days, when the effusion may disappear from the knee-joint, reappearing in other joints. The patient may recover in a week or a fortnight, temporarily or permanently, or may continue for weeks or months with a slight though varying amount of pyrexia at night time, from which, however, he is never quite free, and from which he may at any moment pass into a severe pyrexial condition of an even fatal nature. The symptoms in these mild attacks are similar to those met with in the late stages of severe ones, and seem to be cases in which the primary waves of severe pyrexia have been absent. Every grade of severity is met with connecting the malignant case with one such as has just been described. The effusion does not appear in the joints in any regular order, nor is it symmetrical in its distribution. Occurring during the latter stages of the disease, this condition is very commonly met with among invalids, among the patients drafted to the sanitarium, and during relapses among those sent to duty after apparent cure. As long as a patient is liable to a nocturnal temperature of 99° or 100° F. during any ten consecutive days, so long must he be considered liable to arthritic or other symptoms; for apparently he still has the poison in his tissues and the potential element of any phase of the disease, the virus being only kept in check by the inherent or acquired resistance of the tissue cells. Any reduction in their fighting power, caused by fatigue, insufficient or unsuitable food, exposure to cold, etc., is at once followed by an exacerbation of the disease and a temporary triumph of the virus.

(1) The acute effusion, occurring somewhat early in the disease, is usually confined to one joint, is very sudden in onset and acute in character. The patient may be suddenly attacked in the middle of the night by acute pain in one hip, shoulder, knee, or other joint. This pain, considerable even when the joint is at rest, becomes excruciating on the slightest attempt at voluntary movement, and taxes the strength and patience of the attendant to procure for the patient the least painful position. There is swelling, effusion of fluid into the joint, heat, extreme tension with throbbing pain, but rarely any redness. The symptoms are those of acute non-suppurate synovitis. The application of hot fomentations, warm blankets, and the administration of morphia

may soon relieve the pain and tension, which would otherwise have tormented the patient for many hours. Usually after five or six hours the pain and swelling subside, but it is three or four days before all pain and tenderness disappear. In some cases the relief of one joint is followed by a similar condition in some other joint. The pain is in proportion to the amount of tension present, being most intense and intolerable when it attacks the vertebral or sacro-iliac joints. In such cases the condition of the patient is miserable in the extreme, the slightest jar or shaking of the bed, changing of sheets or clothes, the use of the bed-pan, or in fact the slightest movement, being attended by excessive pain. Happily these joints are rarely affected, and these acute conditions are amenable to treatment. These acute arthritic attacks are accompanied by an appreciable increase of pyrexia (2°-3° F.), which increases and decreases with the severity of the local symptoms.

Salicylates have not the same effect on these complications that they have in the case of rheumatic fever, and it is doubtful whether they have any effect at all. Suppuration has never occurred in any case that the writer has seen or heard of, nor is the condition followed by ankylosis, and though some temporary stiffness of the joint may remain, recovery is the rule. Occurring as they so often do during the decline of the primary acute pyrexial wave, it is well to warn the attendants, for they not uncommonly occur after a more than usually hopeful prognosis has been given, and on a night on which the physician has omitted his evening visit on account of the improved condition of the patient.

(2) Subacute effusion into one or more joints is a common but by no means necessary condition. It is usually met with—(*a*) During the later stages of the febrile attack; (*b*) During febrile relapses after apparent recovery; (*c*) As an early and chief symptom in certain mild and intermittent cases as has been already described. The onset and progress of the effusion is accompanied by slight nocturnal pyrexia, 99° to 100° F., or by a slight increase in any pre-existing pyrexial condition. In the former case the pyrexia appears to be secondary to a local action of the virus on the individual joints. Their common occurrence at a late stage in the attack, often passing from large joints to smaller ones, and finally ending with the phalangeal joints of the face or hands, has given rise to the popular theory that their appearance is the beginning of the end, the disease tending to pass out of the body through the fingers and toes. The condition attacks joints without regard for symmetry or order, nor does it usually remain long with any particular joint (2 to 7 or more days), but its subsidence in one joint is usually followed or anticipated by a similar condition in some other joint on the same or opposite side. This metastasis often passes from large to smaller joints. When affecting the small joints of the hand or foot it usually extends to several adjacent ones.

In the writer's cases the joints have been affected in somewhat the following order of frequency: hip, knee, shoulder, ankle, wrist, fingers, toes, elbows, intervertebral joints, sacro-iliac synchrondrosis, lower jaw, etc.

As in the acute condition, neither suppuration nor ankylosis occur, though in a few cases an affected joint has become the seat of tubercular deposits at a subsequent date. Stiffness of the joints remains for some weeks or months in many cases, preventing soldiers from assuming the kneeling position when firing, etc. This disappears at a later date, so that complete return of function is the rule. The stiffness is probably due to slight synovial adhesions and to prolonged rest in bed. The clinical features are swelling and fluctuation in the joint, pain increased by movement, and occasionally some exudation into the surrounding tissues if the condition is at all long continued.

The condition is somewhat similar to that met with in rheumatic fever, but unlike that disease, the arthritic condition is by no means a necessity nor so usual a symptom. It has often been noticed, too, that those who have previously suffered from rheumatic fever or rheumatism before arriving in the Mediterranean are especially prone to these symptoms when they contract undulant fever. So like rheumatic fever are acute cases with early arthritic symptoms, that the writer has seen such cases erroneously diagnosed as such by medical officers new to the Mediterranean. Other cases have been diagnosed "synovitis of knee," etc., when on admission to hospital in the morning with effusion in one joint their temperature has been found to be normal, in spite of the absence of a traumatic history. Such cases are found to have more or less evening temperature, while the subsidence of the effusion is followed by effusion in some other joint.

The condition of arthritic and tendon effusion may again be compared with that met with, but, on the other hand, much less often, in gonorrhœa, scarlet fever, influenza, and even in enteric fever. In these diseases, however, there is reason to believe that the arthritic symptoms are not necessarily caused by the specific virus of the disease itself. Again, in chronic pyæmia, where a somewhat similar type of micro-organism has found entrance to the body tissues, we find the same swollen joints, but with the difference that in this case the virulence of the poison is sufficient to cause suppuration and its results.

The exact pathology of the arthritic symptoms needs working out, but there is a certain connection between these symptoms and chills received during an attack of this fever that is worthy of notice. In the majority of cases no such connection exists, but in many they follow like cause and effect (*vide* Case 42). Patients who suffer from this fever become most susceptible to changes in external temperature, and seem to feel "every breeze."

The difference between patients who sleep in woollen material and those who wear cotton or linen bedclothes and linen sheets, in the occurrence of arthritic symptoms (and the same may be said of neuralgic pains) is most marked, as is also the comfort derived from flannel next the skin by those already suffering from such symptoms. Again, the writer has noticed that private patients, convalescents, and others treated out of hospital are especially subject to effusion into the hip-joint (and to sciatica), while those in hospital seem less subject to such symptoms, but suffer from effusion into the finger-joints, and to rheumatic pains and stiffness about the head and neck. The greater tendency of the former class of patients to hip troubles he would attribute to exposure while using the chamber ewer, or polished and often draughty water-closet seat, in place of the bed-pan used in hospital. The tendency to similar conditions affecting the hands, head, and neck in all classes of patients he would attribute to variation in covering to which these parts are subject in bed. An effusion into the tendon-sheaths of the right knee, from which the writer suffered, was distinctly caused by an experimental exposure to cold.

In some cases "rheumatism" and stiffness is complained of in the inter-muscular aponeuroses, the sheaths of the muscles, bursæ, and in the periosteal coverings of the tibiæ, ulna, etc. The latter may be combined in rare cases with subcutaneous nodes and acute swellings, with all the local signs of periosteal or bursal abscess, but without any suppurations occurring.

In subjects with gouty diathesis or hereditary history the onset of the fever may be accompanied by a typical attack of gout.

Case 43.—*Gouty diathesis with undulant fever.*—Capt. B., Lincolnshire Regt., age 29; Mediterranean service one year; developed undulant fever of a mild intermittent type on 10th May 1896; furred tongue, severe head and back ache and shooting pains down the legs and arms. On the third day these pains subsided, and he was attacked with acute gout in the left great toe lasting four days, and on the fourth day in the right toe lasting three days. It was relieved by warmth applied locally, and by colchicum and alkalines internally. He had a very strong family history of gout, and had previously been attacked. The undulant fever lasted six months. On admission the temperature was 101·6° F., above which it did not go until the fourth month, when he suffered from a severe relapse.

Case 44.—*Illustrating sacro-iliac effusion at a late stage.*—Pte. S., aged 24, with a good previous medical history, arrived in Malta in the middle of January 1895, after nearly three years' service in Gibraltar. He was admitted to hospital on the 29th of June 1895 suffering from severe undulant fever, with a tendency to extremely high pyrexia out of all proportion to the urgency and severity of the other symptoms. He remained in hospital for seventy-two days, after which he returned to duty apparently cured. On the 9th of January 1896, more than three months later, he was again admitted with a similar form of pyrexia, its height being excessive when compared with other symptoms and with its effect upon his constitution generally. The temperature gradually fell until it reached normal on the morning of the 27th, being under 100° in the evening. On the 31st he complained of severe pain in the sacral region, which became excessive on the slightest movement, rendering the use of the bed-pan or even a change of position in bed most excruciating. There was great pain on pressure over the muscles covering the sacro-iliac joint. This began to subside on the 6th of February, but had become more bearable under hot fomentations and morphia soon after its onset. By the 8th he was able to move in bed without much pain, and though stiff in the back for some time, all acute symptoms had disappeared about ten days from the onset, but was followed by a less acute attack of a similar nature in the left hip ten days later. His temperature did not become permanently normal until the end of March, when he was invalided home to England, nine months after the first onset of the fever. He did not return to duty until after fourteen months from the primary onset of the fever.

Case 45.—*Illustrating early arthritic symptoms.*—Mrs. H., of Malta, complained on 3rd June 1896 of pains in the left hip, temperature apparently normal; on the 4th pain more severe, temperature at 6 P.M. 99°. On the 5th, hip somewhat swollen, painful and tender. On the 6th all the symptoms of synovitis of left hip; evening temperature 100·2°. Rest in bed, belladonna plaster and flannel bandage, salicylate of quinine, gr. v., three times a day. The temperature remained normal every morning, and rose to 99° or 100° each evening. About 10th June the hip recovered, but the temperature continued an intermittent and undulant course until the last week in June, when it rose to 103·4° in a wave, and falling gradually became normal on 30th June. This was followed by complete recovery, but for occasional rheumatic pains following exposure to chills in England during August. The patient left Malta on 28th July.

The affection appears to be situated in the fibrous tissues and ligaments around the joint, the bony and cartilaginous structures being unaffected. Pressure on and stretching of the ligamentous structures is most painful, while this is not the case when the ends of the bones are pressed together, unless such a proceeding increases the intra-articular tension. When the tendons become affected there is usually some swelling and œdema in their sheaths and in the surrounding tissues, with local pain and tenderness on pressure or voluntary movement. The tendons most commonly affected are the extensors of the hands and feet, and the hamstring tendons. These conditions of the joints and tendons are doubtless closely connected pathologically with the conditions affecting the nerves, pleura, bursæ, pericardium, aponeuroses, etc.

Circulatory system.—The pulse is usually slow and firm at first (80-90), even out of proportion to the number of the respirations and the amount of pyrexia present, when these are uncomplicated by other serious symptoms. Later on, especially in malignant cases, the pulse becomes rapid (120-140) and intermittent; and with increasing lung congestion may become small, thready, still more intermittent until the overburdened heart gives out entirely. In malignant cases the condition of the pulse and the force of the heart's action, taken with the condition of the lungs, should engage the constant attention of the medical attendant, for the key to his patient's general condition rests in such watchfulness.

In long-continued cases the pulse often becomes constantly increased in rate (110-120). In these cases nervous cardiac irritability of other parts of the nervous system is of common occurrence, the heart being subject to attacks of palpitation on the slightest exertion, or even under the influence of some trifling emotion.[1] Other symptoms referable to irritability of the nervous vaso-motor system may be present, such as abnormal abdominal (aortic) pulsation.

Hæmic murmurs are met with in anæmic and debilitated subjects towards the end of long attacks and during convalescence. Organic disease is said to be set up in some cases, but the author has only met with it in four fatal instances, where it was not known to be present before the onset of the pyrexia. These cases proved fatal on the 19th (Case 8), 62nd (Case 14), 111th (Case 13), and 154th (Case 11) days of the disease.

In the second case (see "Histology") the disease might not have been antecedent to the fever, but in none was there any reason to connect the post-mortem appearances with the fever in question. In the first two cases the fatal result was directly due to coexisting pericardial effusion, in two it was due to sudden cardiac syncope. Cardiac valvular disease is a most serious complication, though not necessarily fatal, as in malignant cases death is usually due to failure of the heart to carry on the circulation.

Swelling and œdema of the ankles and legs is a common and even severe symptom during convalescence, and much aggravated by standing. It disappears gradually as the anæmia and debility decrease. The writer has only once met with phlegmasia dolens complicating a case of this fever, and occurring during the eighth week of a pyrexial attack lasting fourth months. Resolution was but slowly effected.

The spleen can nearly always be made out on percussion and palpation below the margin of the ribs, and occasionally is considerably enlarged, especially in malignant cases. During the first acute stage it is tender to pressure, and may be painful, but after and towards the end of the second month of long attacks it often shrinks again. The specific organism has been isolated from the spleen by puncture and aspiration during life. Localised but slight swelling of the lymphatic glands may occur. They do not suppurate. Those in the neck and groin are most often affected.

[1] In many cases this irritable condition of the cardiac nerves is most marked and lasts long into convalescence, and it is to be met with to a lesser degree in all cases of over sixty days' duration. In one case (duration 111 days), the news that the patient had been placed under orders to go home to England proved a fatal excitement, and death took place suddenly from syncope, though, except for great anæmia, debility and long-continued but slight fever and a slight mitral murmur, the patient had no serious symptoms at the time.

Epistaxis occurs in a few cases early in the attack, but is most uncommon. Intestinal hæmorrhage is limited to spots of fresh blood in the stools in cases where the lower bowel is affected.

When the pyrexia is at all severe or of long duration the menses are suppressed, and this continues well into the convalescent period. Pre-existing pregnancy is not necessarily interrupted. The lymphatic glands are occasionally swollen and painful, but do not suppurate.

The blood has been microscopically examined by Dr. Thin, the writer, and by numerous other observers, and culture experiments have been made, but no organisms have been found to be present. The coagulability of the blood is said to be somewhat diminished. The red corpuscles diminish rapidly at first, from 5,000,000 to 3,000,000 per cubic millimetre (Bruce), more slowly but steadily later on throughout the pyrexial period, leading to the pronounced anæmia which so prolongs convalescence.

Scorbutic symptoms, during the progress of long cases, have been described. The writer has only seen them occur in one instance, the spongy and hæmorrhagic condition of the gums being due to an excessive use of mercury. He is of opinion that the free use of fresh lemonade, and when possible of fruit, during the long period of attacks has been the means of abolishing these symptoms so rarely met with now. (See "Alimentary System.")

In long cases constipation and continued abdominal congestion may set up a hæmorrhoidal condition of the mucous membrane of the lower part of the rectum. This usually disappears when convalescence becomes established.

Pericardial effusion.—The writer has twice met with instances of pericardial effusion occurring in the course of this fever. Both cases proved fatal, one on the 19th and the other on the 62nd day of the disease. In both cases there were vegetations present upon the mitral valve; in both cases the effusion consisted of clear serum and partook of the nature of hydrops pericardii. No pus was present, but little fibrin, while the pericardium was but slightly congested. The condition was overlooked until the symptoms became suddenly urgent, when the nature of the complication was obvious. It was not relieved by any of the usual remedies, and aspiration was not tried, though it is apparently the treatment to be employed in any future case. The condition was remarkably similar to the common arthritic effusions of this disease, death resulting directly from the amount of serous effusion present, there being no other urgent symptom present of a dangerous nature. Consequently the hope of a favourable result following aspiration should be great. In both cases the writer saw the cases only at the last moment, when they were both quite conscious and sensible. They were sitting up in bed, suffering from extreme dyspnœa, pain in the cardiac region, with restless countenances, on which were written that anxious look of impending death. The pulse was small and feeble, the heart sounds almost inaudible, the area of cardiac dulness largely increased. In both instances there had been a rise of temperature during the previous few days, probably associated with the pouring out of the effusion.

Case 8.—Private W., Royal Berkshire Regiment, age 23, was admitted to hospital on 29th December 1892, suffering from acute undulant fever of about three days' standing, contracted with another case near a burst drain (see "Instances of Outbreaks"). Health during five years' previous service had been very good. On admission his temperature was 103° F., and all through the attack, until his death on 15th January 1893, his temperature was most remittent in character, varying between normal on the mornings of the 7th, 10th, and 16th days, and 104° F. on the evenings of the 8th, 10th, 12th, 13th, 14th, and 18th days of the disease. On admission he suffered from pain in the chest, palpitation, and signs of catarrhal pueumonic consolidation, with profuse expectoration. On the 10th day he suffered from vomiting and increased lung symptoms. On the 14th day he became rapidly worse, suffering from frequent loose light yellow stools, and his temperature rose to 104° F. at 3.30 P.M., from which it was reduced by sponging to 101° F. It began to rise again at 6 P.M., while at the same time he complained of great pericardial pain, dyspnœa, and anxiety. His lungs were considerably congested at the bases with signs of consolidation, his pulse was small, thready, and intermittent. His temperature reached 104·6° F. at 8 P.M., from which it was reduced by sponging to 102·4° F., but the cardiac symptoms increased, and the diagnosis of pericardial effusion was made, but too late for any satisfactory result, and he died somewhat suddenly of heart failure. An apical systolic murmur had been audible from the first, and treatment had been directed towards helping the action of the heart, which was at no time strong, much of the lung stasis being doubtless due to the presence of this condition, and the local symptoms to a great extent at first being put down to this cause.

At the post-mortem examination the lungs were found to be extremely congested, with patches of basal consolidation. The spleen (weight 12 oz.) was extremely congested, and colonies of the micrococcus Melitensis were obtained from it. The liver (weight 50 oz.) was congested and slightly nutmeg. The heart contained a large ante-mortem clot in each ventricle, and there were thickening and vegetations on the mitral valve. The pericardial sac contained 13 oz. of clear serum; the serous surfaces were not inflamed.

Case 14.—Private J., age 22, was admitted to hospital on 8th August 1895. His previous medical history was good. The primary wave was severe, and lasted until the middle of September, when the temperature fell to normal, and remained there for sixteen days until 7th October, when it rose suddenly to 104° F. During this apyrexial period the patient was up and about, and had even for a few days been having solid food. On the 8th his tongue was furred slightly, but he complained of no pain. His temperature was reduced slightly by sponging, and perspiration was encouraged by diaphoretic mixture. On the 9th he seemed better, and on the 10th his temperature fell to 101° F. after a good night, and he seemed to be much improved. On the afternoon of the 11th he for the first time began to suffer from pain in the chest, but did not complain of anything until 6.30 P.M., when his temperature was found to be 103·6° F. He also complained at this time of great pain in the cardiac region and dyspnœa, while his pulse was found to be weak and his heart sounds inaudible. He became very rapidly worse, the dyspnœa increased, the pulse became small, intermittent, and very rapid; he became extremely collapsed, his temperature at 7.30 P.M. being subnormal, and in spite of treatment he died soon after of cardiac failure. Aspiration was not tried.

Temperature from 5th October to 11th October

Date.	Day of Disease.	Morning Temperature.	Evening Temperature.	Bowels.
5th October	56th	97·6° F.	98·4° F.	2
6th ,,	57th	97·8°	98·8°	2
7th ,,	58th	98·8°	104·0°	2
8th ,,	59th	103·0°	103·4°	2
9th ,,	60th	102·6°	103·0°	1
10th ,,	61st	100·0°	101·0°	1
11th ,,	62nd	100·0°	{103·6° at 6.30 P.M. 97·2° at 7·30 P.M.}	2

At the post-mortem examination the right lung did not collapse on opening the chest, the left one did so imperfectly. The entire right parietal sac was obliterated by adherent lymph, sufficiently organised to contain distinctly marked blood-vessels in it. The right lung (weight 33 oz.) was congested and œdematous; the left (weight 23 oz.) slightly emphysematous, the lower lobe being congested. There were 17 oz. of clear serum in the pericardial sac, which was not inflamed. The heart was relaxed and flabby, but the valves were normal. The liver (weight 70 oz.) and the spleen (weight 14 oz.) were congested. The kidneys were congested, and their capsules somewhat adherent.

Should the writer again meet with such a case of pericardial effusion, apparently uncomplicated by other dangerous symptoms, he will most certainly feel justified in resorting to aspiration or other operative measures for its relief. He would refer his readers especially to a recent paper by Dr. William Ewart on some twelve "Practical Aids in the Diagnosis of Pericardial Effusion," reported in full in the *British Medical Journal*,[1] and warn them to be on the look-out for this rare but dangerous complication. The sudden onset of dangerous

[1] 21st March 1896, vol. i. p. 717, and 23rd January 1897, vol. i. p. 185.

symptoms shows the necessity for prompt action, for in neither of the cases reported was the condition suspected until a short time before death, nor was there time in either instance for the medical officer in actual charge of the case to be summoned in time to take action before death ensued.

The site usually chosen for aspiration is the fifth intercostal space on the left side, close up to, or from one to two inches out from the sternal margin, the aspirating needle being inclined upwards and towards the middle line. Others choose the fourth, sixth, or seventh interspace, left side, or even the right side of the sternum, but it will be well to be guided by circumstances after carefully mapping out the extent of the effusion.

Respiratory symptoms.—About the beginning of the third week, or earlier in severe cases, some bronchial cooing becomes audible on auscultation, being most marked posteriorly at the bases of the lungs. Later on, in some 95 per cent, there is evidence of basal congestion, varying in amount according to the severity of the general condition. In malignant cases this is apt to go on to lobular consolidation and hypostatic pneumonia; so much so that this condition is nearly always present in post-mortem examinations of rapidly fatal cases, and has a large influence in bringing about the fatal result. In a large number of cases bronchitis with frothy or more often sticky mucous expectoration is present, and a certain amount of this symptom may persist throughout the pyrexial period of long cases. In such cases it may only be marked by a few fine crepitations, often only at the apices, a few rhonchi, and expectoration of sticky and even blood-stained sputum. These symptoms, with the hectic kind of temperature of such cases, and the copious night-sweats, are often mistaken by the unwary for phthisis. The sputum is, however, not nummular, and does not contain tubercle bacilli, while the pneumonic physical signs are not typical nor progressive. The writer has, however, seen such cases diagnosed as phthisis, invalided as such, and recover before embarkation for England. Others have hurried home to consult specialists with a belief, supported by local medical advice, that they had contracted tuberculosis of the lungs. Indeed, in years gone by writers were in the habit of describing a "Mediterranean phthisis," which yielded wonderfully and generally entirely to treatment.

These pneumonic symptoms, though to a certain extent possibly caused by the direct action of the virus, are due largely to congestion, from inefficient pulmonary circulation, and are therefore most common and severe in those who have previously suffered from pleurisy or pneumonia, or who suffer from organic cardiac disease.

A nervous cough, unaccompanied by expectoration or physical signs, is present in some cases, being worst at evening when the temperature rises, while dyspnœa may occur without any ostensible cause, but is less common.

A form of pleurisy without effusion is not uncommon, leading to permanent adhesions; while pleurisy with effusion may accompany pneumonic trouble, but is not commonly marked. Very rarely excessive effusion into a pleural cavity may occur, but it has never in the writer's experience gone on to suppuration.

Intercostal neuralgia is not uncommon.

In even the mildest cases from the beginning of an attack we find that all patients expectorate some sticky mucus from the lungs, though there be no physical signs present. This is especially notable in the morning, when the accumulation of the night is brought up. This symptom is usually proportionate in severity to the temperature, and varies in amount directly as the pyrexial undulations rise and fall. Where the sputum contains slight streaks or flecks of bright blood, the temperature has usually reached the summit of a wave late in a long attack, and the condition disappears soon after the temperature has reached normal again.

In some cases where cardiac and pulmonary irritability and distress are marked, out of proportion to the amount of the pyrexia, the disease seems to be specially affecting these organs locally or through their nervous supply.

In all cases where such symptoms are present, and very especially in cases where organic cardiac disease is present, or where the pyrexia remains continually high, a close watch must be kept on the lungs, and any tendency to congestion dealt with at once.

Alimentary system.—The tongue on admission is usually swollen, thickly coated with whitish yellow fur on the dorsum, pink at the tip and edges, moist, flabby and indented laterally by the teeth.

These points are accentuated in those who have been for some time suffering from pyrexia, and have been eating unsuitable food before reporting sick. In severe cases the dorsum becomes covered with thick ragged fur, and may for a few days become dry and brown, and even in very severe cases may become fissured and a little blood issue from the fissures. In long-continued cases, during or after the second month, the tongue often becomes glazed, of a dull, raw meat appearance, with patches of its surface denuded of epithelium. The condition of the tongue is roughly an index of the severity of the case, and of the importance of any given rise of temperature. It is an accurate index of the suitability or otherwise of the diet in use, and often gives warning of the necessity for the exhibition of stimulants. High temperature, with serious constitutional disturbance, is accompanied by a dry brown tongue, while, when there is a tendency to hyperpyrexia, the tongue is usually proportionately foul. In the high temperatures accompanying symptoms referable to the central nervous system, there is often little constitutional disturbance, and the tongue remains comparatively clean in spite of continued high pyrexia. The tongue rarely, if ever, becomes quite clean until the disease is over, remaining lightly furred during long but temporary apyrexial periods. It may, therefore, be taken as a rough but useful rule that a fall of temperature to normal will rarely prove permanent unless at the same time the tongue has also become clean. This has an obvious bearing on the question of an increase of diet, or permission to get up for an apparently convalescent patient. At the end of very long and protracted cases, in which the disease is limited to slight nocturnal pyrexia with little or no constitutional disturbance and a clean tongue, it is occasionally found that solid food may be given that would upset other patients whose gastro-intestinal mucous membrane was still in an irritable condition, as evinced by the furred condition of the tongue. This power of assimilating solid food at the end of long attacks is in great contrast to the general gastro-intestinal irritation present in severe cases, and indeed during the initial stages of nearly all cases. Besides the condition of the tongue, other signs of gastric irritation are constantly present during the early and severe stages of the attack. These are loss of appetite and desire for food, foul taste in the mouth, inability to digest any but suitable food, epigastric tenderness in almost all cases, occasionally nausea and even vomiting. Both these last symptoms are increased by unsuitable food, and in a few cases have proved most serious. The epigastric tenderness, and occasionally also pain, is marked, and contrasts with the iliac tenderness of enteric fever. It is felt on pressure over and to the left of the sternal notch, and is increased to the left when, as is usually the case during the first month or six weeks, the spleen is enlarged and tender to pressure. In such cases the area of splenic dulness is proportionally increased, while the spleen may often be felt on palpation below the margin of the ribs, on inspiration and expiration, during the first month or so.

The liver is often tender to pressure and slightly enlarged downwards in severe cases, at an early stage and also towards the end of prolonged attacks, when from continued back pressure congestion, it has become somewhat "nutmeg" in character. Occasionally patches of intestinal congestion may give rise to localised tenderness at various points over the abdominal surface, but such are rare in occurrence.

Epistaxis[1] has occurred in five of the writer's cases; it is an uncommon but early symptom. Bleeding from the gums, combined with a spongy condition, has been described, but has been only met with once by the writer in a case in which the exhibition of calomel was unduly pushed. Its absence is probably due to the use of fresh lemonade and fruit.

Bruce (1889) mentions a case where "on the 94th day of the disease the gums were found to be spongy; the lower half of a dark claret colour, the upper pale and livid.[2]

The pillars of the fauces, the uvula, and tonsils are usually red, relaxed, slightly congested, and dry at the onset of the disease, while

[1] For profuse epistaxis during the eighth week see MacLeod (1897).

[2] See also Davidson's *Geo. Path.* (1892), vol. i. pp. 262 and 264, Veale (1879), and Macleod (1897).

the patient complains of a feeling of constriction. An aphthous film, or grayish translucent coating with small white points over the follicles, is often noticed at the same time over the tonsils. The breath is usually foul, and remains so in proportion to the condition of the tongue and stomach, and to the suitability of the food. There is often some swelling or tenderness, with hardening of the cervical or submaxillary glands. These can be distinctly felt, and vary in size from a pea to a hazel nut.

In non-malignant cases constipation is the rule. In the writer's experience it was marked in 81 per cent of cases; while of the remaining 19 per cent it was combined with diarrhœa in 3 per cent; 12 per cent were normal, and in only 4 per cent was diarrhœa markedly present. In fatal cases, owing to the frequent involvement of the large gut, diarrhœa has been present in 13 out of the 22 cases in which the state of the bowels was noticed, and in many of these it was excessive, the stools being loose and watery in consistence, light in colour, most offensive, and at the end passed involuntarily. In other cases the stools are usually brown, somewhat offensive, and even in severe cases are as a rule more or less formed, and in many cases very hard, scybalous, and yellow or almost white in colour.

Bruce (1889) says: "In 65 cases in which the condition of the bowels was noted, in 48 there was constipation and in 17 diarrhœa."

In severe cases the condition of the teeth and gums may become offensive, from collection of sordes, as in other fevers. In Malta, flies are apt to collect round the mouths of such cases and prove annoying. This occurrence is looked upon as a bad sign by nurses and sick attendants.[1]

The stools are usually, and especially in mild cases, brown, and hard in character. In many cases they are lighter in colour and even scybalous. In all cases they are offensive, and in severe cases excessively so. When diarrhœa is present they become loose in character, but have usually a darkish colour, and a great tendency to be more or less formed, even in cases with many of the characteristics of enteric fever. In certain severe cases, especially when there is involvement of the lower bowel, there may be loose yellow stools, passed frequently and even involuntarily, but they rarely have the pea-soup appearance of those met with in enteric fever.

Tympanites is rarely met with, and is but seldom marked. Occasionally the common tenderness on pressure met with over the epigastric, splenic, and at times over the hepatic regions, may extend downwards, being presumably due to intestinal congestion. It is mostly met with over the sigmoid flexure in cases in which the large bowel is involved, and is with gurgling most rare in the right hypochondrium.

The appetite and powers of digestion decrease almost directly in

[1] See Baxter (1820) who includes "muscæ circa os volitantes" among his serious prognostic signs.

proportion to the severity of the disease. In severe and malignant cases the digestion is almost in abeyance, while in very mild cases, and in the final chronic and intermittent stages of long attacks, the patient often can digest the most unlikely diet, apparently with impunity. The return of the appetite is gradual, and is rarely so marked as is the ravenous desire for food after enteric fever. Its return, combined with the cleaning of the tongue and abatement of pyrexia, is a sign of commencing convalescence. The re-establishment of the digestive powers is very slow after prolonged attacks, and the greatest care must be taken with regard to dietary for a long time after the actual pyrexia has disappeared. Much of this is doubtless due to anæmia, but besides there is much attenuation of the intestines, wasting of their mucous membranes, and loss of function by the digestive glands and organs of a temporary nature, in long cases of this fever.

Urinary and sexual system.—The urine is decreased in amount at first, and in severe cases dark in colour and loaded with lithates. Later on, unless there is much diaphoresis, it may be increased in amount, light in colour, and of low specific gravity. It is acid in reaction, except in a few instances when temporary irritability of the bladder is present. Albumin is rarely present, even in fatal cases. In very prolonged fatal cases a condition of commencing large white kidney has been met with. Albumin is absent from the urine of those suffering from œdema of the ankles during convalescence, the condition depending upon anæmia.

As has been mentioned before, retention may occur in severe cases; and slight weakness of the sphincter vesicæ has been met with during convalescence. Also a temporary difficulty in starting micturition.

In very mild cases sexual desire may be increased, the sexual organs partaking in the generally increased nervous susceptibility. Menstruation only disappears in severe cases, and in those in which anæmia is marked. Attacks of this fever have not caused abortion in pregnant women, in the few instances which have occurred in the practice of the writer.

Attacks of this fever, especially when combined with epididymitis, have been accused of causing sterility. This has not been proved by any facts, while the Maltese are a most prolific race. It is certainly not the case with females. The writer has met with an instance in which a wife became impregnated a month after recovery from a mild attack of this fever (40 days' pyrexia) when her husband was in the middle of a severe and prolonged attack of the same disease, but during a temporary apyrexial period. The pregnancy went on successfully to term.

Epididymitis and orchitis (usually single), occur in about 4 to 5 per cent of cases, and are late symptoms. Such conditions are met with more commonly during relapses after apparent convalescence has been established, and may be acute or subacute in character. Suppuration is most uncommon, but occurred in one of the writer's cases, accompanied by a superficial abscess over the ensiform cartilage, both being apparently accidental and due to causes other than the fever virus.

When acute in nature, the testicle and epididymus swell, in from 24 to 48 hours, to the size of a small orange, are very painful and extremely tender. There may be some redness of the skin and effusion into the tunica vaginalis. The condition has no connection with antecedent attacks of gonorrhœa, and very many men who have suffered from gonorrhœa previously, go through an attack of Mediterranean fever without any testicular trouble. The acute inflammation usually subsides in the course of a few days, leaving the organ hard and slightly tender. Gradually the hardness disappears and the normal condition is returned to, but this often takes a considerable time. The subacute variety is merely a less acute form of the above, the patient complaining of pain and a feeling of weight about the testicle, especially after exertion or exercise. On examination the epididymus is found to be enlarged, and the whole organ somewhat tender when squeezed even gently. A few days' rest and support relieves the distress, though it may return if exercise is taken before it has quite recovered.

As is the case with the arthritic attacks, a certain amount of pyrexia, proportionate to the acuteness of the symptoms, accompanies attacks of this kind.

Cases 46-49.—*Illustrating orchitic symptoms.*—Pte. E., admitted in Malta, June 28th, 1895, suffering from Mediterranean fever, for which he remained in hospital for 125 days. Seven days after his return to duty he was again admitted to hospital with similar pyrexia complicated by acute orchitis, and pains in both hips. During his first stay in hospital he had suffered from effusion into the hip and elbow joints. The orchitis (with epididymitis) ran an acute course, with remittent pyrexia lasting a fortnight, after which the testicle slowly recovered, but he continued to suffer from pyrexial symptoms every now and then for two months longer. Eventually he completely recovered, returning to permanent duty on Feb. 17th, 1896, seven and a half months from the first onset of the fever.

Pte. A., admitted to hospital, August 29th, 1895, with Mediterranean fever complicated with swollen joints, being discharged to duty 43 days after. Five days later he was readmitted for orchitis following the fever, and did not again return to duty until 24 days later.

Pte. M., admitted to hospital, June 23rd, 1895, with a mild attack of fever for 12 days. Readmitted 79 days later with orchitis and pyrexia lasting 13 days. Again admitted with severe Mediterranean fever 12 days later for 70 days, followed by complete recovery.

Pte. F., admitted on July 27th, 1895, with Mediterranean fever for 59 days. Readmitted with orchitis and pyrexia 36 days later, lasting 35 days. Readmitted a fortnight after with rheumatism lasting 19 days.

Pte. E., admitted September 4th, 1895, with mild Mediterranean fever lasting 22 days. Admitted three months afterwards with orchitis lasting 17 days.

Ollivier[1] mentions 27 instances of orchitis occurring in the course of enteric fever. In 7 it set in during the primary pyrexia, in 20 during convalescence, but not later than twenty days from the cessation of the primary pyrexia. In one-fifth of the cases suppuration occurred. Murchison and other works do not mention this symptom, but it is noted by Velpeau (1844).

Complications. — Hyperpyrexia, uncombined with other serious symptoms, may occur at the onset of an attack, at the summit of a pyrexial wave or late in a long case. In these instances it can generally be successfully coped with, unless the patient is very debilitated. It is then not very serious, and is usually followed by a more or less permanent fall of temperature. When combined with pulmonary congestion or consolidation, and with symptoms of failure of the cardio-respiratory circulation, hyperpyrexia is, however, an extremely dangerous and fatal complication at any stage of an attack. This condition usually follows a period of continuously high temperature where antipyretic treatment has been neglected, either early in a malignant attack or during a severe relapse. Only too often in such cases the cardio-respiratory circulation fails to support life in spite of temperature reduction. In a few cases hyperpyrexia is accompanied by severe nervous prostration, and may immediately follow a fall of temperature to normal (accompanied, however, by no improvement in the general condition of the patient) well on in an attack. In these two last instances the pyrexia too often proves uncontrollable to drugs or external application of cold, the patient's extremities and nose become cold and white, his body very hot and probably cyanosed, while his temperature rises steadily from 106° to 108° F. and after death, to even greater heights (112° to 115° F.) These cases almost always prove fatal.

Pulmonary congestion, passing into consolidation, is present in nearly all malignant cases and in all early fatal ones. The bases of the lungs and heart's action should therefore always be carefully watched in all severe cases with high temperature, and treatment of a suitable nature begun early on the first sign of stasis in the pulmonary circulation. In severe cases this condition of the pulmonary circulation often determines the fatal issue. It must, of course, be borne in mind that the state of the heart's action is the great factor to consider in such cases.

Pleuritic effusion may occur and need tapping, but it is rarely in itself dangerous. Empyema the writer has not met with, though it is said to occur.

[1] *Revue de médecine*, Paris, Oct. and Nov. 1883, and in *Practitioner*, May 1884, vol. xxxii. p. 375.

Cardiac failure may occur, weakness and irregularity of the heart's action are not uncommon. Care must therefore be taken to watch the pulse, and meet by adequate stimulation any flagging, especially when there are any signs of pulmonary congestion, during relapses in long cases or when signs of general nervous prostration are present.

The presence of organic cardiac disease is a serious element of danger, weakening as it does the power of the heart to carry on the circulation, and leading in long debilitated cases to danger of sudden death from syncope.

Pericardial effusion is a very dangerous, but happily uncommon complication. In the only two cases the author has met with, the condition was not noticed or complained of until a very short time before death. In both mitral organic cardiac disease was present, though not in any severe degree. Aspiration may in future give better results.

Renal disease has as yet been seldom present, but has proved a serious complication in prolonged cases, and if present would doubtless add greatly to the danger of serious cases.

Anæmia, debility, and bed-sores materially lengthen the periods of both pyrexia and convalescence while leading to danger to life from exhaustion.

Uncontrollable vomiting is a most serious and dangerous complication, happily but seldom met with. In lesser degrees it may seriously complicate severe cases, and need very careful dietary and medication. It is most prone to occur with high temperatures combined with over-feeding.

Diarrhœa, especially when due to involvement of the large gut and when the stools are frequent, offensive, and passed involuntarily, is a serious symptom. Cases in which it is marked not infrequently prove fatal.

Symptoms associated with the "typhoid state," especially dry brown tongue, delirium, and nervous prostration, are serious but not unamenable complications.

Constipation and portal congestion may give rise to hæmorrhoids, but these tend to disappear with convalescence. Anal fissure, of a most painful nature, complicated a case in Malta. A slight operation for the relief of pain, during a somewhat high pyrexia, proved fatal from hæmorrhage, in spite of every attention in hospital. There was no history of hæmophilia.

CHAPTER IV

Diagnosis: From enteric fever; Paludism; Tuberculosis; Hepatic abscess; other suppurative diseases; Rheumatic fever, etc.—*Prognosis.*—*Duration:* Pyrexial duration; Stay in hospital in a non-effective condition.—*Mortality.*—*Morbid anatomy:* Naked-eye appearances based upon accounts of 62 post-mortem detailed examinations, on cases whose duration varied from 4 to 160 days; Division into two classes; Class I., rapidly fatal cases; Class II., longer cases; Descriptions by other authors; Microscopic appearances.

Diagnosis. *From enteric fever.*—Though the writer has had the opportunity of personally observing a considerable number of cases of enteric fever both in England and Malta, besides many hundreds of cases of undulant fever, the following remarks are based on the carefully recorded notes of three hundred cases of the latter fever, whose later history or post-mortem appearances have left no doubt as to the correctness of the diagnosis. This diagnosis in typical cases is sufficiently clear, even to an inexperienced observer. There are, however, cases, and these are unfortunately of the more serious and fatal class, in which there is a great tendency towards passing into the so-called "typhoid state." In such instances it is only by long experience, daily watching, and by carefully weighing every available fact, that a correct diagnosis can be arrived at.

In the first instance, many facts of collective value may be gleaned from the history of the patient. With many exceptions, undulant fever favours individuals in their second, third, or fourth years of residence, and these indiscriminately up to and even over 35 years of age, the 23rd being the most frequent and fatal year among the troops. It occurs mostly during the hot dry months from June to October, when the average monthly temperature is over 60° F.; its prevalence having an inverse ratio to the amount and continuance of the rainfall. Individual cases may as a rule, and more especially during an epidemic, be traced to certain rooms in certain buildings. Enteric fever, on the other hand, favours new-comers between the ages of 15 and 25, occurring mostly after the first heavy rains, and continuing to prevail during the autumn and early winter months. As a rule this prevalence has relationship with some definite area of milk and water supply, distinct from that of undulant fever, except in certain epidemics, when a dual cause appears to be at work.

Passing to clinical points we find that the pyrexial curve is on the whole the most accurate guide. The intermittent waves of remittent pyrexia, varying in number from one to seven (usually three), with a more or less marked apyrexial period between, are very characteristic of undulant fever. Moreover, these waves are of an irregular character, being often combined, especially in the case of the shorter ones, with periods of intermittent (but non-paroxysmal) pyrexia of variable duration—while each successive wave of temperature bears no necessarily definite relationship to the character of the primary attack or to intervening waves. These waves vary in duration from three days to eight weeks, the average being about ten days. The total duration of the pyrexial condition is most indefinite, varying from 20 to 300 days or more, the average being about nine or ten weeks, the only reliable indication of convalescence being a period of subnormal temperature. The resulting anæmia and debility are extreme, causing an average stay in hospital of over 90 days.

This condition is very different from the occasional irregularities from the recognised type met with in enteric fever; for however many relapses may occur, such relapses as a rule bear a definite relationship in character to the primary attack. Nor is the pyrexia of enteric fever often of so prolonged a character, though the writer was once deceived by a case of unusually remittent enteric fever, which died in a relapse, on what appeared to be the 64th day of the disease. At the post-mortem examination there were, besides recent enteric ulceration, signs of previous healed and healing ulcers. Such a case is, however, of most unusual occurrence.

The chief difficulty in diagnosis always arises during the first fortnight of continuously high temperature in severe cases. In the writer's experience, a fall in temperature approaching to normal, though only of a temporary nature, if it occur during the first ten days of the disease, and without adequate apparent cause (such as entorrhagia), is in adults a most valuable indication of undulant fever (see Chart XIII.).

The occurrence, two or three times, of slight epistaxis during the early stages of an attack would raise a presumption of enteric fever, while the occurrence in an adult of entorrhagia to any notable amount is a sure sign that the case is not one of undulant fever. It must be remembered, however, that a spongy hæmorrhagic condition of the gums is occasionally present, at a late stage, in cases of undulant fever, and that hæmorrhoids or colitis may cause a few drops of bright blood in a stool, conditions easily distinguishable from the above.

When the temperature in undulant fever begins to remit there is a great tendency to profuse diaphoresis. This takes place about one o'clock in the early morning, as a general rule, and is sufficiently profuse to necessitate one or more changes of clothes. Though more common at a late stage in the attack when the patient is much debilitated, it is somewhat characteristic at all stages, being uncombined with any rigor or paroxysm.

Constipation, with more or less formed, and even very hard stools, is the rule in undulant fever, while diarrhœa is exceptional in non-fatal cases (three times in 100 cases). In fatal cases diarrhœa is common (13 times in 20 cases); the stools then, however, are usually darker in colour and less fluid in consistency than in enteric fever. As constipation occurs also in about 4 per cent of enteric fever cases, the presence of numerous "pea-soup" stools can be of diagnostic value only in mild and uncomplicated cases.

In undulant fever there is usually an absence of that tumid, swollen condition of abdomen so common in enteric fever (79 per cent), while the pain and tenderness in the right iliac fossa, so characteristic of the latter disease, is generally replaced by a similar condition in the epigastric region, due, it is believed, to a common tendency to gastritis. This may be combined with even nausea and vomiting. The tongue is moist, swollen, and more uniformly furred than in enteric fever, with an absence of the peculiar reddened edges. The area of splenic dulness is more extensive, the spleen more tender, and its lower border more obvious on palpation below the margin of the ribs, the liver being at the same time often slightly enlarged and tender. The face is frequently excessively flushed, and even cyanotic, while there is an early tendency to severe headache and neuralgic or muscular pains. Though slight swelling of the joints may very occasionally occur in enteric fever, it is a common symptom in undulant fever, more especially in the later stages of the disease, passing from one joint to another, but especially affecting the extremities, combined with effusion and occasional redness. Troublesome rheumatic and neuralgic symptoms are very common complications and sequelæ of undulant fever, while orchitis and mastitis may occur.

In undulant fever during life, and more especially during post-mortem examination, the writer has observed in severe cases a characteristic goat-like odour not present in enteric fever, but comparable to those present in typhus and rheumatic fevers. During life this is noticeable about the skin and breath.

Undulant fever has no characteristic eruption, but on the other hand the peculiar rose-rash is seldom well developed in enteric fever cases in Malta, though present in some 70 per cent of English cases.

The reaction given by Ehrlich's sulphanilic acid test for urine has, in the at present limited experience of the writer, given aid in questions of diagnosis. In enteric fever this test has given in twenty instances (including a fatal case with post-mortem verification) a crimson-red or port-wine colour, especially noticeable as a salmon tint in the froth when shaken. This reaction is most intense during the primary fever of the first fortnight, but gradually disappears during the third week. This crimson is precipitated on standing as a greenish rusty-brown mass. In undulant fever, in over 160 instances, the reaction has varied from orange to mahogany-brown, and although the latter has occasionally in reflected light a pink tinge, there has always been a total absence of the enteric red or rather crimson, both in the fluid and in its froth, in cases of varying severity and at all stages of the disease. The precipitate, too, has no green tinge. As this test is applicable to the first and most difficult week from a diagnostic point of view, it should, if it continues to give such satisfactory results, prove of utility. Unfortunately, however, it has two disadvantages, which for the busy practitioner will mitigate its general usefulness. Firstly, it needs freshly-made solutions, which take up time to make, but after a little practice this is reduced to a small minimum. Secondly, the test rests in most cases on a distinction between various shades of one primary colour, these shades depending on its admixture with very small amounts of other colours. This, especially as the colour is red, has proved an insurmountable difficulty to some persons, who, without being colour blind, lack the necessary appreciation of colour.

The following is the method of application the writer has employed :—

SOLUTION A.[1]

Sulphanilic acid .	5 cc. (sat. solution).
Hydrochloric acid .	50 cc.
Water . .	1000 cc.

SOLUTION B.

Nitrite of Soda	95 cc.
Water .	1000 cc.

Keep in separate stoppered bottles.

At time of testing add 200 cc. of solution A to 5 cc. of solution B, add to this mixture an equal part of the urine, and render alkaline with ammonia. Shake well and observe (*a*) the colour of the fluid, (*b*) the colour of the froth, (*c*) after standing for twenty-four hours the colour of the precipitate. A standard red enteric tube may be made with red ink or fuchsine for purposes of comparison.

The sodium nitrite solution should be freshly prepared, the sample of urine freshly passed and acid in reaction, and the fact that morphine gives a similar reaction borne in mind. Hewlett mentions various modifications of this test. Thus Ehrlich mixes the urine with five times its volume of absolute alcohol, filters and tests the filtrate as previously described. Simon adds the ammonia by means of a pipette, so that it forms a layer on the surface, and a coloured ring is produced at the junction of the liquids. Rutimeyer makes his test solution by adding to 200 parts of a saturated aqueous solution of sulphanilic acid, 10 parts of pure nitric acid, and 6 parts of a 0·5 per cent aqueous solution of sodium nitrite. Green claims that the reaction is much more reliable if the test solution be prepared by mixing A and B in the proportion of 100 to 1

[1] See also V. Taksch's *Clinical Diagnosis; Lancet*, 6th Jan. 1894; *Practitioner* for March 1894; and *Brit. Med. Jour.*, 18th Jan. 1896, vol. i. p. 136, etc.

instead of 40 to 1, as originally recommended. He has also established the fact that the addition of various drugs does not interfere with the reaction.

That the crimson reaction has been met with also in cases of advanced phthisis, tuberculosis, extensive malignant disease, and occasionally in measles, pneumonia, typhus fever, acute rheumatism and septicæmia, is true, but as the absence of the reaction is the important point in this question, the usefulness of the test is not materially weakened, but if anything rather strengthened.

The serum reaction test (Vidal), which has been recently employed in the diagnosis of enteric fever,[1] has also been applied to undulant fever by Professor Wright of Netley. He employs serum sedimentation tubes, in which serum from blood, obtained from the patient's finger, diluted with normal salt solution and intimately mixed with a living culture of enteric or undulant fever bacteria. After twenty-four hours the agglomeration and sedimentation of a similar culture, or the diffuse growth of a different one, settles the nature of the disease. The details of the reaction are fully described in a paper by Professor Wright[2]; also a method of applying the test with dead cultivations which can be forwarded in capsules from a laboratory, and so do away with the necessity for the cultivation of the bacteria by individual medical officers in various stations.[3] The technique is as follows:—

A blood-capsule is made by drawing out the ends of a piece of glass tubing (of about a quarter of an inch in diameter) to capillary fineness, in the blow-pipe flame, in such a manner as to leave about a quarter of an inch of the original tubing in the centre. Blood is then obtained in the usual manner by pricking the finger of a patient near the nail. This blood is drawn into the capsule and its capillary ends sealed in the blow-pipe flame. The capsule is then set aside or sent to a laboratory for examination. As soon as the serum has separated from the clot it is ready for use. A capillary pipette is now made by drawing out the end of a piece of glass tubing in the blow-pipe flame. One extremity of the blood capsule is nipped off and the contained serum drawn into the capillary pipette, a mark being made on the tube at the upper margin of the serum to indicate the amount obtained. This serum is then blown into a watch-glass, and is diluted, first, five-fold by filling the capillary pipette four times in succession with normal salt solution (to the same extent as it was filled with serum), and by blowing this salt solution into the watch-glass containing the serum. In this manner any desired dilutions are obtained. It is convenient to work with 5, 10, 25, 50, and 100-fold dilutions of each sample of serum.

An emulsion of living typhoid bacilli or of the micrococcus Melitensis

[1] *Vide American Journ. of Med. Science*, March 1897; *Lancet*, 1895, vol. i. p. 1459 and p. 1464; 1896, 19th Sept. and 19th Dec.; *Brit. Med. Jour.*, 5th and 12th Dec. 1896, Jan. 1897, vol. i. pp. 147, 231; and *New York Med. Jour.*, 31st Dec. 1896, etc.

[2] *Brit. Med. Jour.*, 1897, vol. i. pp. 139, 258. Serum sedimentation tubes can be obtained from Mr. A. E. Dean, jun., 73 Hatton Garden, E.C.

[3] *Brit. Med. Jour.*, vol. i. p. 1214; 1897.

is made in another watch-glass (or that of dead bacteria, sent in a capsule from a laboratory, may be used).

Equal parts of the diluted serum and of this emulsion are now mixed together. This may be done by running a certain amount of the diluted serum into the capillary pipette, and making a mark at its upper margin to indicate the amount run in. A small air bubble may then be drawn into the tube, and next the bacterial emulsion run into the tube to the point already marked. The capillary pipette will now contain equal parts of the diluted serum and of the emulsion, separated from one another by an air-bubble. These are then blown into a watch-glass and intimately mixed.

A drop of this mixture placed on a cover-glass and inverted over a hollow-ground slip may be examined under the microscope. The remainder is again run into the capillary pipette, the capillary end sealed in the blow-pipe flame, and the pipette placed on one side for observation (for convenience in an ordinary glass test-tube). A control tube, containing equal parts of the bacterial emulsion and of normal salt solution, may also be prepared and placed by the side of the original tube for comparison.

Under the microscope the bacteria will soon lose their motility and become agglomerated into clumps, if they have been mixed with the diluted serum from a person who is undergoing, or who has undergone, the specific fever which corresponds to the variety of bacteria which has been employed. In the capillary pipette this agglomeration is shown by a precipitate formed of these agglomerated masses of bacteria, which in about twenty-four hours forms a pellet near the lower end of the capillary tube of the pipette, plainly visible to the naked eye, while the fluid above is clear. In the control tube, or in a tube where the serum has been obtained from a patient who is neither suffering nor has suffered from the specific fever caused by the bacteria employed in the emulsion, no such change occurs. Even where dead bacteria are employed which are eventually deposited at the lower end of the tube, they form a different and evenly-disposed non-flocculent deposit of individual bacteria.

This technique is simple and easily carried out, though a written description may seem so full of details. Where capsules of dead bacteria are used no special bacteriological apparatus or knowledge is required, but only a blow-pipe flame, watch-glasses, and some slight manual dexterity. Professor Wright has described (*Brit. Med. Jour.*, 15th May 1897) a method in which, by the substitution of methylated spirit for ether, the ordinary freezing spray used in hospitals may be employed to obtain a blow-pipe flame. The spray must be finely divided and the spirit fed into the spray with regularity and in sufficient quantity. The glass tube must always be removed from the flame *before* being drawn out into capillary pipettes and blood capsules.

Diagnosis from paludism.—Undulant fever differs essentially from paludism in being non-paroxysmal, by having no periodical or regular apyrexial intervals, by being unaffected by quinine to any great extent, and by leaving the system free from relapses in after years when once the disease has ceased to manifest clinical phenomena for any considerable period. The cases which approach most closely to paludism, clinically speaking, are those cases in which there is a daily intermission, more especially when they occur in countries where ague also exists. There is in Malta no difficulty in distinguishing such cases, and even the question as to whether the patient has previously visited a paludic country or not, is almost a foregone conclusion to one who has witnessed the symptoms of both diseases. In undulant fever of an intermittent type the temperature rises so steadily and slowly that the patient often makes no complaint, or complains of but slight headache and general malaise. There is no paroxysm, and rarely any attempt at a rigor, though when the temperature falls profuse and continued sweating may take place.

In undulant fever the hæmatophyllum malariæ is invariably absent from the blood.

It has been said that undulant fever and paludism can simultaneously coexist in the same subject. The writer has seen cases of undulant fever, in subjects who had previously suffered, in former stations, from paludic infection, exhibit suddenly every alternate day an unusually high temperature of a paroxysmal character. These periodic paroxysms and excessive temperatures disappeared after the administration of quinine, leaving only the pyrexia characteristic of undulant fever. Unfortunately the organism peculiar to paludism has not yet been sought for in these rarely seen cases, but an analogy exists in the relapses of ague which frequently occur in England in paludic subjects after operations or accidents.[1] If the organism is ever found in such cases, its discovery will strengthen the differentiation between these two fevers.

In Malta, where undulant fever is unfortunately far from uncommon, paludism does not exist in these days as an endemic disease, though slight relapses are met with among such of the troops as have previously served in Mauritius, Cyprus, India, and in other countries where that disease is prevalent. Such relapses are readily cured by quinine, and are quite distinct clinically from cases of fever contracted in Malta.

In 1800-1810 we find cases of "malaria" referred by Burnett to emanations from the marsh at the end of the Grand Harbour, but he also points out that large sewage drains opened there also, and stated that he considered that they had much to do with the matter. Hennen in 1825 also speaks of "malarial fevers" arising from this marsh, and from a similar one at Misida, at the end of the Quarantine Harbour, though Davy (1835) throws doubt on this assertion.[2] He mentions that the Capuchin monks of the convent at Floriana, which overlooked the

[1] The writer has seen a case of tubercle of lung with hectic pyrexia similarly complicated by paludism. See also Dr. Patrick Mason in *Brit. Med. Jour.* for 6th Jan. 1896.

[2] 1827, MacCulloch, *Malaria*, London. Note on Malta, said by Davy in 1835 to be erroneous.

former marsh, had a special dispensation from nightly devotions on account of the exposure that these necessitated. These marshes have since been drained, and are now in an innocuous condition. Whatever their effect on the troops may have been in those days, it can never have been great, as we find only very slight admission and death rates from malarial fevers since 1817 (*i.e.* quotidian, tertian, and quartan fevers), and whenever these rates reached a little above the average there was invariably a note attributing these admissions to imported cases from the Ionian Isles or elsewhere. (See back.)

Certain it is that paludism is not at present an endemic disease of rocky Malta, though visitors arriving there seem frequently to possess an opinion that undulant fever is a "malarial disease," and gaze at those who have had experience of the disease with incredulous pity when they attempt to disprove such a theory.

From *phthisis, liver abscess*, and other *suppurating diseases* combined with hectic pyrexia, we have to depend principally upon the presence of local symptoms for our diagnosis. The temperature charts of many chronic intermittent cases of undulant fever are undistinguishable from many which occur in the course of pulmonary tuberculosis. Moreover, in many cases of undulant fever a condition of alveolar and bronchial catarrh is set up, which with slight nocturnal pyrexia may persist for three or four weeks or even months, before actual convalescence is established. This, together with the profuse night-sweats, anæmia, emaciation, and debility so often present, is apt to lead the unwary astray, especially as there may be apical crepitations on auscultation. The writer has seen such cases diagnosed phthisis, and invalided for that disease, but completely recover before they had even embarked for England. In these cases there is an absence of dulness, localised apical flattening and pain, and tubular breathing. The condition is more generally distributed over the lungs on both sides, and is not progressive; the expectoration is strictly mucous, and though even blood-stained is not hard and nummular, and contains no tubercule bacilli. Often it is due to enfeebled circulation and the recumbent position in bed, in which case it is marked by excessive physical signs at the basis of the lungs behind, marking hypostatic congestion. This condition has been called "Mediterranean phthisis."

It must, however, be borne in mind that phthisis is a not uncommon sequela of undulant fever, occasionally appearing to overlap that infection, or follow after it with but a short interval between, and such a condition must be distinguished from that described above.

Cases of chronic hepatic abscess have frequently been overlooked to the detriment of the patient, the case having been considered as one of undulant fever. This is accounted for by the similarity of the pyrexial curve, and the fact that the liver is occasionally enlarged and tender to pressure in the latter disease, while vague (?) pains of a rheumatic and temporary nature are not uncommon in both diseases.

Hepatic abscess is occasionally met with in the Mediterranean, though it is much less common among English troops than it used to be fifty years ago. The liver should always be carefully examined for tenderness or enlargement in cases of continuous or intermittent pyrexia, and constant pain or uneasiness referred to that organ be carefully gone into, lest that early moment so often suitable for successful operation in the case of liver abscess be missed.

Empyema and other suppurating diseases accompanied with temperature are usually easily distinguished from undulant fever, if their cases are properly inquired into, by their localised symptomatology and the history of the case.

The writer has not met with acute croupous pneumonia as an endemic disease in Malta, though he has met with many cases transferred from troop and merchant ships outward bound from England. If the disease exists it is not common, but catarrhal (broncho) pneumonia is a most common and severe complication of undulant fever. As to the existence of acute croupous (lobar) pneumonia elsewhere in the Mediterranean the writer can give no opinion, but does not think that a diagnosis should be difficult to establish, especially when a single lung only is attacked. He has, however, seen cases landed from ships whose temperature after the fall by crisis has on account of pleurisy or empyema simulated the intermittent pyrexia of this fever. The history and physical signs were sufficient for diagnosis to be certain.

An effusion into a single joint can be readily distinguished from *traumatic synovitis*, by the presence of pyrexia at least in the evening, and the absence of a history of traumatism.

The early gastric symptoms are distinguished from simple *dyspepsia* by the presence of pyrexia, though the writer has frequently known a mistake made in diagnosis owing to neglect in omitting to take the patient's temperature.

The rheumatoid and neuralgic symptoms following attacks of this fever must be carefully distinguished from other conditions associated with similar painful symptoms, as the latter are apt to be overlooked unless a careful physical examination be made in each case. The writer has known extensive spinal caries thus missed; while he was once handed over a case of sarcoma extensively involving the ischium, anterior muscles of the thigh, and extending noticeably into the abdominal cavity under the peritoneum of the iliac fossa. This case was said to have recently suffered from undulant fever, and to be at present attacked with sciatica, the result of that fever. The physical examination made on transfer of the case at once disclosed, both to his former attendant and to the writer, the real nature of the case, which was still more evident on the post-mortem table somewhat later, in both this and the preceding case.

The writer has not met with true *rheumatic fever* in Malta, though he has more than once seen cases diagnosed as such, which subsequently proved to be undulant fever. He has only personally met with two cases of undulant fever which could be said to resemble rheumatic fever, in which early joint effusion was combined with somewhat high pyrexia, a condition not often met with in undulant fever. Even in these two cases a correct diagnosis was not difficult.

As a general rule in undulant fever, the joints are rarely affected early in the attack, but when this is the case the temperature is usually low, intermittent, and bears little proportion to the amount and severity of the arthritic condition. The joints, when affected, are rarely so painful as in rheumatic fever, except in those cases where one joint is acutely swollen and the temperature is high. In this later event the pain and tension soon gave way to appropriate treatment. The patient has not that dread of movement, or of having his bed shaken, so characteristic of rheumatic fever patients. There is not the same constant sweating and acrid smell about the patient; the sweating in undulant fever, though often profuse, being associated with definite falls of temperature. Cardiac and pericardiac affections are rare in undulant fever, and even when organic cardiac disease has been present, there has been reason to believe that it existed prior to the onset of the attack. Pericardial effusion has not been mentioned by other writers, and was only present in less than 0·2 per cent of the author's cases. Cardiac murmurs were present in less than 0·5 per cent of his cases, while they are said to occur in 20 to 80 per cent in cases of rheumatic fever in England (Fagge). Lastly, salicylic acid and its salts have little or no effect upon the pyrexia or other symptoms of this fever.

Prognosis.—With regard to danger to life and hope of ultimate recovery the prognosis in this fever is a very favourable one, the case mortality being about 2 per cent.

A previous history of tubercular, cardiac, or pulmonary disease (pneumonia, pleurisy, etc.), or the presence of organic cardiac or renal disease, of concurrent anæmia, phthisis, syphilis, etc., or of great nervous excitability, all indicate a serious prognosis. The great majority of deaths occur during the first or second month of the disease, and are mostly due to a train of circumstances which has led to hyperpyrexia, pneumonic congestion (with perhaps consolidation), and failure of the heart's action. Of those dying at a later date (less than 25 per cent), many die in a severe relapse associated with a similar combination of hyperpyrexia and cardio-respiratory failure, others from syncope. Hyperpyrexia when uncombined with failure of the cardio-respiratory circulation can usually be controlled, but a combination of these two conditions, unless energetically treated from their first appearance, have only too often proved fatal. This is very evident in the reports of post-mortem examinations on severe cases. We cannot, therefore, but view any condition likely to interfere with or retard the cardio-respiratory circulation, as a serious symptom, becoming the more so as the pyrexia increases in amount and severity.

In other cases which have proved fatal at a later date, we meet with organic cardiac disease, pericardial effusion, pleuritis, or empyema, anæmia, debility, exhaustion, and intercurrent phthisis as causes of death.

The cases which most often prove dangerous are either those which commence with a tendency to continuously high pyrexia, with early signs of pneumonic congestion, or those in which the patient is anæmic with a highly excitable nervous temperament.

Obese plethoric patients more often suffer from malignant symptoms, bear the fever worse, and are more prone to pneumonic congestion and consolidation than those of a spare and lean build.

It has been said that those who have previously suffered from a tendency to "rheumatism" are more prone to the rheumatoid and neuritic symptoms of this fever.

The appearance during an attack, of feeble, insufficient, irregular or intermittent cardiac action, of pericardial effusion, pneumonic congestion, pleuritis, renal disease, persistent vomiting, severe diarrhœa from involvement of the large gut, excessive or continuously high pyrexia with a tendency to dry brown tongue, and other symptoms of the so-called typhoid state, of great anæmia, debility or bed-sores, one and all call for constant attention and a guarded prognosis.

A dry tongue at any stage of the disease is always a serious symptom; a cleaning tongue, especially when associated with a fall of temperature, a most satisfactory condition.

Arthritic and acute neuritic symptoms rarely last long, and ultimately subside. The former may, however, leave some temporary stiffness, and though the joints never suppurate, they have been known to become the seat of subsequent tubercular deposits; the latter may leave a tendency to neuralgic symptoms on exposure to chills, etc. Gouty arthritis may be brought on in persons subject to that diathesis. Chronic neuritic affections may persist for some time (1-12 months), even after pyrexia has disappeared, and thus give rise to after admissions to hospital for sciatica, neuralgia, rheumatism, etc.

Pyrexia that is uncontrollable by cold applications (generally the result of want of early treatment) is almost invariably fatal.

Convalescence is usually rapid when once fairly established, but anæmia, œdema of the ankles, nervo-muscular debility, cardiac irritability, shortness of breath, and feeble digestion may remain for some time in cases in which the pyrexia has been unusually severe or prolonged.

With regard to the length of time that a patient may expect to be incapacitated from active work, prognosis is unfavourable and unreliable. The average time spent on the sick list by soldiers treated in hospital (including time spent at the sanitarium or in hospital in England after invaliding) has been from 70-90 days, but this duration varied between wide limits. While some patients returned to duty at the end of a month, many who were invalided to England were away from duty for a year, others from a year and a half to two years, before final recovery.

No definite rule can be laid down, but the pyrexia of cases of the undulant type with severe onset may usually be expected to end during the second month, and be fit for work between the end of the third and the sixth month, but there are many exceptions. Very severe cases, though more dangerous to life, are on the whole less prolonged. Intermittent and mild cases vary within very wide limits, while they are unfortunately just the cases that are usually the most anxious to know when they may expect to recover.

Thus the writer has separately treated the husband and wife of two separate families simultaneously attacked during the spring. Both of the husbands were officers, of similar rank and mode of life; and all four individuals suffered during the first two months from pyrexia of a similar type and severity. With one family this pyrexia lasted, in the case of the wife for two months, in the case of the husband for ten months. With the other family, in the case of the wife for one month, in the case of the husband for eleven months. The wives suffered from mild intermittent pyrexia, some arthritic effusion, were confined to bed, and dieted early in the attack, and were transferred to England before the hot weather. The husbands did not at first wholly give up work, were not sent to England until the hot weather was nearly over, and arrived for an unusually damp and wet September. Their temperature was intermittent and mild for the first three months, and then became undulatory and severe, returning to an intermittent type before recovery.

In all outbreaks of this fever the individual cases have varied greatly in type, duration, and severity.

It is therefore never advisable to give an opinion upon the probable duration of any individual case. At the same time, while inculcating and encouraging patience, the patient's spirits should be stimulated by the hope that it may soon end. As a general but not invariable rule, a gradually falling pyrexial undulation with markedly remittent temperature is more favourable than a rapid fall. A *subnormal temperature lasting for a day or two*, and following an intermittent temperature or gradual fall, when accompanied by a *clean tongue* and general improvement, is very often a sign that pyrexia is to cease, even though the patient himself may not feel in very excellent spirits. The afternoon and evening temperatures are the only ones on which an opinion can be based, as the morning temperature may be subnormal for days or weeks while the later ones vary in their height above the normal line.

What the remote effects of this fever are it is impossible to say, without further data than are at the disposal of the present writer. We find, from microscopical examination of the tissues of prolonged cases, that changes occur, due to the constant and prolonged action of an irritant poison, producing a "fibrosis" in certain organs. Though this is not great in amount, yet it is a change that cannot be beneficial, and which in greater amount leads to danger in such conditions as chronic alcoholism and paludism. Whatever its effect may be on the ultimate prolongation of health and life, it is one that has not been complained of as yet among officers and long service soldiers, or among civilians living in its endemic area. In these days of short service but little is known of the old age of the private soldier, but though very many cases of undulant fever are annually invalided to England, but very few are discharged from the service on account of permanent unfitness.

Duration.—There are two points connected with this question, namely, the duration of the active disease, *i.e.* the pyrexial duration, and the length of time spent in hospital on account of the effects of the fever.

Disregarding doubtful non-fatal cases of under three weeks' duration, the author has found the pyrexial duration of 372 cases in which it was noted to be as follows :—

TABLE XIV.

1-20 days (fatal cases) .	5	75
21-30 ,, . .	70	
31-40 ,, . .	65	154
41-50 ,, . .	50	
51-60 ,, . .	39	
61-70 ,, . .	36	88
71-80 ,, . .	34	
81-90 ,, . .	18	
91-100 ,, . .	20	39
101-110 ,, . .	8	
111-120 ,, . .	11	
121-130 ,, . .	8	14
131-140 ,, . .	...	
141-150 ,, . .	6	
151-160 ,, . .	2	
	372[1]	

To the above must be added, in certain cases, the unnoted relapses for which they were subsequently admitted into other hospitals, or from which they suffered at the sanitarium, or after being invalided from the island. It may be safely said that the average pyrexial duration exceeds 60 or 70 days, while cases have been known to exceed 300 days. (Bruce, one case, 18 months; Veale, one case, 2 years; author, one case, 277, two cases over 300 days, and two for 2 years.)

On a similar principle the time spent in hospital in Malta by 844 cases has been :—

[1] Average pyrexial duration about fifty-eight days.

TABLE XV.

1-20 days (fatal cases)	10	214
21-30 ,,	204	
31-40 ,,	153	378
41-50 ,,	119	
51-60 ,,	106	
61-70 ,,	72	159
71-80 ,,	57	
81-90 ,,	30	
91-100 ,,	26	59
101-110 ,,	21	
111-120 ,,	12	
121-130 ,,	12	28
131-140 ,,	5	
141-150 ,,	11	
Over 150 ,,	6	
	844	

In these are included 26 fatal cases, of which 10 died at an early stage in the disease. Also 401 cases sent to the sanitarium at Citta Vecchia for change of air (average stay there one month); and 142 cases invalided home to England. Moreover some of these cases subsequently relapsed in other stations.

Taking these three latter items into consideration, it would appear that the average time spent in hospital by cases of undulant fever contracted in Malta is from 70 to 90 or more days, while cases with sciatica have remained non-effective over a year and a half. Long cases can scarcely be said to have completely returned to their original state of health until an interval of from 12 to 24 months, while many seem to take years to completely shake off its effects. Of these 844 cases only 275 were sent straight back to duty from hospital, and many of these relapsed.

Bruce gives the time in hospital as an average of 90 days, Moffet 9 to 12 weeks, Guiffré between 15 days to 28 weeks.

Mortality.—Bruce and many others estimate the death-rate at about 2 per cent of cases attacked. During the six years spent by the author in Malta, the mortality varied greatly from year to year in relation to the strength of the garrison, but averaged fairly constantly slightly over 2 per cent of cases attacked.

Morbid anatomy.—The following remarks are based on the reports of 62 post-mortem examinations on soldiers (duration of disease 4 to 156 days), recorded in the military hospitals in Malta, at 15 of which the writer was present.

These morbid appearances depend, apparently, to a great extent on the direct effects of the virus or its products on tissues of the human organism. The post-mortem naked-eye appearances in acute and rapidly fatal cases are those of intense congestion, especially marked in the internal organs. While those met with in chronic cases, fatal at a later stage in the disease, are those of long-continued irritation of the tissues. In the following description the writer will endeavour as far as possible to divide the cases into two such classes.

Of these 62 recorded cases, 27 belong to the rapidly fatal class, 18 to those fatal at a later stage, and in 17 the duration was not mentioned.

CLASS I.—*Acute and Rapidly Fatal Cases* (27)

These comprise nearly all the cases which die during the first four weeks of the disease (some 60 per cent. of fatal cases), the fatal result being apparently due to the direct action of the virus, or of its products, on the patient.

Brain.—In ten cases in which this organ was examined, the meninges, superficial veins, and choroid plexus, were congested in nine, the greatest intensity being in early cases. In a few cases there was effusion into the ventricular spaces. In one the condition was described as normal.

Heart.—The muscular walls are described as normal in all except one case, when they were said to be "flabby" (duration 12 days). In three cases there were vegetations on the mitral valves, presumably in two, and probably in one case, of previous origin. In one of the two cases there was also fatty infiltration present, and in the last case extreme pericardial effusion was present (duration 19 days).

Lungs.—These were invariably congested at the bases, especially behind. In many cases this hypostatic congestion had gone on to lobular consolidation and œdema, but though small portions might sink in water, the whole lung floated in those cases tested by the author. Of fifteen cases in which the condition was clearly noted, there was considerable congestion with lobular consolidation of the bases of both lungs in eleven; a similar condition of the left lung, with congestion only of the right in one case; the remaining three cases having their lungs congested without consolidation. The condition is one of hypostatic congestion passing into broncho-pneumonia, with consolidation in lobular patches, with much serous exudation into the bronchial tubes, which latter are often injected. The bronchial glands were enlarged in proportion to the pulmonary lesion.

Pleuritic adhesions are mentioned in six cases, in three of which they are described as "old" (duration of cases 4, 7, and 8 days); in three they are described as of "recent origin" (duration 8, 13, and 14 days).

Liver.—Congested, and somewhat enlarged and increased in weight, in very acute cases; in a few cases not altered in appearance.

Spleen.—Enlarged, the average weight of twenty-six cases being 19·9 oz. (10-44). It has always an extremely congested appearance, being dark red or even red-black in colour, and of these twenty-six cases nine were much congested, eleven were soft and extremely friable in texture, while six were so broken down as to appear almost diffluent. This latter condition is very characteristic, the spleen in some cases appearing like a large clot of venous blood, in other and more extreme cases as a bag of semi-fluid blood. This appearance has been described as "broken-down and rotten."

Alimentary canal.—Patches of congestion were present in twenty-four cases out of twenty-seven. These were present in the stomach in six, in the duodenum in six, in the jejunum and ileum in nineteen (one very severe), and in the colon in eleven instances (two very severe). This congestion followed the arborescent distribution of the vessels of the stomach and intestine, and produced a dendritic appearance when held up to the light, the congested veins, some a quarter of an inch apart, looking like leafless trees. It is not confined to, nor constant in any particular spot, and has no relationship to Peyer's patches, though occasionally one of these patches may happen to be situated on a congested area. Similar congestive patches have been met with in enteric and other forms of abdominal disease of an acute nature, and while they form part of the general internal congestive condition, they can scarcely be considered as typical lesions, nor specially characteristic of this fever. The mucous membrane is often swollen and softened. Peyer's patches are unaffected, except that when there is extreme intestinal congestion one or two of these glands may appear to be slightly prominent (twice in twenty-seven cases), but there is no condition present in any way approaching the lesions found in enteric fever. In no case was ulceration present.

The congestion met with in the colon is more characteristic of the disease, being occasionally of an inflammatory character and combined with œdema of the mucous membrane. It appeared in some cases to decide the fatal issue, and in the sixty cases, in many of which the duration is not given, it was noted as being present in twenty-two instances, in eleven of which it is described as very severe. A similar condition was specially noted by Oswald Wood in 1876. The condition reminds one of the early stages of dysentery, but the clinical course of such cases, fatal or non-fatal, is different. The mucous membrane is swollen, softened, and œdematous in large patches, livid and even purple with congestion, and the solitary glands may be prominent. In long cases which present this condition we have usually to attribute death to the effects of a severe relapse complicated by this local lesion, which approximates such cases to the acute rapidly fatal cases of Class I.

In six cases only were the mesenteric glands enlarged, in which the duration of the disease is noted, and in these cases such enlargement was probably due to the excessive congestion of the large and small intestines present in all these cases. Enlarged glands are mentioned in thirteen of the sixty cases, in each of which cases intestinal congestion was present, and in ten of these the congestion may be said to have been excessive.

Kidneys.—These are in some cases congested, especially about the pyramids and Malpighian corpuscles, in others apparently normal.

CLASS II.—*Cases Fatal at a Late Period in the Disease* (18)

In these cases the fatal issue is generally the result of heart failure from intercurrent mitral disease; of broncho-pneumonia or other complication acting on a debilitated and enfeebled constitution; or of a sudden exacerbation of acute febrile symptoms. Such cases, besides the signs of the local and immediate cause of death, show signs of chronic irritation of the tissues similar to that met with in certain forms of chronic poisoning. The duration of these cases was from 32 to 156 days, so that some of the cases which died during the acute stage of their first relapse are included.

Brain.—In only five instances does this organ appear to have been examined; in one (duration 117 days) there was effusion and softening; in another (duration 44 days) "there was slight serous effusion into the arachnoid space and lateral ventricles"; in another (duration over 31 days) the "meninges were congested"; while the remaining two were normal. There is an absence of mention of the intense congestion met with in acute and very early cases.

Heart.—This, though usually described as normal, is in five instances termed "pale and flabby"; in one there were mitral vegetations (111 days); in another (156 days), in which the organ was "soft, flabby, and small"; there was a small aneurysmal dilatation above the posterior left semi-lunar valve, vegetations on all the semi-lunar valves, and some old pericardial adhesions; in another (62 days) there were 17 oz. of clear fluid in the pericardium, without any apparent cardiac lesion. In the last three cases death occurred suddenly on account of heart failure.

Lungs.—As in the former class, these are usually congested at the bases, and in four cases patches of consolidation were present. The condition is not, however, nearly so severe as is the case with short acute cases. In only two cases are the lungs returned as normal.

In five cases there were pleuritic adhesions of long standing, in two adhesions of recent origin, and in two cases there was pleuritic effusion present.

Spleen.—This organ is invariably congested in appearance and increased in weight. Leaving out two cases whose time in hospital only just exceeded one month, we find that the average weight of the spleens of fourteen long cases was 14·4 oz. Of these three were firm in texture (duration 58, 72, and 53 days; weights 9, 12, and 11 oz.), eight softened, and of these two were "diffluent." The softer spleens occurred in those who died during acute relapses.

Liver.—Of twelve cases in which the condition of this organ is noted it was described as normal in two, congested in five, pale in three, fatty in one, and nutmeg in two, both of which were complicated by cardiac disease. It was in nearly all cases increased in weight.

Alimentary canal.—Of eighteen cases (duration 32 to 156 days), but four were free from mention of congestion. These are scattered about indiscriminately, and though somewhat constant in their presence, were not as a rule nearly so intense as in the former class. In two cases there was the severe congestive appearance of the colon, that has already been mentioned in Class I.; in a few long-continued cases the intestines were sunken and attenuated.

In one case (duration 88 days) there was a small superficial ulcer in the cæcum, and a shelving ulcer with irregular and ragged edges in the colon; three or four of the Peyer's patches were slightly congested, and one mesenteric gland had suppurated, this latter condition probably depending upon an abrasion or small ulceration which was present. A case published by Bruce in the *Practitioner* of April 1888 (duration 53 days) had also ulceration present, and was thus described: "The ulcerated condition was found 36 inches from the ileo-cæcal valve upwards. In this space there were four patches of ulceration. The first 4½ inches above the valve and opposite the mesenteric attachment was oval in shape (one-third by one-quarter of an inch), and divided into two by a bridge of mucous membrane. The edges were thickened and undermined, and forming the floor could be seen the circular muscular layer. This ulceration did not seem to correspond to a Peyer's patch, but was evidently formed on a loop of blood-vessel. No change could be seen on the peritoneal surface. The other three patches of ulceration were in Peyer's patches. They had each the same character. There was no thickening of the edges or undermining, but the substance of the gland had fallen out in small oval and round patches, so as to give a serpiginous character to the ulceration. In addition to these four patches there were many minute losses of substance evidently corresponding to solitary glands. It was noted that immediately above the ileo-cæcal valve there was a large Peyer's patch which was neither thickened nor ulcerated, and appeared to be healthy." In addition to these, Peyer's patches are described as slightly enlarged in one case (duration 40 days), but no ulceration was present. In another case (duration 58 days) Moffet, at Gibraltar, says: "A few of Peyer's patches were prominent in lower third of ileum, while one or two higher up presented a 'shaven beard' appearance, the mucous membrane was soft, and the coats of the small bowel were attenuated and atrophied; no ulceration nor cicatrices of old ulcers were seen." This case died during the first acute relapse, on the 58th day. Another case in Malta had an ulcer upon the posterior wall of the anal sphincter (duration 46 days).

Of 62 cases, these are the only ones that had any ulceration resembling enteric fever, and in only two of these was the ulceration sufficiently like to need discussion. In the first case the ulcers had neither the locality nor the appearance of enteric ulcers, and in the second case (Bruce) the ulceration appeared to depend upon accidental causes other than the true enteric virus. Moffet's case, of which full notes with temperature chart are published in the *Army Medical Report* for 1889, was certainly not enteric in nature. Besides these cases, Chartres mentions one (duration 18 days), in which the intestines were normal except for "two very minute points of abrasion of the apices of Peyerian glands which were somewhat more pronounced than usual." This case, together with one of short duration in which the author found two small superficial ulcers (like abrasions) not situated on any Peyer's patch, have not been included among the 62 cases quoted, on account of the element of doubt that they might introduce.

The losses in continuity in these cases were more of the nature of abrasions than of specific ulceration, and taking into consideration the softened and congested condition of the mucous membrane, and in the long cases the atrophied and debilitated state of the intestinal tract during the long-continued pyrexia associated with intestinal irritation and marked constipation, we have not far to go for a solution of their cause. While remembering that enteric fever has a peculiar specific and typical form of intestinal ulceration, we must therefore bear in mind that non-specific losses of continuity of surface of the intestinal mucous membrane may occur in undulant fever, being in these cases (as was doubtless the slight enlargement of Peyer's patches in the case mentioned) of accidental occurrence, and like bed-sores, having no direct specific connection with the disease. In the many post-mortem examinations that the writer has made on cases of enteric fever in Malta, he has never had any difficulty in identifying the specific intestinal lesions of that disease, which lesions differed in no way from those met with in England and elsewhere; and he has no hesitation in saying that the case he mentions above, in which two small ulcers were present, had none of the characters of true enteric fever; while sixty of the total quoted cases had not the slightest trace of ulceration apparent in the alimentary tract.

Squire (1886), when describing cases of so-called typho-malarial fever at Suakim, mentions that intestinal ulceration, when present, was "not such ulceration either in site or character as that of enteric fever."

In four cases the mesenteric glands were said to be somewhat enlarged.

See also ten or eleven cases mentioned by Guiffré (1893), collected from various sources.

Squire (1886) gives the general pathological appearances in cases of typho-malarial fever at Suakim, as follows:—

"General injection of the mucous membrane of the alimentary canal, often most marked in the duodenum and upper jejunum, but affecting at different times the whole length of the tract. With this fulness of the vessels there may be ecchymoses under the mucous membrane at various parts in the intestine.

"When ulcers are found they are generally irregular in shape, and do not select the closed glands of the intestine.

"The mesenteric glands are often enlarged.

"The spleen is generally enlarged; and the liver frequently congested."

For detailed descriptions of post-mortem examinations see Cases Nos. 2 to 15, Chapter II.; Nos. 3, 7, 8, 10, 14, 15, 21, 24, Chapter III., and No. 13, Chapter IV.

Microscopic appearances.—With the exception of the spleen there is nothing to be seen microscopically in the tissues that can be said to be characteristic of this disease. The appearances in acute rapidly fatal cases are those of acute pyrexia, with local congestions and hyperanæmias, the result of the irritating poison circulating in the body. In long chronic cases the appearances are those of long-continued toxic irritation of the body tissues. Owing to the high temperature of the Mediterranean, during the summer months, when these cases occur, section cutting is very difficult, so that there is a great want of further and more accurate histological investigation.

Bruce states: "On making a section through a Peyer's patch and examining it under a low power, the serous, muscular, submucous, and mucous layers are found to be unthickened and almost normal in appearance. The epithelial layer is continuous over the surface of the gland. Under a high power morbid changes are found restricted to the mucous and submucous layers, and consist in a slight proliferation of the cellular elements. On examining the large endothelioid plates of the glandular tissue they are seen to be somewhat swollen and proliferating, and there is a slight proliferation of the adenoid tissue. There is proliferation of the cellular elements of the lymphoid tissue of the mesenteric glands, the reticulum is very delicate, and appears in places to be almost obliterated by the increase in the number of the cells; there is some proliferation of the endotheliod plates, and they are in a condition of cloudy swelling. The Malpighian bodies of the spleen are enlarged from an apparent increase in the number of the round lymphoid cells; the endothelioid plates of the marginal sinuses are proliferating and swollen; a condition of intense congestion is seen in the section; the sinuses being enormously distended with blood; there is marked exudation of small round cells along the lines of most of the venules. The liver is congested, the cells in a condition of cloudy swelling, and there is an infiltration of small round cells in the interlobular fissures. The kidney is also congested, and in a state of glomerular nephritis."

Bacteriologically he mentions the appearance of single micrococci scattered throughout splenic sections in enormous numbers; while micrococci similar in appearance to these are found in smaller numbers in the liver and kidneys.

The writer has also observed the micro-organisms peculiar to this fever, in cover-glass preparations of fresh splenic substance, shortly after death, in five instances, in two of which they were extremely numerous. In other cases they were not noticeable, though cultures on agar-agar were obtained by inoculation. As no agent, by which the stain can be fixed in the micrococci while the tissues are being decolorised, has yet been discovered. These cocci have not been carefully studied *in situ*, but when they were visible they appeared to be in a free state in the extra-cellular fluids. As they have been grown as pure cultures from the spleen by inoculation on agar-agar in twenty-five instances, from splenic blood obtained during life in two instances, and from the spleens of inoculated monkeys after death in three instances, there can be little doubt that the spleen is one of the places where the micro-organism is invariably present in cases of this fever, a fact further probable when we consider the naked-eye appearances of the spleen at post-mortem examinations. In the liver and kidney it has been found, and we must next search for it in the lung, intestine, cerebro-spinal system, and in the swollen joints, before its pathology can be placed on a sound footing. It has been found in the circulating blood of the inoculated monkey, but not in that of man.

In acute cases examined by the writer he has observed the microscopical appearances described by Bruce as present in the spleen, liver, Peyer's patch, and mesenteric gland.

With regard to chronic cases, Dr. Hewlett, of the British Institute of Preventive Medicine, has very kindly cut and stained sections of the organs of Case No. 13 (duration 111 days), from specimens sent to him by the author.

Case 13.—Aged 25 years. Mediterranean service two years. Admitted 14-5-95 from a barrack where an outbreak of this fever was occurring at the time. Previous history good. Admitted with the usual symptoms of Mediterranean fever of sudden onset. On May 24th signs of hypostatic basal pneumonia of the right lung appeared and persisted until June 9th, when resolution set in, and there was a temporary abatement of symptoms until June 18th, when there was a pyrexial relapse of about a month in duration. On June 29th a large abscess formed in the left groin and was opened. Between June 18th and July 14th another abscess formed on the back of the head and was evacuated, and many boils in various regions of the body required incision. At the end of July these abscesses had healed and the patient was better, while no more boils or abscesses occurred. On August 20th he was emaciated, debilitated, and extremely anæmic, his lips being almost colourless. He also suffered from intractable sciatica. A systolic murmur, thought to be hæmic, was audible at the apex of the heart. About August 24th he became worse; muscular tremors were constantly present, and the pulse became flapping in character. On the 29th he died suddenly of cardiac failure, after 111 days of pyrexia.

Post-mortem examination three hours after death. Body greatly emaciated, post-mortem rigidity well marked. Hypertrophy of the left ventricle of the heart, with warty vegetations on the mitral valves; weight, 12 ounces. There were recent adhesions between the parietal and visceral pleura at the base and posterior part of the right lung. The lower portion of the right lung was consolidated to some extent and weighed 26·5 ounces; the left lung was healthy and weighed 17 ounces. The right bronchial glands were enlarged. The liver (weight, 72 ounces) was much congested. The kidneys (weight, 10·5 ounces each) showed the characteristic changes of "large white kidney," there being strands of connective tissue between the pyramids. The spleen (weight, 15·5 ounces) was much congested, soft, and friable. The intestines were much attenuated as regards their walls, but were otherwise quite healthy, there being no congested patches. A few mesenteric glands were slightly enlarged, but Peyer's patches appeared normal. The pericardium contained from 4 to 5 ounces of serous fluid. Small portions of the lung, liver, spleen, kidney, mitral valve, mesenteric gland, and a Peyer's patch, were placed in equal parts of alcohol and water for twelve hours. They were then transferred to absolute alcohol (frequently changed) for three days, and then sent in absolute alcohol to Dr. Hewlett.

The case was of the undulatory type, the pyrexial waves lasting 30, 27, 7, 13, 6, and 8 days, with some irregularity towards the end.

Dr. Hewlett embedded the specimens in paraffin in the ordinary manner, cut sections with a rocking microtome and stained them with Ehrlich's hæmatoxylin and eosin.

They show the following appearances:—

Heart.—The small vegetation on the mitral nerve has become nearly fully organised into fibrous tissue, and though it is still infiltrated with round cells undergoing change, it cannot be of very recent origin.

Lung.—The perivascular and interalveolar tissue is infiltrated with round cells (leucocytes). The air vesicles contain large catarrhal cells and shreds of fibrin, indicative of catarrhal pneumonia.

Liver.—Neither fatty nor fibroid changes are present. There is cloudy swelling of the liver cells, which have stained badly and show granular degeneration of their protoplasm.

Spleen.—Beyond a larger proportion than usual of lymphoid tissue there is apparently nothing abnormal.

Peyer's patch.—The epithelium is continuous over the surface of the gland. There is slight infiltration and increase in the lymphoid cells. Otherwise the section of the intestine through a Peyer's patch appears to be normal.

Kidneys.—There is cloudy swelling, granular degeneration and loss of nuclei in the lining epithelium of the tubules, pointing to tubular nephritis. In places there is infiltration of round cells into the intertubular connective tissue, with commencing interstitial change. The glomeruli are normal.

These appearances are not in any way specially characteristic of undulant fever, but are rather those of severe and prolonged pyrexia, acting on the tissues of the body.

Professor A. E. Wright, of Netley, has also cut sections of the spleen, liver, kidney, and brain, of Case No. 14 for the author. These showed the same signs of continued tissue irritation, much marked in this case in the brain, and in and around the tubules of the kidney.

CHAPTER V

Prophylaxis: Period of prevalence in endemic area; Nature of suitable clothing; General hygienic measures; Notification; Disinfection of stools; Prevention of pollution of soil; Flushing and disconnection of house-drains; Avoidance of proximity to drain ventilators; Extravasation from house-drains; Flushing of main drains; Cementing of ground-floor, living-rooms, etc.; Leaking cesspits in porous soil; Discharge of sewage into tideless harbours; Dry-earth system, supervision of; Disconnection of rain-water pipes, sinks, etc., in the open air; Avoidance of polluted ground for camping purposes; Prophylaxis on board ship; Vaccination. — *Treatment:* No specific drug known; Remove patient from insanitary surroundings; Dust from soft stone flooring; Nursing and night attendance; Cotton sheets, etc.; Confine to bed during acute stages; Avoid fatigue, worry, and chills; Fresh air; Absorbent clothing; Bed-pan and night stool; Dietary; State of tongue; Severe cases not to be overfed; Milk, source of, and amount; Peptonised milk; Lemonade, lime-juice, and fruit; Eggs and albumin water; Beef juice, beef tea, etc.; Soda-water, lime-water, tea, coffee, etc.; Ice; Calves' foot jelly, chicken quenelle, soups, light puddings, etc.; Tobacco; Stimulants; Drugs; Constipation; Diarrhœa; Record of stools; Bladder; Teeth and gums; Mosquitoes and flies; Prickly heat, sudamina, boils, bed-sores, etc.; Diaphoresis and change of patient's clothes; Pneumonic, pleuritic, and cardiac symptoms; Fever pains, headache, sleeplessness, cerebro-spinal irritation, neuritis, arthritic effusion, hyperæsthesia of the feet, and atrophy of muscles; Moderate regulation of temperature; not to exceed 103° F. unchecked; Antipyretic drugs condemned; External use of cold water advocated; its advantages; apply early in attack, and with regularity; Patients differ in response to external cold; Mode of application; Amount of supervision necessary; Excessive reduction of temperature deprecated; Results of application; Friction of extremities combined; Tepid daily sponging of skin; Management of convalescence; Certain drugs; Quinine, bismuth, arsenic, hydrocyanic, carbolic acid, boracic acid, chlorine, mercurial preparations, aconite, colchicum, eucalyptus, turpentine, salicylates, antipyrin, antifebrin, phenacetin, resorcin; Invaliding with change of air and scene.

Prophylaxis.—Until the disease has been eradicated, those who visit localities in the Mediterranean where this fever prevails, for mere pleasure or in search of health, will do well to limit their stay to the period from November to April (inclusive), during which period there is little or no undulant fever. From the beginning of the hot weather, which usually commences during May, until the sirocco winds of September and October are over, all children and women who can afford a change are better away from the infective area, in the more bracing climate of Switzerland, the Italian Alps, England, or elsewhere.

When business, duty, or pleasure calls strangers to the Mediterranean at any time of the year, there are a few simple points which they rarely realise, but which natives regularly practise. The sleeping suit (be it pyjamas or night-dress) should be composed of absorbent material, such as flannelette, Jaeger, cotton-wool fabric, or flannel. Wear also similar material next the skin during the day, however little else is worn, and remember that the dampness of the climate and its sudden changes of temperature make the Mediterranean a cold and chilly place, a fact little realised by those who have not visited it. When visiting its shores in winter, do not leave rugs, furs, and warm clothing behind. When likely to be out after sundown, especially when driving, warm wraps should be taken, as the change from bright and warm sunshine to the evening cold is sudden and often great. The same is necessary when the harbour has to be crossed at night. Into the ordinary hygiene of every-day life it is unnecessary to enter, as every one should understand the necessity of avoiding excessive exposure to sun, fatigue, etc., the supervision of their milk and water supplies; the avoidance of overcrowding, and the necessity for an adequate supply of fresh air in dwelling-houses. It is not, however, out of place to remark that those of the garrison who take exercise in the fresh air of the country during summer, are healthier and less liable to attacks of fever than those who habitually remain in the vicinity of their barracks, offices, or houses in town.

The main point to dwell upon, if indeed we are correct in our surmise, as to the actual cause of the fever, is the avoidance and subsequent eradication of existing localised infective areas. For this purpose every case admitted to hospital or notified as existing in private houses, should be as carefully inquired into by their attending or district medical officers, as is at present done in the case of enteric fever among the troops. Notification, which is in force in Malta, should be made compulsory in all places where the fever exists. For this purpose a printed form should be used and filed for future compilation of results. In the Army each district medical officer should keep a book or plan in his inspection room, having a space for every room in barracks, in which the simple entry of the date on which each case was admitted would cause little trouble, and be a guide to the localised distribution of cases, and soon lead to the detection and eradication of infection foci. The writer, by roughly following out such a plan, and by tracing each case occurring in the barracks under his medical charge to the bed it occupied, has not only discovered unsuspected insanitary conditions of a gross nature, but has found his opinion of the fæcal nature of the fever confirmed over and over again. This system with some variation, if applied to many other diseases also, would soon lessen their occurrence and the inefficiency and expense they involve. There is a great tendency in military medical reports to give the sickness which occurs in various regiments and corps, rather than that which occurs within the definite areas which they occupy. The fact, so carefully recorded in our published annual blue-book, that this or that regiment when in Malta seven years ago, suffered severely from enteric or S. C. fever, etc., is of little value to us now, since we do not know what barrack they then occupied. What is urgently needed in each garrison, is a record of the sickness in each barracks and barrack-room, with its probable cause, a brief account of remedial measures taken, a plan of the drainage, water-supply, and an account of the milk-supply, etc., kept up to date. This would be a sort of medical history sheet for each barracks, similar somewhat to that at present kept for each soldier. These and other sanitary records should be kept in some central office such as that of the principal medical officer, and be available for the inspection of those concerned, while in large districts or stations a special sanitary medical officer (who, for a very slight addition to his pay would soon qualify for a diploma in public health) in charge of such records, and with a separate office and clerk, would investigate and eradicate much of this and other preventible disease.

The notification report should specify—

(1) The number, name, rank, age, army and Mediterranean service of the sufferer, as is at present done in Malta.

(2) The barracks, room, and bed he has occupied during the two months previous to the onset of the disease, and what previous admissions have been noted from the same locality. If married, whether any other member of the family has been attacked.

(3) The general habits, occupations, and character for sobriety of the sufferer.

(4) Any insanitary conditions to which he has been exposed, which may have a bearing on the case.

(5) Date of apparent onset.

Any small extra expenditure that may be necessary to work such a system, would soon be repaid over and over again in the Army by saving lives of officers and men, the replacement of whom, to say the least, is a serious financial loss; the saving in non-effective pay, and in diets, extras, and stimulants in hospital; and in civil life by saving the bread-winners of families from long periods of absence from work, etc.

A modified form of this scheme might equally apply to civil communities, and by the knowledge gained by such notification, the efforts of the civil sanitary department in preventing the occurrence of this disease, by sanitary advice and control, would prove most beneficial both to individual families concerned and the community at large.

If the theory of the causation of this fever by aërial emanations from soil (or drains, etc.) previously contaminated by the evacuations of those suffering from the disease prove correct, there are many prophylactic measures that we should adopt. The evacuations of those suffering from the fever should be disinfected before being discharged into the house-drains, or should be burnt. This will prove a large question, as we have to deal with a disease having an extremely long duration when compared with enteric fever. Moreover, owing to its often insidious onset, its occasionally long apyrexial periods, and to the fact that patients are often up and about, though still liable to slight rises of temperature, it follows that many cases of this fever are leading for various periods an ordinary life, though possibly their evacuations are of an infective nature. Care must be especially taken that such ambulatory cases do not make a habit of fouling ground in and around houses, barrack-rooms, and camps. Such habits are unfortunately not uncommon among both the native inhabitants of these parts of the Mediterranean garrisoned by England, and among the soldiers themselves. The only way of guarding against such pollution is to prevent both the healthy and unhealthy from such habits. This is provided for in Malta by law among civilians, and a little more activity on the part of the police would work great improvements. It is further prevented in many places by paving such spots as are liable to frequent pollution, and many of the streets, pavements, and squares, with asphalte or cement, suited to the climate; and more especially by providing urinals, etc., in suitable quantities, in the towns, for public use. These improvements to the porous and dusty soil of the towns of the Mediterranean, are beneficial for many reasons besides that under discussion, and should not be stinted. In the Army the same precautions can be even more easily applied, and are most important, for there we have a community of men all more or less of a susceptible age, and who are constantly being encamped on ground close to and around barrack-rooms or on which troops have been previously encamped. Facilities should be given to men to carry out instructions, by providing urinals in suitable places, instead of placing them all together at one end of the barracks, as is often the case. This particularly applies to large barracks, and to such places as the canteen and sergeants' mess. Again, the urine tubs for night use should, besides being themselves kept clean, be placed in such a position as not to contaminate the ground beneath them. At very small expense indeed the space on which they are placed can be cemented, and if possible be supplied with a slope and a small trapped drain, disconnected outside. This allows of the ground being properly washed down every day. Those who have seen the flat paving stones (usually themselves of a porous nature) taken up, disclosing the filth which collects beneath them in such situations, will not doubt the necessity of this measure. A light should also be placed near the spot on which these tubs are kept, so that men may be able to see their position, and use them instead of the ground between, as is too commonly the case where they are placed in the dark, outside the barrack-room. They should further be emptied under *very* reliable supervision, as the soldier will invariably use the easiest means of getting rid of their contents, rather than the most suitable, unless well looked after. Usually the nearest surface-water drain is made use of, and the writer has even seen them emptied down grids, collecting water for tanks set apart for ablution and cooking purposes.

It should be hardly necessary to point out the need for adequate flushing and disconnection of house-drains, but unfortunately in these countries water is not too abundant during the hot weather, while the crowded nature, at any rate of Malta and Gibraltar, leads to a close proximity between dwelling-rooms and latrines. Flush-out apparatus with waste-preventing flushing gear, arranged with a sufficient fall to procure the maximum of work with the minimum quantity of water, are being gradually introduced and give excellent results. Unfortunately flushing is too often done by emptying water down the latrine by hand, in the houses of the lower classes. From laziness where water drainage is in force, and from a desire not to fill the cesspit in other situations, this proves a most faulty method. The disconnection of the house-drains from the general drainage system is a most important point in the crowded cities of the Mediterranean. Latrines are for want of space often in close proximity to bedrooms, placed in enclosed air-shafts or yards, on the small verandah of the only window, or actually communicating with bedrooms by a door or (as the writer has seen on several occasions) by a room brick-ventilator intended for a fresh air inlet! In hot weather there is a considerable amount of sewer-gas to escape, and if precautions are not taken, syphons may be forced. While providing free ventilation to cesspits, house, and main drains, it is very necessary that shafts should be carried well above the roofs of houses and kept away from all neighbouring windows. In towns such as Valetta and Gibraltar, where a very large number of houses are crowded into a small space, and where from the hilly nature of the ground the roof of one house is very often on a level with the windows of those in front or behind, much difficulty is experienced in effecting this. So many cases have, in the opinion of the writer and others, occurred in rooms opposite such drain ventilators that visitors and others should be careful to ascertain when taking a house, flat, or rooms, that no such dangerous and possible cause of infection exists in their proximity. Where house-drains are unavoidably carried across yards or under cellars, any dampness that might indicate leakage should at once be inquired into. Main drains cannot be too well flushed in hot weather, and where fresh water is scarce or limited in amount, and salt water close at hand, it would appear reasonable that some means of utilising the latter might be made available as has been done in many of the English towns lately. As leaking and ruptured drain-pipes have so often contaminated the subsoil of houses and yards in Malta, owing to the extremely porous nature of the soil, it has proved practically advantageous in many places to have the floors of cellars, ground-floor rooms, and yards rendered with cement or other impervious material. The writer is of opinion that all ground-floor rooms used for sleeping purposes should be so treated, and in many of the barrack-rooms so treated this has proved of great value in lessening or removing sickness from this fever. In many cases this has been applied to streets, pavements, and public squares with advantage. As has been mentioned already it is a great improvement in hospital wards over the usual dusty paving of soft stone.

In the porous soil of Malta cesspits have not proved a success in neighbourhoods where there are any number of houses close together, as however carefully they are built in the first instance, the temptation of allowing or producing leakage has proved too strong to the native, on account of its saving the cost of frequent emptying. Unfortunately, however close these houses may be to the open sea, they continue to build cesspits, until by their number and close proximity a subsoil pollution of so great an amount has taken place as to cause a danger to the community at large. At this stage the institution of a general water-drainage system has become a costly matter, and one to which the existing landlords are not inclined to contribute. It seems a pity that in the case, at least, of growing watering-places and suburbs of large towns, some system is not instituted when these are in their infancy, at which time there should be little if any difficulty in getting each landlord to contribute his share of the expense when building a new house. We must remember, however, the lesson of the past, and carry all such systems to the *open* sea, and not into the tideless harbours of the Mediterranean, as has been too often the case.

Where the dry-earth system is in use, it must be under careful supervision, not only as regards the cleanliness of the pails in use, but also as to final disposal of the material. The writer has found a covered surface-water ditch full of such matter, which a contractor, to save himself the trouble and expense of removing, had thrown down a neighbouring grid in barracks. This covered ditch ran behind some married quarters, where unaccountable cases of fever were occurring. In barracks the contractor for emptying dry-earth pails usually visits at an early hour, and before the men are about, so that special supervision must be arranged for. The ultimate disposal of this material in crowded places and in such a place as Malta, where the soil usually only has an average of from six to ten inches thickness, needs consideration. This soil also has but little activity in the dry hot weather. It is necessary that the power of growth and future mischief of such germs as those of enteric and undulant fevers, which appear to be able to lead a saprophytic existence in some soils, should be carefully ascertained. It is only with such knowledge in our possession that we can scientifically discuss the possible merits or demerits of disposal of sewage by means of the dry-earth system, or of sewage farms on any large scale. Of this knowledge we at present are deficient.

Rain-water pipes from roof, etc., must be disconnected from foul drains, in the open air, over suitable traps, or they may prove dangerous in dry weather by becoming drain ventilators. The same may be said of sink, bath, and overflow pipes, which only too often are either connected directly with drains, or are disconnected indoors instead of in the open air, or have only a forceable syphon between. People living in England scarcely realise the closeness of these to living rooms in such a town as Valetta, where the average population is estimated officially as 75,883 to the square mile; while that of the whole of Malta is as much as 1600 to the square mile. To a less degree this is the case with Gibraltar.

Care must be taken not to camp on ground liable to pollution, and this especially applies to those tents used in barracks in Malta during hot weather to relieve the barrack-rooms, which must not be placed on or near to ground liable to pollution, nor near to drain ventilators. The writer has seen many cases of this fever admitted to hospital from tents unsuitably erected in such situations.

As to prophylaxis on board ship the writer can give no opinion, but must leave to his colleagues in the Royal Navy and mercantile marine the elucidation of this subject. As all cases of this fever (other than relapses) are said to occur within a reasonable period of leaving port, it seems probable that the disease is not causally connected with the ship itself nor with its food or water supply. It would, therefore, follow that the prevalence of undulant fever on board ship is due to some factor connected with either the situation of the ship in harbour or to the visit of its occupants to the shore. It would be interesting to know whether Burnett's remarks on the difference of fever prevalence in ships in dock or in the creeks, from that of ships in Bighi Bay (see back, Chapter II. p. 63), still holds good; and whether those who sleep on shore when in harbour suffer more than those who remain habitually on board. The possibility of danger arising from eating harbour shell-fish, from bathing in polluted harbour water, and from using it for washing down decks, etc., has already been pointed out (Chapter II. p. 65).

Lastly, it is possible that some form of vaccination may be discovered that may render susceptible troops immune from attacks of this fever, if only for a time, as in these days they do not remain as a rule long within the endemic area of the Mediterranean. In this hope we are much encouraged by recent experiments made on monkeys by Professor Wright of Netley, in which he has, by artificial inoculation of dead cultures of the micrococcus Melitensis, been able to confer upon monkeys not only a high serum sedimentation power with regard to that micro-organism, but also a power of at least inhibiting the growth of the micro-organism of that disease in their system. Moreover, these dead though still poisonous cultures, without being in any way dangerous, appear to confer on monkeys as effectual an immunity as living ones.[1]

Treatment.—There is no drug of a specific nature at present known which will cut short an attack of this fever by its action on the virus, as does quinine in ague, and mercury in syphilis. We have, therefore, primarily to treat a pyrexia which, except perhaps at the end of an attack, we can do little to directly shorten by means of drugs. Not infrequently when the pyrexia is dying out, and the virus is apparently making its last stand, its final disappearance is synchronous with the

[1] *Brit. Med. Journal*, 1897, vol. i. p. 258, and note on p. 259.

administration for a few days of quinine or some other germicidal drug. Whether this is accidental coincidence, or due to the action of the drug administered, it is difficult to say. We find, however, that for this reason various drugs are vaunted as specifics, which not only fail to cure other cases at a similar stage in the disease, but which, when administered during the acute stages, when the virus is, so to speak, in possession of its full fighting powers, not only have no effect upon the virus itself, nor are able to shorten the duration of the attack, but in most instances actually increase the severity of local alimentary symptoms, and also the general febrile condition. In numerous cases, after much ineffective medication, recovery has followed the cessation of all medicinal treatment.

We can, however, do a very great deal towards mitigating both the general and local effects of this pyrexial condition, and towards the lessening mortality due to hyperpyrexia. We have, secondly, to treat the various localised morbid conditions which arise. Lastly, we have to consider the best means of recovery from the anæmia, debility, tissue irritability, and other conditions left by the fever, after all pyrexial symptoms have disappeared and the virus has been completely subdued.

Our first aim should, therefore, as is the case with enteric and many other acute fevers, be to place the patient under the most favourable circumstances for nature (*i.e.* the individual tissues of the affected subject) to effect her own cure, and at the same time to alleviate and ward off complications and sequelæ.

Although many cases will do well with careful nursing and dietary alone, it is a great mistake to think that this is all that is necessary; for we each find that as our experience increases our deaths decrease or are postponed, our cases become milder and shorter, while complications become less frequent and severe. Expectant treatment is very apt to develop into *laissez-faire* in so prolonged a disease.

On arriving in Malta, Army medical officers have, as a rule, to treat numbers of cases of this fever almost at once, and not unnaturally ask those with former experience for advice in the matter. They rarely obtain more than a suggestion that they should consider them as cases of enteric fever, and treat them as circumstances should appear to require. As it is these severe cases with a tendency to the "typhoid state" that require the most active treatment, in the absence of any authoritative advice on the subject, this suggestion comes to be useful, under the system that half a loaf is better that no bread, but leaves much to be found out at the expense of each medical officer's early cases. The writer's treatment, as detailed below, leaves much to be desired, for while dealing with a fever which, like paludism, has an indefinite duration, he is unable to cut short or restrict that duration within fixed limits, and is only able to a certain extent to control and curb its virulence. This, however, is a valuable power to possess, and the fact that the writer has more confidence and satisfaction and less anxiety in treating his present cases than he had six years ago, leads him to hope that the following remarks, while assisting new comers to the Mediterranean, may be a nucleus on which others with more experience may build up a more perfect system of treatment in the future.

It is, first of all, advisable that the patient should be removed from the neighbourhood of any insanitary surroundings which may have been connected with the origin of his attack. If, as the writer believes, this fever is caused by an aërial organism of a fæcal nature, which enters the body by way of the inspired air, it is evidently unwise to let him inspire a larger dose than is necessary. Theoretically speaking, until a patient has acquired absolute immunity from the disease, a new dose of the poison would be supposed to predispose him to a relapse. Practically speaking, it is found that patients who show no signs of improvement while treated in their own beds in their own insanitary rooms, improve rapidly when removed to another house, or room, or to an hospital. Again, as has been already mentioned, patients who go back to the same bed in the same barrack-room in which they developed an attack of this fever, often have subsequently to be admitted to hospital with symptoms of the same fever, after from one to three months of apparent recovery. Many of these cases look suspiciously like instances of re-infection. Soldiers when attacked with this fever are at once invariably sent to hospital, with the best results.

Officers do best in hospital, while women who are treated in hospital, do better than those treated in their own quarters. Though a great deal of this may be due to the better nursing and care which is met with in hospital practice, there is something more than this, and the writer has often been able to date improvement in a case from the day on which the individual changed a room or house. This is a preventive rather than a remedial measure.

The room in which a case is treated should, if possible, be large, so as to allow of plenty of fresh air being available. This is not a mere platitude, but a necessity proved by experience. As the patient has to remain in the same bed or room for eight or more weeks, during that time his pyrexial condition will be materially affected by the temperature, moisture, etc. of the air he breathes. The lofty ceilings of many of the hospital wards and private rooms in Malta make them admirably suited for the treatment of these cases, though unfortunately the extreme density of the population makes large and lofty rooms the exception, except in the houses of the rich. The soft stone floors so generally met with in Malta are exceptionally badly suited to the treatment of these cases, for not only are they extremely absorbent and difficult to keep clean in a sick-room, but give rise, when swept, to a cloud of finely powdered stone dust, which predisposes cases to the common pneumonic troubles so often dangerous to life in this fever, and aggravates such symptoms when present to an extreme degree. This was most marked in the large Military Hospital in Valetta, where the floor of the fever ward was formerly of soft stone, giving rise when swept to a cloud of dust. In 1894 the floor of this ward was relaid in cement, and the improvement in the decrease in frequency and severity of pneumonic complications in undulant fever cases, occupying the same beds, was most marked. When, as is often the case, it is necessary to treat cases in rooms with soft stone floors, these should be either oiled, painted with silicate or other paint, or carefully sprinkled with damp tea leaves before being swept. While promoting free ventilation, and providing for as much fresh air as possible, precautions must be taken against draughts, on account of the tendency to rheumatic or neuralgic complications which frequently follow exposure to sudden chill in the course of this fever. A trained nurse is advisable in all cases, and is indispensable in severe cases, and it is especially during the night and early morning that an attendant is required in even mild cases. All sheets and pillow-cases should be of cotton and not linen. It need scarcely be mentioned that a single bed, with a firm spring wire mattress under the hair matress, without sides or foot-piece, is the most suitable; that it should be approachable from all sides; while unnecessary furniture would be better elsewhere than in the sick-room. An air or water-bed is often necessary in severe or emaciated cases.

The patient should be confined entirely to bed during the acute stage, and while the tongue remains furred, or acute neuralgic symptoms combined with pyrexia are present. Usually it is best to keep the patient in bed until pyrexia has ceased for some ten days, and the clean tongue and temporary subnormal character of the temperature curve gives promise of permanent recovery. Many a relapse may be traced to the patient having been allowed up prematurely and injudiciously. Thus a case in 1892 relapsed almost fatally after being allowed up for a short time in the afternoon of Christmas day, though before that time she was improving daily. It is often extremely difficult to persuade the friends of a patient to keep him in bed during an apyrexial period, though the patient is generally more amenable, and only experience can teach the medical attendant when a relapse is not to be anticipated. There is, however, a not uncommon exception to this rule. In the late stages of some cases that have dragged out their monotonous length, and show little variation from normal in the morning and 99°-100° F. in the evening, when the tongue is fairly clean and the patient has some appetite, it is often advisable to allow him to be up in a chair or sofa for a short time each morning, or later in the afternoon between 4.30 and 7 P.M. The exhilarating feeling of being "well enough to be up" is beneficial, and more than counteracts any depressing feelings if the patient is not allowed to tire himself. When the weather is suitable the patient may in such instances often be placed in a chair, on a sofa, or have his bed moved on to a verandah; but on no account must this be allowed in acute stages, or in a draught, nor must he be left in the open air as late as sundown. The writer has seen most severe relapses and distressing rheumatic symptoms arise from neglect of these precautions. It may practically be said that in the absence of draughts the more fresh air the patient gets the better. The writer has been in the habit of advising his patients not only to keep their windows open, but to be actually in the open air as much as possible during the milder and more chronic stages of the fever, and especially during convalescence. Great care must be taken, however, that in following out this advice the patient does not fatigue himself when moving out of doors. When the weather is warm, it is better for him to lie on a couch out of doors than to move about in a bath-chair or carriage. Not only is it more fatiguing to sit up in these conveyances, but when the patient leaves his home, he is not able to return at once to bed when he feels at all tired. All through the treatment of this fever there is a happy medium to be achieved between healthful stimulation of the nervous faculties and the depression which follows fatigue or tissue irritation from injudicious medicine, dietary, or other treatment. This happy medium can only be achieved by experience combined with common sense, applied to each individual patient; nor can any rules be laid down that will be found suited to any large section of cases, unless the physician is prepared to modify his treatment according to circumstances and personal idiosyncrasies. The excessive severity of the initial symptoms met with in those who have attempted to "fight off the disease," is comparable with those relapses which follow over-exertion during the progress of an attack, or with the temporary rises of temperature which follow the afternoon on which friends are allowed to visit their friends in hospital, or the depressing dampness of a sirocco wind. In short, the leucocytes have their battle to fight, and we must be careful not to draw their attention from the work by other calls on their exertions, but assist them to expel the foe we are unable ourselves to subdue. The writer's cases have suffered much less from the distressing neuralgic and rheumatic symptoms of this fever since he has made thin flannel, flannelette, or the new forms of cotton wool or Jaeger, the routine clothing of those under his care. The soldier in hospital wears what is given to him without complaint, while most officers abroad wear flannel pyjamas, or are willing to do so if such are recommended to them. With ladies, women, and children the case is different, and the most tactful and firm persuasion is necessary before they can be induced to discard the linen or cotton night-dress for one of woollen or other absorbent material. Besides the strong feeling of habit and precedent, there is the awkward fact to combat against, that the latter can rarely be made to look as pretty as the many forms of elaborately trimmed cotton or linen night-dresses. This feeling should, however, not be allowed to interfere with this most useful point in treatment, for not only are the acute arthritic or neuralgic symptoms most painful, but intractable sciatica has been known to cripple strong men for a year or more after the pyrexial condition has entirely ceased. For men the usual suit of pyjamas, made large, is suitable, while for women and children some form of combination garment is really the most useful. The combination form of garment is invaluable for children, as they are very apt to throw off the bed-clothes and remain uncovered, though it has the disadvantage over the pyjama suit of being more difficult to change. Though many women positively assert that their skins will not stand flannel, flannelette, or other absorbent material worn in this way, it is found that any feeling of discomfort complained of at first wears off with wonderful rapidity, and the majority of patients continue to wear these absorbent night-dresses permanently after recovery, at any rate while abroad. The comfort of this form of garment, be it night-dress or suit, will be most evident when the profuse and debilitating night-sweats of this fever begin, for a linen or cotton garment will be saturated in a moment, nor will the patient be comfortable until after the diaphoresis is over, in spite of constant changing. An absorbent garment reduces this discomfort to a minimum, prevents chills after changing, and is most grateful and comforting to the patient whose temperature has recently fallen with the outbreak of the perspiration. On account of these profuse night-sweats, not only will an attendant require to be ready to change the patient's night-clothes and sheets during the night, or early morning, even several times, but a good supply of these articles should be in readiness for this purpose. Here, again, the superiority of woollen or other absorbent material comes in, for articles of this description can readily be dried or washed in the house, and again be ready for use, thus minimising the number of garments necessary. The greater the number of night-clothes and sheets available, the greater the comfort experienced by the patient. It is difficult to insure comfort to the patient unless he has at least six, or in long cases eight or more night-suits, four to six sets of sheets, six pillow-cases, and a spare blanket and pillow, besides those in use on his bed, while under these circumstances he will require to have facilities for drying and washing these at home when necessary. In summer a light blanket should be folded and placed at the foot of the bed, so that the patient can pull it up at any time. In certain cases with neuralgic or arthritic symptoms, as will be mentioned again, it is desirable to discard the sheets and place the patients between blankets.

The use of the bed-pan should be enforced in severe cases, and during the acute stages of all cases. Later on, when the patient can be safely allowed to use the night-stool, he must not be compelled to go to it through draughts or the outside air, and he should protect his hips with a blanket from the cold, as these joints are so often the seat of acute effusion and pain, of sudden onset, and attributable in many cases to direct chill. An enema syringe is often required, and the usual feeders, lamps, and other paraphernalia of a well-regulated sick-room.

During convalescence a comfortable arm-chair will be used for some time, while in hospital the writer's cases have derived the greatest benefit from a chair in which the patient has been able to wheel himself about, as it combines an interesting and larger amount of exercise with a minimum of exertion.

The general principles of dietary laid down for enteric fever cases are applicable to a very large extent to cases of undulant fever.

Though ulcers are not present in the intestines, the mucous membranes are in a very irritable condition, and the digestive functions are out of order, in proportion to the severity of the pyrexia. Moreover, any foreign bodies present in the alimentary canal, such as undigested food, unsuitable and unnecessary drugs, etc., considerably increase any irritability present. On the other hand, want of food or suitable nourishment has a most depressing and harmful effect on the patient. Here again we are placed between two fires, and have to find that suitable middle course between over-feeding and starvation, the attainment of which is one of the most important points in the successful treatment of this fever. A rough rule of great value is that a patient's power of digestion is usually inversely in proportion to the severity of his symptoms. It may seem almost unnecessary to mention that the patient's tongue is the surest guide to the state of his alimentary mucous membrane, and therefore an index of his digestive powers, but it is strangely true that this important point is frequently forgotten. Thus the writer has often seen cases whose tongues were brown, dry, and cracked, in the condition well known as the "typhoid state," with or without vomiting being present, plied with milk and other forms of nourishment at intervals of increasing frequency, with a painfully mistaken kindness on the nurse's and physician's parts. Such cases he has found at the post-mortem examination to have their stomachs enormously distended with undigested food, a condition which must have seriously handicapped the action of the adjacent heart and lung, at a time when these were battling their hardest to keep the failing circulation at work. Experience has taught us the nature and amount of food that fever cases can digest, and though many improvements may be made in the food-stuffs available, there is no doubt that it is quite wrong to suppose that the worse the patient becomes and the higher his temperature rises, the greater should the amount of food be. In fact the reverse is the case with regard to the quantity of food required. The writer would lay special stress upon this point, not only because its importance has been proved over and over again by clinical experience, but because there is a great tendency to this practice on the part of many nurses and of all untrained friends. They feel an increasing necessity for action as the patient becomes more seriously ill, while this is the part of the treatment that they have more especially under their control. It is, therefore, well for the physician to lay down definitely not only the nature of the food to be given, but also the exact amount that should be sufficient for the twenty-four hours, with the time of administration. Many cases whose breath has been unusually foul, whose tongues have been undesirably dry and brown, or who have been subject to vomiting, and whose general condition and pyrexial elevation has been unsatisfactory, have at once improved on the amount of their nourishment being lessened, or its character made more suitable to their digestive powers. Any excess of milk and undigested curd, besides acting as an irritating foreign body, also gives rise to fermentative changes in the alimentary canal, which cannot but increase the already irritable condition of the mucous membrane.

In practice it is found that fluid food is the best during the acute stages of the fever. Milk, as fresh and pure as possible, should form the chief part of the patient's diet. Solid food should be withheld in ordinary cases until there is an absence of gastric irritability, and an indication of a probable cessation of acute pyrexia of a permanent nature. A clean tongue, an attempt at an appetite, if combined with a subnormal temperature for one or two days, followed by a normal temperature of ten days' standing, is a fairly sure sign, and would justify a return to solid food in moderation. An exception may be made to this rule in long-continued cases, whose tongues are clean, and whose only disabilities are debility, anæmia, and a slight rise of temperature every evening to 99° or occasionally to 100° F. To allow such patients up for part of the day, and to give them some interesting and light though solid food in moderation, promotes a hope of recovery which is in itself a powerful and beneficial mental stimulant. To such patients poached eggs, well-boiled chicken or white fish, bread and milk, or milky pudding are often beneficial, and at any rate do no harm. They must not, however, be given potatoes, crusts, pastry, or other forms of indigestible food, while the tongue must be watched for any indication that food is improperly digested. The patient's inclination for food follows very closely his capabilities for digesting it, especially from a quantitative point of view. Such a course of action in well-chosen cases, when combined with stimulants and a careful avoidance of fatigue, often enables patients to throw off the remnants of the pyrexial condition, which before seemed unending. In acute stages, however, such treatment would invariably be followed by a relapse, hence it must be only exceptionally allowed and cautiously applied. In the countries where this fever occurs, goat's milk is always obtainable, cow's milk being less commonly used. As goats can generally be brought to the patient's house, or to the hospital, and there milked under supervision, their milk is to be preferred to the more doubtful cow's milk, which is only obtainable from a distance. In Malta there are many more persons drinking reputed cow's milk than there are cows in the island for this supply, and as cow's milk and the milk of goats milked away from the house is usually cheaper than that obtained under supervision at the door, there is little doubt that it is better and safer to use milk that has been milked straight into private vessels at the door, under personal supervision, than any other. In the latter case we are able also to inspect the goat and its milker, and are only subject to the trick of giving the goat salt in its water, so that by increasing its thirst and causing it to drink a large amount of water the vendors sell inferior milk in larger quantity. Goat's milk thus obtained, in clean and well-scalded vessels, is excellent in quality and admirable for the purpose. It does not taste unpleasantly of the goat unless kept for an unusually long time, or allowed to ferment. This milk should be given fresh, while any that is to be kept should be pasteurised or sterilised,[1] and kept in the ice chest (especially in summer and during sirocco winds) until wanted. In hospital this is easily managed, while in private practice a simple form of steriliser may be readily procured (Soxhlet's, Aymard's, etc.), or made locally at small expense. The lengthy duration of this fever, the necessity of having the milk free from fermentation, and the great digestive superiority of milk pasteurised at a comparatively low temperature over boiled milk, makes such an outlay of time, trouble, and expense trivial when compared with the results obtained.

Having procured a supply of fresh pasteurised or sterilised goat's milk, we come to the question of the *amount* required by the patient in the twenty-four hours. As a general rule three pints of good milk is sufficient for a very severe case, in its acute stages, for twenty-four hours. This may be increased in amount in less severe cases until a maximum of five pints is reached. This is not meant to include the total fluids given, but only the amount of milk necessary. In very severe cases even three pints of milk may not be digested, and in some cases pure milk does not seem to be digested at all with ease. In such cases peptonised milk (combined with beef juice and similar food-stuffs), in small quantities at a time, seems to meet the case. It would appear in such cases as if the digestive functions were almost in temporary abeyance, when the temperature is very high.

In ordinary mild cases, however long in duration, milk is well borne and digested (up to four or five pints), and when the tongue is cleaning, and the patient begins to take an interest in his food, and shows even some attempt at an appetite, rice milk may be given. This is prepared by boiling two ounces of best Bengal rice with three pints of milk. To this may be cautiously added bread and milk, custard pudding (equivalent to half an ounce of sugar, one egg, and half a pint of milk), sago, rice, and other milky food.

When vomiting is present the greatest care has to be taken to give the patient only such food as he will be able to retain. In these cases peptonised milk is especially useful, and with it bismuth in large doses, beef juice, albumin water, and champagne are, as will be further explained, our chief remedies. A portion of milk should be given to the patient *the first thing in the morning.* This should be the rule as long as any temperature or debility remains, and it will be especially appreciated when the patient is showing signs of recovery, at which time he will be found to feel miserable and low-spirited at that time of the day.

Next to milk, fresh lemonade, or some such substitute, is necessary. Not only is the patient likely to be for a long period without vegetable food while milk is his staple diet, but a scorbutic condition has been described by many early writers as occurring in the later stages of long

[1] See articles on this subject by Drs. Johnstone-Campbell and Hunter-Stewart in the *British Medical Journal*, 6th September 1896, vol. ii. p. 623, for details.

cases. This scorbutic condition has also been associated with purpura. The writer has only once met with a scorbutic condition among the many cases treated by various medical officers in Malta, and in this case the condition of the gums appeared to be due to an excessive use of mercury. The absence of such symptoms he would attribute to the universal system of giving these patients two or more pints of lemonade, made with freshly squeezed lemons, every day; each pint being equivalent to one large lemon and three-quarters of an ounce of sugar. When lemons are unobtainable two ounces of lime-juice have been substituted. Besides this, the writer has been in the habit of allowing very mild cases, convalescents, and cases that have reached the late and chronic intermittent stages of the pyrexia, fresh grapes, oranges, strawberries, bananas, and other fruits in season, skins and stones being, of course, discarded.

Added to these articles of food, eggs are valuable in various ways. During the acute stages egg flip, made with the yoke of an egg beaten up with milk, with sugar, and brandy, and flavoured if desired with a pinch of nutmeg, is a valuable and acceptable form of nourishment. This may be given twice a day with benefit. The white of these eggs, mixed with water and flavoured with cinnamon, peppermint, or other aromatic, makes a useful form of albumin food of a fluid character. In the later stages eggs lightly poached or scrambled may safely be used as a stepping-stone between fluid and solid dietary. During convalescence eggs for breakfast cooked in various ways are most acceptable to patients after their long course of milk.

Beef juice is a most valuable form of nourishment for those severe cases whose digestive faculty is almost in abeyance, or who suffer from obstinate vomiting. In bad cases it is occasionally the only form of food that can be retained, and in many cases the writer has seen great benefit follow its use. In cases of obstinate vomiting this form of food has tided over a crisis, until an abatement of symptoms has been accompanied by an increased tolerance for food, and a return of digestive activity. The writer has prepared it as follows:—

One pound of fresh beef, free from fat, and finely minced, is mixed with eight ounces of soft water, six drops of hydrochloric acid, fifty to sixty grains of common salt, and after being well mixed is allowed to stand for three hours in a cool place. It is then pressed through a hair sieve, and taken cold or slightly warmed.

Beef tea, beef essence, beef extract, etc., though stimulating, can scarcely be called nourishment,[1] as there is little but the extractives and meat salts left in them. They appeal, however, to the popular mind, and, if well made, are stimulating, and form a change from the dull routine of milk and egg flip, greatly appreciated by those who have had to undergo a course of such diet. They appear to have no bad effect on ordinary

[1] *Practitioner*, Nov. 1881. p. 343, etc.

cases, unless there is a tendency to diarrhœa, in which case they are distinctly prejudicial, and where this is at all excessive, such food may even be termed dangerous. In those cases in which a congested or inflamed condition of the great gut is present, where vomiting occurs at all frequently, where excessive pyrexia is accompanied by failure of digestion, foul breath, and dry brown tongue, or where diarrhœa is present, beef tea is incompatible with successful treatment. With regard to the various essences of beef, chicken, etc., none are so well borne as beef and chicken jelly. The best are neutral in reaction, pleasant in taste, and have a jelly-like consistence when kept at a sufficiently low temperature. The alkaline essences that are issued to army hospitals are not so well borne. In mild cases, beef tea in the evening about 7 P.M., when the temperature is falling, is a welcome form of stimulant, and during convalescence may be given at 11 A.M. with advantage, varied by strong soups. The amount of fluids taken should not be restricted, as the surface loss from perspiration is generally great. Soda-water in a syphon may be placed by the bedside for use as required both by day and night. Lime water added to the milk is of value where there is gastric irritability, but is undesirable in other cases on account of its constipating effects. Tea, coffee, and other beverages may be given as desired.

Ice in small pieces is grateful in the hot weather, when sucked at intervals, especially where the mouth is inclined to be dry. It will also be needed in warm and sirocco weather, for preserving milk and other food; and where there are severe cases, for direct application, as will be described later.

Calves' foot jelly, though possessing little or no nutritive value, helps to vary the diet, and is a harmless form of solid food.

In intermittent cases, and during the period just before recovery in long cases, food is generally taken well during the morning, and during the evening, when the temperature has fallen previously, but solids are badly borne during the rising and maximum of pyrexia, usually between 1 P.M. and 6 P.M. As the patient's digestion begins to become stronger in its action and his appetite to be established, chicken broth and soups with bread or toast may be added to the poached eggs, custard and farinaceous puddings. These may be cautiously increased to chicken quenelle, chicken cream, bread and butter without crust, crumb-bread soaked in milk or soup, white fish, and well-boiled chicken or fresh game.

Chicken panada or quenelle is made by soaking the crumb of a French roll, a few rusks, or some stale bread-crumb in hot milk, and placing it in a clean stew-pan with an equal quantity of the breast or wing of a roast or boiled chicken (or a chicken that has been used for broth) previously pounded in a mortar. Add a little chicken broth and stir over the fire for ten minutes or so.

Crusts of bread, potatoes, and oatmeal should be withheld until convalescence is undoubtedly established. In regulating the diet, the state of the tongue and bowels should be carefully noted, for these will infallibly indicate the wisdom or otherwise of the course adopted. The greatest care must be taken in serious cases, as one day of injudicious dietary may make a great difference in the patient's general condition, or in a case that is mending, may cause a serious relapse. It is easier to regulate the diet of convalescents in this fever than it is in enteric, as there is usually an absence of that ravenous appetite which is occasionally the undoing of promising cases of the latter disease. A great deal of care is, however, necessary in dieting convalescents, as the anæmic and enfeebled state of the mucous membranes of the alimentary tract renders them deficient in function for a considerable period after the pyrexial condition has subsided; and it is only by judicious dietary that they can be educated into health, nor will the general anæmia and debility of the body decrease unless this point be carefully attended to.

Tobacco is best withheld from the majority of cases until convalescence is well established, and in all cases where cardiac irritability is present.

Stimulants.—These are very necessary in severe cases, where the digestion being in abeyance, artificial support other than that to be obtained from food is necessary. Under such circumstances a larger amount of alcohol is oxidised in the system than is the case during health; but the amount given in each individual case should not be in excess of that amount which the patient is able to oxidise without having to noticeably excrete alcohol by the lungs or kidneys. When the temperature runs high stimulants are generally needed, and in those cases where signs of nervous exhaustion with a moderate temperature are present they may require to be pushed. Where cardiac failure is present, or the pulse is feeble, stimulants are needed, and a favourable result is often due to their judicious administration. No definite amount of stimulants can be laid down, the condition of the pulse and tongue in each individual case being the best guide to the amount necessary for that particular case, and the effect of stimulants on the rate and character of the pulse should always be carefully noted. In long chronic cases a small amount of alcohol daily is very beneficial, and also during convalescence. The most valuable form in which to administer it is undoubtedly brandy, provided it is good in quality. It may be given in milk, arrow-root, egg flip, soda-water, etc., commencing with two ounces a day and increasing as desired. The early morning (2-6 A.M.) is a time when stimulants may be given with advantage, though this is often overlooked. If brandy is not liked, whisky, moselle, or champagne may be substituted, the last being one of the most valuable forms of stimulants we possess for these cases. Where there is obstinate vomiting or extreme exhaustion, good light dry champagne with a little soda-water may tide over a crisis and save a patient when in an almost hopeless condition. In cases where only beef juice and iced champagne can be retained, there is hope while the circulation is kept going and the lungs are not choked up with passive congestion. As the case progresses and improves, port wine, Graves, or claret may be gradually substituted for the brandy, and when convalescence is established good stout, ale, or burgundy is beneficial.

When we realise that most severe cases die from failure of the circulation, with consequent passive congestion of the lungs, we see plainly that much may be done to accelerate the circulation by increasing the force of the heart's action and so clearing the lungs, and ultimately lessening the work that the heart has to do. On the judicious administration of stimulants (alcohol and ammonia) we greatly rely when endeavouring to attain this necessary object.

In the early morning and at any time when the temperature is subnormal or the patient seems fatigued, a small dose of whisky or brandy is beneficial. Also before sponging or packing.

From a drug point of view there cannot be said to be any specific form of treatment applicable to this fever, as no drug or other medical agent, having a germicidal action on the organism, has been discovered.

From its clinical analogy to paludism one should anticipate the discovery of some such drug, but many and various have been tried without effect. There would appear to be a possibility in favour of the future discovery of some antitoxin treatment.

The fact that the administration of quinine, calomel, carbolic acid, and other germicides has frequently been followed by convalescence within a reasonable period in certain cases of this erratic fever, has led to the advocation of many specifics. These have generally been advocated by comparative new-comers, and have unfortunately failed to hold their own in any way. When the writer began to treat these cases he administered iodide of mercury to three cases of chronic intermittent pyrexia which had for a considerable time withstood treatment. All three cases recovered at once in a most satisfactory manner, and a specific appeared to have been discovered. The writer has failed, however, to cure any further cases with the same remedy. It is a fact, however, that the date of recovery of some chronic cases, dates from the day on which quinine, arsenic, or other germicide has been administered; whereas these drugs have no effect on the majority of these chronic cases, and have a most prejudicial effect on acute cases by aggravating pre-existing gastric irritation. The only explanation is that those cases which recover on the administration of a germicide, would have recovered in any case, or that, either by its tonic or germicidal action, the drug in question may have been of some slight assistance to the human organism, without having any irritating effect on the mucous membrane, in a case which was on the eve of recovery. Individual drugs will be noticed later on.

So far therefore we have laid down—

(1) That the patient should be transferred from insanitary to sanitary surroundings, and supplied with a suitable nurse.
(2) That he should be confined to bed during the acute stages of

the disease, be clothed in absorbent material, and be protected from chills.

(3) That it is of the utmost importance that food and stimulants should be judiciously administered.

It will be further shown that it is necessary—

(4) That the natural processes of excretion, the respiratory, and cardio-circulatory equilibrium should be carefully maintained.

(5) That the temperature should be moderately regulated.

(6) That special treatment is necessary to meet certain symptoms when they arise.

(7) The effects of certain drugs will be discussed, and the advisability or otherwise of change of air and climate dealt with.

In the great majority of cases constipation is present and should be relieved. In a few cases, and those usually of a severe and often fatal type, there is diarrhœa, which if at all persistent is a symptom requiring much consideration.

On admission to hospital any existing constipation should be at once relieved. For this purpose nothing works better than a good dose of calomel combined with powered jalap, or pulv. jalapæ co. If, however, there is any doubt as to the diagnosis between this fever and enteric fever, a castor-oil or simple enema should be used instead. This will often bring a high temperature permanently down. The bowels should be further kept open every other day by the above means, or by doses of compound liquorice powder, cascara sagrada, Hunyadi water, enemata of glycerine or soap, etc. Castor - oil internally is not satisfactory on account of the constipation which so often follows its use. The free use of these remedies at an early stage in the disease seems to mitigate its severity, and to lessen the necessity for their constant use during later stages of the fever. As diarrhœa seems to be often associated with a congested condition of the large or small bowel, such treatment tends rather to prevent than to produce diarrhœa, if used with due caution.

In late stages, when the tongue is fairly clean, stewed prunes, baked apples, etc., are useful in relief of constipation.

Slight diarrhœa, dependent on the condition of the small bowel, is often due to improper food, such as beef tea, excess of milk, etc., or of drugs, such as quinine. In both cases it may be cured by removing the cause and giving lime water with the milk, arrow-root, and if necessary some astringent, with a small dose of opium, or if more severe a pill of lead and opium. Occasionally it is combined with a foul tongue and mouth, possibly tympanites and evidence of gastric and intestinal fermentation, in which case small doses of calomel ($\frac{1}{4}$ to $\frac{1}{2}$ a grain) or grey powder (gr. j.) with sugar of milk, twice or three times a day, often suffices.

The mixture used in Malta for slight diarrhœa dependent upon the condition of the small gut is :—℞ Pulv. cret. aromat. gr. xviij., Tinct. catechu gr. xxv., Tinct. opii. ♏vj., Aqua chloroformi ad ℥j. M. et F. misturam, to be given as required.

When dependent on the condition of the large bowel this diarrhœa is harder to treat. The diet having been attended to, enemata of starch and opium must be frequently administered. These enemata should be made with sufficient boiled starch to produce a consistency like cream, be given warm, and retained as long as possible. At the same time a Dover's powder at night is beneficial. Irrigation with a solution of boracic acid has been advocated.

A record of all stools, with colour, amount, and character should be kept by the nurse, as their appearance, especially in early stages, is a valuable guide to diagnosis, and in all stages as to the state of the intestinal mucous membranes.

The bladder must be watched in severe cases lest retention be missed; while any irritability which may be present is usually removed by the administration of acetate of potash, soda-water, saline diuretics, and attention to diet.

The teeth and gums must be attended to, especially in severe cases, when the breath has a tendency to become foul, the tongue brown and cracked, and the teeth covered with sordes. Such a condition is mostly met with where the diet has not been judiciously regulated, or the temperature has been allowed to remain continuously high. In the former class of case undigested and unsuitable food ferments in the stomach and gives rise to these symptoms. The remedy is to regulate the amount and nature of the food, and to give the patient bismuth, while small doses of calomel, about $\frac{1}{4}$ to $\frac{1}{2}$ a grain, two or three times a day, or salicylic acid in 5 or 10 grain doses, have been recommended to bring about a more healthy condition of the stomach. In these cases the stomach is usually very irritable, and does not tolerate stronger forms of antiseptic treatment, such as boracic acid or iodide of mercury, quinine, arsenic, etc. They are very badly borne, and appear to do more harm than good. Reliance should be placed on methods of treatment which tend to improve the condition of the stomachic mucous membrane, the most important of which are bismuth and suitable dietary, such as peptonised foods, fresh beef juice, champagne, etc.

A return to a more normal condition on the part of the mucous membrane proves the strongest and most reliable form of antiseptic treatment we possess.

The local use of glycerine and borax, lemon juice, etc., to the tongue and gums, or of mouth washes such as rose water, Condy's fluid in weak warm solution, or a solution of carbolic acid (1 in 100) mixed with tincture of myrrh, glycerine and water, are useful as deterrents against local fermentative growths. Where tartar collects on the teeth and they become loose in the gums, a weak solution of sulphate of copper may be used with a tooth-brush.

In summer a mosquito net is often necessary to keep off the swarms of flies which inevitably collect round patients whose mouths and breath are not sweet. A plate of quassia chips in water helps to reduce their numbers if placed on the bedside table. In clean and well-kept hospitals in the Mediterranean, the common house-fly can usually be kept down, except about these severe cases, when their numbers are almost an indication of the severity of the case. In the country houses, and in the less clean houses of the lower classes, they prove a worse pest than the notorious mosquito, and breed with enormous rapidity during the summer months in any house refuse or roadside filth that may exist. In Valetta and other towns where the roads are paved and regularly swept, these and the venomous sand-fly are less numerous, and may be kept from the sick-room by attention to cleanliness, and by carefully arranging for the room to be darker than the outside air during the first half of the day, by closing the blinds or jalouses from 6 A.M. to about 4 P.M. according to the direction of the outlook from the windows. Those who are new to the Mediterranean must also bear in mind that mosquitoes breed with great rapidity in any water that is allowed to stand about during the hot weather; so that the jugs and water-bottles must be emptied every morning and refilled, indoor tanks kept covered, flower-pot saucers banished from the neighbourhood of the sick-room, and garden tanks stocked with gold-fish. Though long familiarity breeds contempt, one musical mosquito within the net, will often prove a great nuisance to a patient, and bring about a sleepless night, while the effect of their bites on new comers is often most unpleasant. Worse still is the sand-fly, as its minute size gives it access through most netting, while small-meshed netting, by restricting the flow of pure air, is very hot. The various incense-burning cures are only efficacious while actually burning, while little short of anointing the exposed surfaces and the feet and ankles with eucalyptus or paraffin oil will stop them from biting. At night a light within an open window attracts both mosquitoes and sand-flies, which when numerous may keep the patient awake for hours.

Prickly heat and sudamina may be largely prevented by due attention to the skin, by careful changing of clothing after perspiration, and by daily sponging of the surface with tepid water to which vinegar or acetic acid has been added, and afterwards dusting with powder. When present the affected surface should be frequently washed with soap and water, bathed with boracic acid solution, and carefully dried but not rubbed. If the irritation is excessive, it may often be allayed by a surface coating of some unirritating soap, applied by damping a cake of soap and gently passing it over the affected part. This coating should be left on until the next washing with boracic acid. Such treatment will often procure sleep for a patient, when otherwise he would be the victim for hours of increasing sleepless irritation. When sudamina become pustular they should be pricked, squeezed, and washed frequently with boracic acid solution, care being taken that the surrounding skin is well washed. When boils appear they are the result of an infection, by a separate organism, on an enfeebled constitution, and should be treated on sound surgical principles. Evacuation, followed by a dressing of boracic acid lint, soaked in warm boracic acid solution, and kept damp by a covering of gutta-percha tissue and a bandage, proves most satisfactory. The great point is to get rid of the pus, to deter the growth of the organism without using antiseptic solutions whose strength will in any way irritate or lessen the fighting power of the enfeebled and anæmic skin. At the same time the healthy skin all round the boil should be well washed with boracic or even stronger antiseptic solutions, to prevent the not uncommon spread of the organism to other spots along the surface of the skin. Thus the writer has seen a crop of boils on the inside of one thigh affect the opposite thigh, by direct contact for want of a protective dressing. It is very necessary that boils be attended to, for though of slight consequence in themselves in healthy individuals, in subjects who have become enfeebled and debilitated in the course of this fever, they may become the starting-point of bed-sores of a most intractable nature. The same treatment is useful in the case of the small abscesses which are occasionally met with.

The greatest care should be taken to guard against the formation of bed-sores, for so emaciated may patients become, in the course of this fever, that the skin covering their bony prominences is very prone to suffer, and must therefore be carefully watched. It is well to institute a routine practice by which all patients are rubbed with spirit and water or other hardening agent, and treated with oxide of zinc, starch, etc., from the beginning of the attack. When emaciation is present, air or water beds and suitable cushions should be employed, suspicious points protected from pressure, and actual sores treated early.

In severe cases, in the acute stages, the patient's skin is often hot and dry, when it is advisable to promote elimination by means of some diaphoretic mixture. This should be given warm at night with a little brandy, and an attempt made to promote a perspiration at about the time at which it would occur if the case were less severe. In these cases also a routine practice of sponging the surface of the body with tepid water, with some ammonia, vinegar, or acetic acid added to it, two or three times a day, is comforting and beneficial.

In the majority of cases, however, there is more to complain of from excessive sweating than from the reverse. When this occurs (usually but not necessarily in the middle of the night) the patient's sleeping clothes, sheets, and pillow-case will require changing once, twice, or oftener. A supply of these articles, well dried, aired, and warmed in cold weather, should be ready at hand. A spare dry pillow should be kept in reserve until the sweating has quite ceased, and then substituted for the one in use. The patient should on no account be allowed to remain in his damp clothes, and he should be protected from chill during any changing operations. It is not advisable to attempt to check the perspirations by means of drugs, as they appear to be beneficial in their action, except perhaps in long-continued cases where much debility is present, in which case they have a depressing effect. Want of cleanliness and attention to the dryness of the patient's buttocks, and to the changing of soiled sheets, are common sources of bed-sores.

Lung troubles are aggravated by dust and draughts, and by feeble circulation or heart's action, as has already been mentioned. The maintenance of an equable temperature of the air of the sick-room is advisable, and even the variation in temperature and air humidity which accompany the use of punkahs over the beds of patients, has been found in Malta to increase the frequency of neuralgic and lung complications, nor does the freshening of the air achieved by the use of punkahs compensate for their prejudicial effect on these cases. Congestion of the lungs is best treated by stimulating expectorants such as sal volatile, alcohol, etc., and by the application of a flannel jacket to the chest. When severe and when consolidation is present, jacket poultices followed by a cotton-wool jacket, have a most beneficial effect, but it must be remembered that this condition is usually the result of stasis from enfeebled circulation, and should be treated early by appropriate means. The lungs should, therefore, be carefully watched and measures taken directly congestion appears, to prevent matters going further towards consolidation. In some cases it may be that the virus directly attacks the lungs, as pneumonic symptoms are so very common in this affection, and it is in these cases that warm applications, by their stimulating effects, work the greatest relief. Cold sponging, by reducing temperature and stimulating the lungs and heart, indirectly aids in preventing pneumonic congestion.

The chest should be strapped when intercostal neuralgia or pleurodynia are present, and a warm woollen vest worn next the skin. It is always advisable for patients to wear a short flannel jacket during the day, at which time their chest and arms are not covered by the bedclothes as at night. Pleuritis should be treated on general principles.

The dry irritable cough occasionally met with is very difficult to alleviate. Ipecacuanha, squills, and small doses of opium may be tried.

When organic cardiac disease is present great care is necessary. The heart and lungs must be carefully watched, and stimulants applied early, before pneumonic congestion appears. The same care must be taken when the heart shows signs of weak action or flagging. In these cases much may be effected by the judicious use of alcohol. Stimulants should not be given until some symptom clearly indicates that they are needed, and then with some definite object in view, and in sufficient quantities to effect that object. They are too often given as an almost routine practice in this fever, and when most required have not the same effect as when they are reserved until really required. General principles must guide in their administration, but they will be found most useful when symptoms of heart failure occur during the summit of a pyrexial wave. If the heart can be kept at work for a few days it will usually recover its equilibrium again when the temperature falls. The slowing of the pulse, following cold sponging and the internal administration of alcohol in these cases, is a valuable rest to the heart. Small doses of strychnia and digitalis are also useful in these cases, especially when signs of palpitation or intermittent heart's action are present. In many cases the writer has known digitalis improve the pulse and tide over a most critical period. Strychnia and iron are also good cardiac tonics in long cases, where there is a tendency to irregular action of the heart on slight exertion.

The initial cephalalgia, and that occurring during an attack whenever the temperature rises higher than usual, should be treated by local application of cold-water rags or ice.

The so-called fever pains, the headache, and sleeplessness so often met with at the beginning of an attack, are best treated by a draught of bromide of potassium and morphia at night for the first two or three days. It increases the comfort of the patient, allays the pain, anxiety, and mental irritation attending the onset of severe attacks; and while by inducing sleep it improves the general condition of the patient in many ways, it need seldom be continued, as the habit of sleeping under novel pyrexial circumstances is soon acquired. A small dose frequently increases the nervous excitability, and fails to produce sound dreamless sleep, so that a full dose should be given, when a draught is given at all. For the ordinary soldier a drachm of liq. morph. hydrochlor. with 20 to 30 grains of bromide of potassium, in water, is suitable. For officers and females a smaller dose may suffice.

During the course of an attack, mostly when the temperature is rising at the beginning of a wave, hypnotics are occasionally necessary. In the majority of cases sulphonal or a Dover's powder will be found the most suitable remedies. In very severe relapses, however, and when there is a tendency to "typhoid symptoms," the first-mentioned draught may be given; and when there are marked abdominal or intestinal symptoms, opium may prove of value.

When peripheral or other symptoms are referable to central cerebro-spinal irritation, bromide of potassium should be given in fairly frequent doses. When such symptoms are due to an acute attack on a definite portion of the nervous system, morphia gives great relief when given during the few days on which the pain is most acute, for by lessening the acute pain it allows the patient to rest in some fixed position and obtain sleep. Those who have lain awake at night, with the throbbing, gnawing pain of such attacks, altering their position in bed every few minutes without gaining relief, can only thoroughly appreciate the blessing of sleep during the height of an acute attack of this nature. Where there have been symptoms of severe cerebral irritation or intercranial pressure, the use of the ice-bag with iodide of potassium have given relief. In a very severe case the inunction of the trunk with mercury ointment produced marked but only temporary relief. A catheter may be necessary in such cases.

Acute neuralgia of peripheral nerves, due apparently to local inflammation, the acute inflamed bursal swellings, and swollen joints, are best treated by at once placing the patient between blankets, and locally by hot fomentations, hot arm or foot baths, etc. This application of moist heat, as hot as the patient can bear it, should be continued until the pain and tension are relieved or bearable. After this, local applications of opium and belladonna, or equal parts of the liquid extract of belladonna and glycerine, give relief. The whole of the affected part should be wrapped in cotton-wool or flannel bandages, and placed in a position of rest in such a way as to prevent those muscles from acting which are inserted into, or adjacent to the inflamed parts. When the nerves of the limbs are affected, flannel drawers, or vests with sleeves may be worn.

Flannel or woollen material next the skin and warm clothing should be worn for some months after the pyrexia has ceased, especially in cold and changeable climates, as patients are liable to attacks of neuralgic pain on exposure to cold, for a considerable period after apparent recovery.

When the pain and tenderness of inflammations of nerves, joints, bursæ, etc., remain in a chronic condition, massage, counter-irritation with liniments or blisters, electricity and warm baths, are useful. A visit during convalescence to some warm mineral or sulphur baths has proved beneficial. Such patients also like to have some sort of liniment to rub with; those used mostly in Malta have been the linimentum sapon. co.; equal parts of the linimentum bellad. and linimentum camph. co.; or equal parts of the linimentum opii. and linimentum sinap. co.

If joints continue to give pain on movement, or do not return readily to their normal size, a Scott's dressing (ung. hydrarg. co. on strips of lint, under strapping) often does good. Passive motion, massage, or rubbing with some simple form of stimulating liniment, serve to relieve stiffness. Some pain, however, often remains in certain nerves, such as the sciatic, until the general health has improved and the anæmia disappeared. Attention should, therefore, be especially directed towards this point, and the patient suitably dieted, given plenty of fresh air, and some form of tonic. Cod-liver oil, Blaud's pills, small doses of arsenic (provided no gastric irritability exists), or iodide of potassium, may be beneficial.

For the excessive pain and hyperæsthesia which occasionally affects the soles of the feet, nothing has given so much relief as soaking the foot or feet in cold water, or in a wrapping of cold-water bandages. If a basin of cold water is securely fixed at the bottom of the bed, or on a chair close by, the patient, without leaving his horizontal position in bed, can by bending his knees place a foot in the basin and keep it there as long as necessary.

Regulation of temperature.—"In a moderate regulation of the temperature" lies the secret of safe and successful treatment, until the discovery of some specific germicidal remedy. The temperature should never be allowed to remain continuously high for any length of time, for in such cases, when dangerous symptoms actually appear, the patient will be found to have lost the strength necessary for combating with the disease. A fatal result due to hyperpyrexia at an early stage in the disease is almost always due to an early neglect of this precaution.

Pyrexia is only one of the symptoms of this disease, and though it is the most constant one, it does not appear to be in itself dangerous when not excessive, that is to say, when it does not rise above 103° F. Above 103° F., especially if it remain continuously above that point, pyrexia of itself becomes a source of danger, either by reason of its exhausting effect upon the nervous system when long continued, or by reason of its excessive height being incompatible with life, causing death from the direct effects of hyperpyrexia, as is the case in a large proportion of fatal cases treated by the expectant method. We find by experience that a routine practice of keeping the temperature below 103° F. and so approximating severe cases as far as possible to those of a milder type, abolishes mortality early in the attack, largely diminishes the total mortality, avoids to a great extent the more serious complications, and does not add any bad symptoms to our cases when due care is taken in carrying out the treatment. When antipyretic treatment is carelessly or unscientifically carried out there is often much harm done, but this may be said of many other forms of recognised treatment. Again, there appears to be a certain amount of liability to shock and other undesirable symptoms when such treatment is carried to excess, by the temperature being brought down too much or too quickly at any one time. This can, however, be easily avoided if proper care be taken. Cases whose temperature remains below 103° F. rarely give cause for alarm, but when severe symptoms do arise in such instances the cases belong to one of two classes :—(1) Cases of long standing, with possibly cardiac complications, which are suffering from extreme anæmia with nervous and cardiac debility. In such cases any strong emotion, excitement, or nervous shock may cause serious and even fatal symptoms. (2) Cases comparable with instances of ptomaine poisoning, in which the alarming symptoms are due to the presence in the blood of non-pyogenous, but even more fatal toxins. Whether these substances are formed by the micrococcus of undulant fever, or by other micro-organisms in the tissues, or whether they are formed in the intestine and absorbed into the blood from there, we cannot say. In such cases we have to support the circulation and general strength of the patient by every means in our power, and any attempt at the administration of antipyretic treatment against a symptom not at the time excessive, is not only unscientific in the extreme, but is followed by serious if not fatal nervous depression and collapse.

In ordinary cases, in which the temperature does not rise above 103° F., direct antipyretic interference is, in this fever, in the present state of our knowledge, theoretically uncalled for, and while *practically* it does not appear to advance matters, it may obscure the early pyrexial indication of the onset of some local complication. Cantani[1] even suggests (as indeed Sydenham taught) that moderate pyrexia has a beneficent effect in the progress of a fever; and that by diminishing the virulence of the cause and aiding phagocytosis, it has a kind of sterilising effect.[2] Hare says that "moderate fever has been proved to be in itself harmless. Hyperpyrexia is of itself harmful. Moderate pyrexia has a useful function to perform in the body in the presence of an infection."[3] It is the experience of all those who have suffered from severe or long attacks of this fever, that they feel much more comfortable and less depressed in the afternoon when their temperature is moderately high, than during a period of normal or subnormal morning temperature, and that a fall to normal of a permanent nature is most depressing. As we have already mentioned starvation can be carried to greater lengths in those suffering from pyrexia than in those with normal or subnormal temperatures. Moderate pyrexia would therefore appear to the author, both personally as a sufferer and in his patients, to have a direct or indirect *stimulating* effect, while a reduction of marked amount is followed by temporary nervous depression, a condition we wish to avoid in those suffering from acute pyrexia, and who have still their battle to fight.

Although it has not yet been *proved* that moderate pyrexia, *per se* (apart from the action of the virus and its non-pyogenetic products), has an injurious effect upon the tissues, or that a certain amount of temperature is necessary for the production of immunity, the writer can scarcely think that pyrexia, even if necessary in fever infection, is more useful or less harmful to the tissues than is inflammation to the healing of a wound, though, like the latter, it may be necessary to combat microorganisms when present. Certain it is, however, that high temperatures are injurious to the delicate central nervous tissues, and that very high temperatures are incompatible with life. We must therefore steer a rational course between needless and harmful interference and life-preserving treatment. As long, therefore, as a case remains mild, from a pyrexia point of view, it will be better to withhold symptomatic antipyretic treatment, until some germicidal antipyretic is discovered, in the realms of materia medica or serum-therapy, for this fever, with an action similar to that of quinine in ague or mercury in syphilis.

In cases whose range of temperature exceeds 103° F. there is danger to the patient from the action on his nervous and other tissues of this pyrexial symptom alone, in direct proportion to the height of that temperature and to the length of time during which it is maintained. Such danger, it may be to life, can only be avoided by early and syste-

[1] *Trans. Int. Med. Congress*, Berlin, 1890.

[2] Hale White, *Brit. Med. Journal*, November 17th, 1894, vol. ii. p. 1093. Dr. Munk, in a lecture by Sir Dyce Duckworth, *Brit. Med. Jour.* vol. ii. p. 258, August 1st, 1896.

[3] *Therapeutic Gazette*, Feb. 15th, 1896. See also Roy, "Protective Mechanisms," *Brit. Med. Journ.* vol. ii. p. 310.

matic reduction of temperature by artificial means. Of the various means at our disposal nothing answers so well as the external application of cold by means of water, nothing is more unsatisfactory than the action of the various antipyretic drugs at present in use. For we must remember that mere elevation of the temperature is not to be attacked as if it were itself the disease, but to be considered rather as a rough index of the intensity of the activity of the virus or of the sensibility of the individual to its action. Nothing is more certain than that the administration of depressing, and even toxic, antipyretic drugs as a routine practice is to be most strongly condemned. These drugs should be confined to two conditions, and even then, as will be shown later on, with certain restrictions in the case of different drugs. (*a*) During the first few days before the patient has, so to speak, become accustomed to his pyrexia, when a dose of some antipyretic drug, while reducing the temperature, also brings on a refreshing perspiration, followed by a relief of headache and the much-needed sleep—a condition which can also be obtained by means of tepid or cold-water sponging. (*b*) With certain exceptions in some conditions of hyperpyrexia early in an attack. Individual antipyretics will be dealt with in the section on drugs.

In the method of temperature reduction by the application of external cold by means of water, we have a most flexible agent, capable of being applied in various ways, at various temperatures, and applicable to every case. This method has all the properties of the various antipyretic drugs, has none of their many disadvantages, and above all, besides reducing the temperature, it goes farther, and by its stimulating effects upon the respiration, circulation, metabolic and eliminatory processes, it has a direct action upon the cause of the fever, thereby having a somewhat specific effect. By aiding in the removal of toxic substances from the blood it leads to an abatement in the severity of the attack, an increased resistance and fighting power on the part of the patient, and a state of equilibrium among the various organs of the body, thereby giving the patient an absence of dangerous symptoms in the present and a reasonable chance of recovery in the future. In fact, this useful form of treatment may be said to have the following properties when employed to obtain a moderate and safe range of pyrexia. Besides the small amount of actual heat it removes from the surface of the body, by its action on the large capillary and glandular integumentary surface of the body it promotes excretion and elimination. By its powerful reflex action upon the numerous cutaneous nerves it stimulates the respiratory centre, producing full and strong respirations in place of frequent and shallow ones, so helping to clear the lungs and increase the oxygenation of the blood. By the same action it also stimulates the cardiac centre, gives rest to the over-burdened heart by causing a stronger and less frequent action, and by accelerating the circulation, removes stasis in the lungs and other internal organs. The improved circulation and oxygenation of the blood promotes metabolism, and carries the leucocytes to all parts of the body, while the increase in blood-pressure and local capillary blood-supply in the kidneys, lungs, etc., promotes elimination of noxious products. This last point has been proved in other fevers by the experimental researches of Juergansen, Roque, Weil, and others. They find that the amount of urea and toxicity of the urine and of carbon dioxide in the expired air are largely increased during such treatment, which is not the case with antipyrin. The improvement in the condition and clearness of the mental faculties, the refreshing sleep, the improved digestive powers, and the permanent abatement of excessive pyrexia which follows this treatment in undulant fever, cannot but be due to a similar action. Lastly, the avoidance of the dangerous toxic effects of hyperpyrexia upon the higher nerve centres is a most valuable property of the cold-water treatment.

During the last six years the writer has employed this treatment extensively, and though he has to regret many instances in which he either neglected it or began its application at too late a point in the attack, he has not once met with a case in which he regretted its rational application, but, on the contrary, believes that many of his severe cases have to thank such treatment for their recovery. He has not used baths, as they necessitate a considerable amount of labour on the part of attendants and are more worrying to the patient, while sponging, ice-water towels or sheets, and packing, have been found to adequately meet all cases.

In applying the antipyrexial cold-water treatment do not wait until a fatal result is anticipated, but begin the treatment as early as possible, and let it be carried out systematically and whenever necessary, avoiding a spasmodic or intermittent administration. In many cases it is sufficient to lay down that the temperature be taken three times a day, viz. at 9 A.M., 2-3 P.M., and 6 P.M.; or at 9 A.M., 5 P.M., and 8 P.M.; and that the patient be then sponged with tepid, tap, cold, or iced water according to circumstances, if his temperature be at or above 103° F., and until it has been reduced to 102° F., or slightly below. It is found by experience that all patients do not respond to the application of cold with equal readiness or rapidity. Thus while tepid sponging is sufficient in one case, tap, iced water, or even ice packing is necessary to produce similar results in others. In some cases the temperature falls slowly, in others more rapidly, and in rare cases with such extreme rapidity that unless care be taken, before it is anticipated it may fall below normal, and warm blankets, hot bottles, and stimulants be necessary to bring about reaction. It is therefore wise to restrict iced water and the use of ice packs to experienced and reliable persons only, though the majority of nurses may safely sponge with tap or tepid water. A little brandy may be given, before sponging or packing, to many patients with advantage. The temperature should be taken immediately before the sponging is begun, and every three or four minutes during the operation, unless the effect of external cold on the particular individual is well known, when it need probably not be taken quite so frequently. As soon as the temperature has fallen two or three degrees, provided it be below 103° F., the sponging should be discontinued, the patient dried and placed in a warm, dry sleeping suit. In any case the temperature should be brought down to about 102° F., but not below 101° F. In ordinary cases of high temperature a great deal more success is obtained by bringing it down two or three degrees at a time than by bringing it down a greater amount, the maximum amount of advantage being reaped with the least amount of disadvantage. Certain it is that success is *not* gained by bringing the temperature down to normal or thereabouts, whereas the moderate course, without causing any bad symptoms, refreshes the patient, braces his nervous system, relieving headache and delirium, promotes tegumentary, respiratory, and urinary excretion, causes the heart's action to become stronger and less frequent, increases the force of the respirations, avoids the dangers of hyperpyrexia, and is usually followed by a refreshing sleep. Usually this artificial reduction of temperature is followed by a slight reactional rise from an hour to an hour and a half afterwards. This is more marked in cases where the artificial reduction has been excessive, while in those in which it has been moderate as recommended, the after-rise is rarely much or long continued, but is followed by some perspiration, sleep, and a permanent reduction of pyrexia.

The clinical appearances would lead one to believe that a certain amount of pyrexia is a necessary and so to speak normal condition in this fever, and that the constitution is able to successfully combat with such a condition. When, however, for some reason or other the pyrexia gains the upper hand, the balance of equilibrium is destroyed, and it becomes an open question as to whether the patient or the fever will prove the stronger. By bringing the temperature down by artificial means within safe limits, we give the patient's heart and other tissues rest and renewed strength, and at the same time restore equilibrium. The rest which is given to the heart is a most valuable point in the treatment, for if the failure of this organ to pump the blood through the lungs, and indeed to beat at all, that is the immediate cause of death in cases whose fatal issue is dependent on high temperature. A lessening in frequency of one beat a minute is equal to 1440 beats in the twenty-four hours, which is equivalent to a valuable rest when the diminution in the number of beats per minute can be expressed in two figures. The stimulation of the respiratory centre and increase in the strength of the cardiac action not only help to clear the lungs, and by raising the blood pressure and increasing the circulation to carry off waste and noxious products by stimulating excretion, but also by so doing causes a lessening amount of cardiac work to be necessary, and so leads to the establishment of a permanent state of equilibrium between the heart and its work. The beneficial action of the treatment on the nervous system is shown by the replacement of delirium, nervous excitement, or insomnia, by a refreshing and quiet sleep; while the return to consciousness from hyperpyrexial coma is too well known in other diseases to need description here.

The writer has obtained excellent results by sponging his cases with tepid, tap, or iced water according to the height of the individual's temperature and the manner in which it reacts to treatment; while in severe cases, and when acute hyperpyrexia has been present, he has employed ice packing. The actual manner of application and the form of treatment applied is a matter of experience and opinion, and the medical attendant must be guided as to whether he will employ sponging, packing, or bathing, by his own knowledge of the treatment, by the reaction of the individual patient to cold, and above all by the amount of reliance he is able to place in the nurse or other attendant at his disposal. The writer has made a rule of invariably being present when the ice-pack is to be used, but has been able, in the case of hospital patients, to trust sponging with tap or even iced water to a reliable nurse. Too much care cannot be taken when giving directions in these matters, and the effects of treatment on the pyrexial curve should be most carefully registered on the chart as a guide to further treatment. The effects of following out published forms of treatment in an irrational and dangerous manner was most apparent in a case of this fever, complicated with double catarrhal pneumonia, which, the writer was told, was treated with ice on one lung and hot jacket poultices on the other! Though both are acknowledged forms of treatment, the combination of the two at one time was followed by fatal results.

It is well at all times to avoid chill when applying this treatment, and as patients are prone in this disease to pneumonic troubles, the writer usually avoids applying ice or ice water to the chest except in severe cases where prompt and heroic treatment is necessary. Usually the legs, arms, and abdomen prove sufficient surface for the application of sponging or ice-water towels. In some cases the application of towels to the arms and legs is soon followed by a reduction of temperature, while a few cases are met with in which one ice-water towel on the arm or leg has made a difference of two or three degrees in short time. With these last-mentioned cases the susceptibility to antipyretic treatment is so great, that a full ice-pack or a moderate dose of antipyrin may be followed by serious collapse. Though these cases are uncommon they should be borne in mind.

As an aid and guide to treatment, the writer has been in the habit of drawing a dark line along that marking the level on the chart of a temperature of 103° F. This marks the point between a safe and unsafe temperature, and though arbitrary in nature, proves useful. It is better not to mark it in red ink, nor to tell the patient much about its use, as in this fever patients are apt to watch their chart, when allowed, with absorbent interest, and to suffer detrimental worry on account of its many fluctuations and relapses. The addition of a "danger line" to their calculations would not add to their comfort. From the same point of view all mental worry and excitement should be avoided, such as the frequent or unnecessary visits of friends, business and official work, etc., for, as has been shown, these all tend to elevate the temperature. The effects of the damp sirocco wind in elevating the temperature has been also mentioned.

When applying this treatment, whether sponging, pack, or baths be the method in use, friction in the form of surface massage or rubbing is a useful addition, as it assists in promoting the cutaneous capillary circulation and excretion.

Patients vary very much in the way in which the pyrexia of this disease affects them. One patient may be seriously ill at 102° F., another may not appear to be much affected by a temperature of 104° F. These points must be borne in mind and allowance made for special idiosyncrasies when moderating pyrexia, though as a general rule the arbitrary line at 103° F. will be found to divide moderate from excessive temperature.

This moderate regulation of temperature must not be confounded with the tepid or warm-water sponging which every patient should undergo each morning. It replaces the morning bath when the patient is confined to bed. It is most necessary, on account of the profuse diaphoresis, to keep the skin in order and to promote its healthy action. In hot weather and during the moist Mediterranean sirocco (or Levanter, etc.) winds it may often be beneficially repeated in the evening, as it makes the patient comfortable and ready for sleep. As pyrexial symptoms diminish, and the morning temperature remains normal, the patient may be allowed to take a warm bath, at his leisure, about 10 A.M., if the weather is cold, before a fire.

The chief point during early convalescence is to guard against relapses. It is impossible to say when a patient is safe in this respect, as relapses have been known to occur after one or two months of apparent convalescence.

Over-exertion, either mental or physical, is probably the most frequent cause of relapse; chills, accidental catarrhs, sore-throats, etc., less common exciting causes.

The first aim should be to provide the patient with clean country air. The locality should be inland and somewhat bracing, but sheltered from the coldest winds, and free from damp on account of the tendency to neuralgic sequelæ in this disease. Change, of scene and locality, often proves a valuable mental stimulant. With due regard to the avoidance of fatigue, damp and cold, the patient should be in the open air as much as possible. This can usually be managed where there is a garden, and abroad where there are usually verandahs to the hospitals and houses. In the Mediterranean the weather is warm enough for this at most times of the year during some part of the day; but in England it is difficult during the damp cold weather of autumn and winter. In the former place, again, the heat of summer and the depressing sirocco winds are prejudicial to convalescence. This question is again dealt with in the section on invaliding. A great number of patients improve largely in health and often lose their fever during a voyage to England.

Besides the mental stimulation of going home, these patients spend a great part of their time on deck, in clean fresh air, in a situation where fatigue can be altogether avoided. The writer cannot help feeling that this has all to do with their improvement in health, the actual fact that they have left the place where their fever was contracted, a point insisted on by many Maltese practitioners, having but a small significance. Patients sent home to England from the Mediterranean during the depressing heat of the summer (*i.e.* before September) do well, but of those sent home during the autumn and winter, the same cannot be said. The most favourable months for recovery in England are from the beginning of June to the end of August, to which may often be added the month of May. The corresponding favourable months in the Mediterranean, especially in the sanatoria of Italy and Sicily, are from the middle of October to the end of April.

Diet must be carefully attended to especially in prolonged cases, in which the anæmic and irritable mucous membranes and torpid liver must be gradually coaxed into activity. Too great a quantity of food should not be taken at one time. To a liberal supply of milk, eggs, fruit, game and fish, should be added the usual plain meals in moderation. A glass of milk before rising, a cup of soup in the middle of the morning, and a glass of milk by the bedside, should be provided. Above all, let meals be supplied *punctually* at fixed times. An occasional whisky with water or soda, when indicated, is useful, and burgundy or stout are often beneficial with meals during convalescence.

Mental work should be put aside if it causes the slightest tendency to worry, irritation, headache, or even difficulty in mental concentration. Exercise is very beneficial in strict moderation, and like food it should be taken in small quantities at a time. Riding and cycling should not be indulged in until convalescence is well established. There is a great temptation when cycling to go too far from home, to over-work up hill, etc. Again, when there is the least tendency to occurrence of pyrexial rises, these by masking the sense of fatigue lead to the patient doing more than he would otherwise do, and so increasing the pyrexia and risking a relapse. Gentle walking exercise is best at first, and infinitely better than driving or bath-chair exercise. The walk can be accurately measured from a hundred yards onwards, while when driving, the patient is apt to find the sitting position fatiguing when some way from home, whereas when walking he will scarcely get far from home when liable to such fatigue. He can rest at frequent intervals, and even arrange to be driven the short distance home if necessary. Walking, moreover, has a therapeutical effect on the circulation, the muscles, bowels, etc. Personally, when convalescing after a long attack the writer preferred rest in the open air with short walks, to any carriage or bath-chair exercise. While exercise is being taken in small quantities as often as advisable, rest, both mental and physical, should be taken in large quantities. All meals should be taken in bed at first, and breakfast also, until the patient is quite strong. His reading should be of a light nature, and while his temperature is above normal he should be read to rather than read himself. Many patients find wool-work, embroidery, or games of patience with cards, help to pass the time without causing undue mental fatigue.

Warm clothes should be worn (especially when there is a tendency to subnormal temperature) with woollen material next the skin. Patients sent home from the Mediterranean must be provided with warmer clothes for wear when nearing England. For a considerable time they will feel every change in the weather, and unless due care be taken to protect them from chills, obstinate sciatica or other neuralgic condition may be set up and prove most intractable. They must study the weather, and dress accordingly. Pain and stiffness in the joints and tendons, especially after remaining long in one position, cause much trouble at first in patients who have been long confined to bed. It is much relieved by wearing warm clothes, boots rather than shoes, massage or soaking in hot water at night. It gradually wears off with moderate exercise, especially cycling, at a latter stage in convalescence. Tenderness of the soles of the feet is also very marked at first after a lengthened stay in bed. They may be hardened by soaking in alum and water.

Hair that has fallen out will gradually return with improved health. The scalp should not, however, be allowed to get too dry, and should be treated with some stimulating and mildly oleaginous wash.

Preparations of iron are useful when anæmia and tendency to œdema of the ankles are present. The writer usually administers iron in the form of Blaud's pills to convalescents, with apparently good results. Easton's syrup is also useful. The last preparation, or strychnia alone in small doses, will be found beneficial where there is a tendency to palpitation on exertion or to nervous exhaustion. Stomachic and bitter tonics often improve the appetite and general health, a useful one being nitro-hydrochloric acid (freshly prepared) with the compound tincture of gentian, before meals. The writer has been in the habit of administering small doses of quinine (two to five grains of the bisulphide three times a day before meals), after all tendency to active pyrexial symptoms and gastric irritation have disappeared. This drug, which during the acute stages of the fever does more harm than good, during real convalescence appears to have its uses. There is then no gastric irritability to aggravate, while as a tonic it seems to give tone to the stomach, heart, and nervous systems in these small doses. It appears to have a further action on the temperature curve of a steadying nature. If the temperature be carefully taken during convalescence, it is found, especially after long attacks, to vary during the day even in cases in whom the body-weight has reached or exceeded the normal. In the morning it will be found to be below 98° F., and in the evening, and more especially after cycling or such other exercise, to reach even 99° F., the total variation of from 1° to 2° being as great as is often present in intermittent cases during active disease. This variation is, however, mostly below the normal line, and may continue for months after all pyrexia due to actual infection has quite disappeared, and in persons whose temperature before the attack had been found by actual and prolonged observation to maintain a constant level. The amount of this variation is proportionate to the physical (and in some cases the mental) exercise taken; the maximum height following the exercise, the minimum height (or maximum of fall) following this rise as a sort of reaction. This variation is also associated during and after the fall by a proportional amount of fatigue or nervous exhaustion. It does not appear to depend upon the pyrexial effects of infection, nor to be due to the action of the micro-organism of the fever in any way, but to a weakening of the nervous mechanism of body-heat regulation, when it is acted upon by external conditions. The exact pathology of this pyrexial variation would prove a difficult question to determine, but the inability to maintain an exact level under all circumstances, after being, so to speak, out of regular working order for a long period (from three to twelve months or more), is comparable with the debility of the rest of the body, and its inability for a time to resist strain upon any of its mechanism whether simple or highly complicated.[1] Whatever it is due to, these small doses of quinine seem to have a steadying effect and so to be beneficial. The writer has also an opinion, based upon a number of cases treated with and without this drug, that it helps in preventing relapses to a certain extent. In the form of compressed tabloids it is easily carried about and administered.

Again, when all signs of gastric irritation have disappeared the writer has administered small doses of arsenic to a number of cases. They increased in weight and their anæmia decreased, no untoward symptoms arising. In these the drug appeared to be responsible for some of the improvement, when their progress was compared with the cases left without drugs during convalescence.

Action of Certain Drugs

Quinine.—So prevalent is the idea that there must be a "malarial" taint at the root of Mediterranean fever, and so universal has the use of quinine for "fever" become among the laity, that it is not surprising that this drug should have been frequently tried as a remedy for this fever, in spite of failure after failure. The writer has employed it in various doses and ways without any specific result being obtained, the fever going on unchecked in spite of continued administration, and in acute cases its administration has usually been followed by an increase in severity of the symptoms. This has been the experience of other observers, who with the writer limit its use to the convalescent stage, when it may occasionally be useful as a tonic.

Marston (1861) says: "Quinine almost invariably disagrees with the patient during the earlier stages of the disease." Guilia (1871) says much the same.

[1] For somewhat similar variation in temperature during health, see Croonian Lectures 1897 (Dr. Hale White), *Brit. Med. Journ.* June 26th, etc.

Boileau (1865) says: "Quinine was given occasionally during convalescence. I believe, however, that this medicine might be banished from Malta without much loss to the station."

Chartres (1865) says: "In prescribing quinine in this disease, and having fairly tried it during remissions under many forms and in various combinations and doses, I confess to have met with much disappointment; its antiperiodic power was almost nil; its tonic or restorative properties extremely doubtful. In heroic doses it was positively detrimental."

Oswald Wood (1876) says: "Quinine appears to possess no remedial qualities in this fever."

Veale (1879) says: "Quinine has been given in doses varying from three to eighty grains per diem, but without beneficial effect. Indeed, the large doses do more harm than good."

Surgeon Gipps, R.N. (1890) says: "Quinine in this disease is absolutely useless, and in fact worse than useless. This is agreed to by all observers. There is already sufficient gastric irritation present without administering a bitter drug dissolved in an acid; added to which it has not the slightest effect on the fever."

Bruce (1893) says: "As the result of many observations on the action of this drug in Malta fever, I can assert that quinine has absolutely no beneficial influence whatever, and if pushed, as is too often the case, is deleterious."

Many others who have treated this fever in Gibraltar, Cyprus, Italy, and elsewhere, have published similar remarks, while the opinion of medical officers that the writer has met with in the Mediterranean have with few exceptions coincided with these views. The tendency to spontaneous cure, when it has coincided with the administration of this or any other drug, has led some persons with a limited experience to lay stress on a particular drug, the more extended use of which has proved its inefficacy. The writer is convinced that this has been the case with the above few exceptions, an opinion based on a personal acquaintance with the practitioners in question.

In the writer's experience quinine in its various forms has had no specific action on the virus of this fever. In acute cases with gastric irritability large doses are vomited, while moderate doses increase the irritability and general depression, and so do more harm than good. In less acute and intermittent cases it appears to have no beneficial effect, while its continued absorption into the blood has a paralysing effect upon the leucocytes, limits oxygenation, metabolism, and excretion (Mitchell Bruce). Its antipyretic effects in this fever are slight, transitory, and in most cases unmarked, while its antiperiodic effects are nil. Where in severe cases it does good, there is apparently a certain amount of septic absorption from the intestine going on, its antipyretic effects being in inverse ratio to the pureness in type of the fever. This is the case whether the drug is administered by the mouth, rectum, or hypodermically. Its action in this fever is somewhat similar to its action on the pyrexia of so-called hectic fever. The only instances in which the writer has found it of use have been in the very late stages immediately before convalescence, in which the appetite has been established, the patient allowed to have certain solid food, and to get up for a time each day, when small doses (two to five grains at most, twice or three times a day) have assisted in steadying the temperature, and stopping the very slight nocturnal rises which seem to almost have become a habit. In such cases, without causing gastric disturbance, it has had a tonic effect, improving the appetite and digestion, stimulating the heart and circulation, and by so increasing the general bodily health has aided the patient in throwing off the small remains of the fever. Quinine has a similar tonic action during convalescence when the febrile stage has ceased.

Bismuth in the form of the subnitrate (most easily taken in capsules), is a most valuable remedy in the gastric derangement that is to be met with almost invariably in acute cases of this fever. It has a sedative and astringent action on the mucous membrane locally, and so by allaying the gastric irritation promotes digestion, and by this means improves the general health and strength of the patient. It should be given to all cases in which there is a foul, coated tongue, with offensive breath, pyrosis, and other signs of imperfect digestion. Many of these gastric symptoms appear to be due to fermentation of imperfectly digested food, as does much of the occasional diarrhœa. The remarkable way in which this condition often yields to doses of from ten to twenty grains of the subnitrate of bismuth given three times a day, combined, in very severe cases with high temperature, with small doses of pepsin or with peptonised milk, has led the writer to believe that this drug has some further action than that of a local mechanical sedative. This experience has received support from the recent writings of Carles,[1] Gayon, and others; and by the fact that such small doses as ten to fifteen grains repeated three times a day have almost if not quite as much effect as very large ones. Carles explains its action as follows:—"In contact with water it has a tendency to split up into the oxide of bismuth and nitric acid. In the stomach, the oxide, which is in excess of the acid, has firstly a detergent effect upon the mucous membrane, precipitating the mucus; and secondly, a germicidal power. The nitric acid has a tonic, astringent, and special antiseptic action (Duclaux). In the intestine it meets with sulphuretted hydrogen gas, which converts it into black sulphide, liberating a further portion of its acid, which is partially transformed into nitrous fumes, the antiseptic action of which has been proved by Giraud and Pabst. For this action to take place satisfactorily, the subnitrate must be pure and unmixed with the carbonate, and should be as finely powdered as possible."[2]

Whether this adequately explains the undoubted benefit met with clinically from the administration of this drug it would be rash to

[1] *Archives Clinique de Bordeaux*, February 1896.
[2] *Brit. Med. Journal*, 14th December 1895, p. 1483, and 4th April 1896.

surmise, but the writer can strongly recommend its use. The effects which follow its administration are almost as great as those following the use of many internal antiseptic remedies in this fever, so that whether it acts directly as a germicide, or indirectly by aiding the germicidal action of the tissues, it matters little clinically. As it does not by its direct action stop the course of the fever, but only mitigates its intestinal or gastric symptoms, it is probable that its action is on the accidental fermentative organisms rather than on the virus of undulant fever proper, so that without being a specific drug it has its uses. It is of no avail in the late chronic stages of protracted cases, whose pyrexial range is low, and whose gastric symptoms are slight. It has the great advantage of being unirritating, and therefore does no harm, which cannot be said of many drugs often given in this fever.

Arsenic acts as a gastric irritant, and has no antipyretic or anti-periodic effects on this fever, but rather the reverse (see Case 42). Its use is contra-indicated in all cases during the febrile stage. It has occasionally been used as a tonic, and for sciatica after convalescence has been well established.

Hydrocyanic acid should not be given for gastric irritation, as locally it only paralyses the stomachic nerve endings, and rather hinders than encourages improvement in the digestive powers of that organ; while internally it acts as a depressant on the respiratory and cardiac centres, the reverse of what is required in severe cases.

Carbolic acid, carbolates, and iodide of potassium, have all been used without specific effect.

Boracic acid internally has been given by the writer in many instances with doubtful effect in a few, and with none in others. Its good effects were probably due to the promotion of intestinal asepsis rather than to any specific action on the virus. In solution it has been advocated as a remedy, in the form of local irrigation, for involvement of the large bowel.

Chlorine has not appeared to do any good.

Salol has no effect on the pyrexia, as might be expected in a local intestinal antiseptic.

Aconite is contra-indicated from its depressant effect upon the heart and circulation generally.

Colchicum does no good, and is a gastric irritant and respiratory depressant, but has proved useful in small doses, combined with an alkali, in attacks of gout complicating this fever.

Eucalyptus has been tried by Tomaselli and Bruce, but neither found it of any use. The same may be said of *turpentine*.

Salicylic acid is a stomachic irritant and a cardiac depressant, salicylate of soda or quinine much less so. On account of the arthritic and neuralgic symptoms of this fever and its consequent clinical resemblance to acute rheumatic fever, for which disease these drugs are held to be specific remedies, there has been a great tendency to administer them in cases of undulant fever. They have, however, no specific effect on the virus of the fever, and a doubtful effect on the local rheumatoid symptoms, and their use has been condemned by Rumno, Tomaselli, and Bruce. In small doses salicylate of soda has appeared of use in cases where fermentative changes were going on in the gastro-intestinal canal, while *salicylate of quinine* is well borne, and its administration in numerous cases has been followed by no appreciable ill effects. The writer has been in the habit of giving the latter in small doses three times a day, under the impression that it has kept off and alleviated the rheumatoid complications. The administration of salicylic acid or the salicylate of soda as a specific routine treatment for this disease is not only unscientific, but has proved actually harmful in severe cases.

Antipyrin (phenazone) has been largely employed. Though it reduces the temperature it has no effect upon the cause of the fever; it does not rest, but often has a powerfully depressant action on the heart, especially in severe and critical cases, and at the same time it reduces the urinary and respiratory excretions. It is an uncertain and even dangerous drug in this fever, and its use should be confined to single doses in strong subjects during the first few days of the attack. At this period, although it reduces temperature, promotes perspiration, relieves headache, and procures sleep, the same results may be obtained with even greater advantage by means of the external application of cold water, while a more exact effect and measurable reduction of pyrexia can be obtained and the heart's action improved.

Antifebrin (acetanilide) should not be used.

Phenacetin is preferable to antipyrin, and may be employed in cases where that drug is inadmissible with greater safety. It produces profuse perspiration, fall in temperature and general (but temporary) relief from discomfort, but the heart's action is not improved, while the temperature frequently rises again to its original level a few hours after.

Resorcin has been used by the author without result.

Invaliding.—In Malta out of 844 cases of this fever among soldiers, 401 (47·51 per cent) were sent to a sanatorium, 142 (16·82 per cent) were invalided to England, and 275 returned straight from hospital to their duty. Among officers the proportion was much higher. In the Royal Navy a much larger proportion of men are invalided to England for the effects of this fever. The question of the advisability or otherwise of leaving the country in which the disease prevails, as a remedial measure, is therefore one of importance. The naval authorities and many of the local practitioners advise patients to at once leave for England. Many others deny the necessity of change or its efficacy as a remedial measure.

Thus we find in the *Naval Annual Blue-Book* for 1886: "A large proportion of the cases sent to hospital were subsequently invalided. Indeed, according to my experience, when a man has suffered severely from this fever he becomes liable to constant relapses, and is not likely to make a complete recovery or be fit for his ordinary duty until he has been removed from the station."

Again in 1887: "Indeed, according to my experience, when a man has suffered from a severe or moderately severe attack of this fever it is hopeless to attempt to keep him on the station, and the sooner he is sent home the better it is for himself and for the efficiency and economy of the service."

This was practically the opinion of those naval medical officers present in the island during the writer's stay in Malta, who had to do practically with the subject. It must be remembered, however, that such a practice is less troublesome to carry out than that of continuing to treat the cases, that it is most suited to the limited naval hospital accommodation, and that there are greater facilities in the Navy for sending men home at all times than there are in the Army. A rigid adherence to the letter of such treatment is liable, however, to carry inexperienced medical officers into grave trouble through errors in diagnosis. Two such cases have come under the writer's notice, where such an error led to most unfortunate and fatal results. In the first case a woman was sent for change of air to Gozo, where on arrival the expected accommodation was found to be deficient. This necessitated a somewhat prolonged drive, in the course of which she fainted, and soon after died. Then and then only it was found on post-mortem examination that she had been suffering from enteric fever, a perforation having brought about the fatal result. The other was the case of a civilian gentleman, who, believing that he was suffering from undulant fever, left Malta hurriedly after a few days' pyrexia, only to die of enteric hæmorrhage a day or two after arrival in England.

The custom in the Army is to give local hospital treatment a fair trial first, and only to invalid such cases as appear to be unable to shake off the effects of the fever without a change. They are rarely sent away during the first two months of the disease, while the majority are kept longer in Malta. This is due to a great extent to the fact that accommodation in troop-ships for invalids is only available in the winter months, at which time the fever is little prevalent; while passages are only provided in private packets when certified as absolutely necessary. This is the other extreme, and frequently invaliding is either left until a very late stage, or invalids who have passed a Board, for change to England, are kept waiting for a Government passage for so long a time that the change comes too late to be beneficial.

Those who treat the disease among invalids sent to England describe many of them, especially during damp and cold weather, as dragging out a weary indoor existence of relapses and rheumatic complications, often for months. Other cases are described as recovering after a few days at sea. Certain it is that cases neither do well in England in the cold of winter, nor in the Mediterranean during the heat and the enervating sirocco winds of the summer. Much of the good effect of change depends on the exhilarating effect on the mind of leaving foreign service for home, on the bracing effect of the fresh air at sea, and on removal from the area of infection.

The last effect can usually be obtained by removal from the infected area to the hospital or elsewhere. One of the writer's sisters, who was sent for six weeks to Italy for change, without material result, recovered from the day she arrived back in Malta. It is certainly not justifiable to send *acute* cases away from the comforts and attentions of home or hospital to the fatigues of travelling, the doubtful comforts of foreign hotels, and away from skilled and friendly advice and help, for the sake of an over-estimated specific treatment by change of air. Many patients have been recommended change to places where the same fever is known to exist, being told that they cannot recover until they leave Malta! The beneficial effects of change of air and environment, especially during convalescence, is not to be denied, but the trials of a sea voyage or overland journey should not be encountered until the acute stages are over, nor until an enteric diagnosis has been excluded. During the winter new attacks, and those still suffering from attacks contracted during the autumn, do very well in Malta, provided they are moved away from the immediate neighbourhood of infection. During convalescence a change to the dry atmosphere of Cairo, or to the hill towns of Italy or Sicily, is most beneficial. During the autumn and winter cases are best away from the rigors and indoor confinement of the English climate. During the spring and summer cases do *not* do well in Malta when at all severely attacked. At such times every case of over a month or six weeks' duration should be inquired into, and everyone who appears to be bearing the fever badly should be invalided and sent home as soon as he is in a fit condition to travel safely. At this time of year the effect of even a few days at sea is most noticeable in the improved general condition of the patient. Those of long duration (three months and over), with much anæmia and debility, will get well much quicker and more thoroughly if sent away to a cool climate at that time of year. When they have arrived in England or elsewhere, a dry and slightly bracing inland place should be chosen, which is not at the same time exposed to cold winds. Patients do not throw off the fever satisfactorily in relaxing or low lying seaside places, and are liable to neuralgia or rheumatic complication and sequelæ in damp or cold places. The duty of Army medical officers is to avoid reduction of the fighting strength of the Army on account of sickness, as far as is possible, with due regard to the rights of the individual and the expenditure of public money. The writer believes that this would be best effected by invaliding to England during the spring and summer, all cases of this fever, in which at the end of five or six weeks (an enteric diagnosis having been carefully excluded), the fever appears to have a strong hold upon the patient, and to show no signs of cessation, or in whom there is much anæmia or debility. A change to a sanatorium would suffice during the autumn and winter, provided the above course was adhered to from May to September. Could a hospital ship be available for conveyance of naval and military invalids from the Mediterranean to England during the spring and summer, after the usual trooping season, it would repay expenditure and be of the greatest service.

To sum up:—

(*a*) Do not invalid patients until a sure diagnosis has been made; nor until the most acute stage is over.

(*b*) Invalid freely during the spring and summer months to England or such similar climate, choosing a dry inland place, bracing without being cold.

(*c*) Treat patient during autumn and winter in the Mediterranean, in sanitary surroundings, sending them if necessary during convalescence to some dry, bracing place within the neighbourhood. A change to Civita Vecchia or Gozo is often of use during convalescence in Malta; or further afield to Taormina or Gergenti in Sicily, to the Italian lakes, Switzerland, the Tyrol, or the Nile.

(*d*) It is very necessary that change of air should be accompanied by relief from mental work, worry, or physical discomfort. This with careful dietary and cheerful surroundings are the chief beneficial items of the change.

INDEX RERUM

INDEX NOMINORUM

www.ingramcontent.com/pod-product-compliance
Lightning Source LLC
Chambersburg PA
CBHW031744230426
43669CB00007B/478
9783742830647